The Middle Schoolers' Debatabase

75 Current Controversies for Debaters

The Middle Schoolers' Debatabase
75 Current Controversies for Debaters

Rhiannon Bettivia

and

National Forensic League

international debate education association

New York & Amsterdam

Published by:
International Debate Education Association
400 West 59th Street
New York, NY 10019

We would like to thank Angela Gunn and Isabel Patkowski for their contributions to this project.

Library of Congress Cataloging-in-Publication Data

Bettivia, Rhiannon.
   The middle schoolers' debatabase : 75 current controversies for
debaters / Rhiannon Bettivia ; and National Forensic League.
      p. cm.
   Includes index.
   ISBN 978-1-932716-57-3 (alk. paper)
   1. Debates and debating--Study and teaching (Middle school) I.
National Forensic League (U.S.) II. International Debate Education
Association. III. Title.
   LB1572.B48 2011
   808.53--dc22
                                    2010046605

Design by Kathleen Hayes
Printed in the USA

Contents

Preface

The Middle Schoolers' Debatabase: 75 Current Controversies for Debaters provides an introduction into the wonderful world of debate for students, coaches, teachers, and parents. This volume gives general information necessary for beginning debaters and their coaches to get started with debate and argumentation and presents 75 debate topics that will interest and challenge middle school students.

Unlike other debate resource books, this volume is designed specifically with the needs and capacities of middle schoolers in mind. This focus has guided every aspect of the book's development—from the design, to the hints for debaters, to the topics included. Topics and motions have been chosen for two reasons: first, to appeal to interests and experiences of middle schoolers; accordingly, a very large number of the topics involve school and environment. Second, to help introduce students to domestic and international issues with which they may be unfamiliar. Each entry contains a topic and motion; an introduction; information on debating the motion; pros and cons; additional sample motions that could be argued with similar research; and web links.

Topics and Motions

Entries in this book are organized by topic for ease of reference but begin with a specific motion. A motion is included because narrower motions (rather than broad topics) are more common in middle school debate. For most middle school students, the research required for each debate will be entirely new; the narrower motions make the research less daunting, particularly as the task of including and excluding information is one that middle schoolers can struggle with.

The motions are also broader than might be seen in a typical middle school debate tournament—where motions might focus on items of local interest. Broad motions are appropriate for a more general audience and also force debaters to define and narrow, skills important in debate. In many cases, I purposely chose vague terms like *schools* and *government* or *good* and *bad* to demonstrate the kind of work that students need to do in defining a motion.

Introductions

Each topic includes a short introduction that provides the debater with enough context to understand the pros and cons and very broadly set out parameters for possible research. Showcasing the controversy helps students understand why they should debate a topic, helping them to realize that debate is not abstract but addresses contemporary problems and issues.

Debating the Motion

This section aims to help students learn how to prepare for debate. It includes information for both teams about how to approach the motion and structure research. Subsections specifically address how the proposition and opposition might prepare their side. Because middle school students have difficulty seeing "the big picture," we offer broad suggestions that will start students thinking about possible approaches and develop their own plans. The information in these sections is deliberately very general so as to encourage critical thinking.

Pros and Cons

Sample statements that might be made by either side of the debate are provided. The pro side will have statements on which the proposition or affirmative teams might build arguments; the con side will provide the same for the opposition or negative teams. Each pro is matched with a con for the purpose of demonstrating clash. Because young debaters have difficulty synthesizing, each pro and con begins with a summary statement highlighting the theme of the argument. The pros and cons address the motion, but because they are argument stems, not arguments, they can also be used for similar motions.

Other Motions

This section will be helpful to debaters but will also help new leagues and coaches who are looking for motions. The *other motions* section includes additional motions that can be argued and debated using the same research and the same framework provided by the *debating the motion* and *pro/con* sections. Other Motions might simply involve flipping the burden from defending something as good to showing it is bad or it might reimagine the motion as about ethics or policy adoption when it was about harms and benefits. Regardless, debaters can use the argument stems from the pro/con section with just a small shift in the emphasis.

Related Motions

The *related motions* section is aimed at providing debate motions that connect to the topic and could be pursued using the same or similar research but would require a shift of framework or assumptions away from the hints that were given in the *debating the motion* sections. In this section, the research a student did for the original motion could still be used, but the debate itself would be about something different and thus would require new cases, counter cases, and arguments. The related motions are also generally aimed at offering a bigger challenge with more difficult motions or topics included—where multiple related motions are provided, they are generally listed in order from least to most challenging.

Web Links

Where possible, *web links* references sites that provide balanced information or important background on a topic as well as sites supporting one or the other side of an issue. Sites were selected because they are age appropriate for middle schoolers.

I hope that *The Middle Schoolers' Debatabase* will be a helpful tool for debaters, encouraging them to explore contemporary issues and providing them with the basics of debate that will last through many years of debating.

Enjoy!

Rhiannon Bettivia
President, Big Apple Debate League

Introduction to Debate

Why Debate?

You have lots of extracurricular programs to choose from—these, in turn, compete with other activities you might want to do, for instance, talking with friends, surfing the web, or playing soccer. With so many choices, why choose debate?

Debate offers you many benefits. The most obvious are academic. These benefits probably are most important to your parents and teachers, but, as you mature and think about your future, you will find them valuable as well. Participating in debate makes you a better thinker and communicator. The skills you develop while debating will improve your classwork and test scores. The communication skills you refine will help you present your point of view when discussing a paper with your teacher or when negotiating with your parents for a higher allowance or later curfew. Having debate on a high school or college application will also increase your chances of getting into the school of your choice: admissions committees understand that debaters know how to think and reason and will be able to attack their work with zeal and competence.

Debate's benefits are often fun. Debate is a very social activity. You get the opportunity to hang out and talk with your classmates in preparing for a tournament. You and your friends and teammates get to spend time surfing the web to find evidence to support your arguments. Finally, you get to travel and meet new people. Debate tournaments take place and debate camps for middle school students are located all over the world. For your own league, you might travel to a dozen new schools in a year; during the summers or other long breaks, you may travel to prestigious Ivy League universities or to Europe and Asia. Best of all, you travel with your teammates and have the opportunity to meet hundreds of other students from different schools, cities, and countries. These are people you might never have met otherwise—it is not uncommon to find a lifelong friend in a debate teammate or, more commonly, in a worthy debate opponent who impresses you with her skill. The opportunities for socializing are many and they can help you find a group where you feel a sense of belonging outside your own school.

Debate also contributes to your personal growth and sense of self. For most students, a lot of life entails being told what to do by adults. When debating, however, you are the center of attention and everyone listens while you suggest plans to solve real problems that policymakers and politicians grapple with every day. Speaking publicly and convincingly will help you develop self-confidence, plus nothing feels as amazing as finding out you've won against a particularly impressive and hard-to-defeat team.

Finally, debate is fun. Tournament day is exciting, with hundreds of kids competing, often in a new and different environment, and the conversations and laughs in rounds are often topped off with something that universally excites all middle schoolers—lots of big trophies for the best speakers and teams.

What Is Debate?

A common misconception is that debate is just a couple of people arguing over some subject. In fact, debate offers a highly structured environment in which two individuals or two teams, often called the proposition or affirmative and the opposition or negative, take turns presenting speeches in favor and against a specific topic proposition called a *motion* or *resolution*. Debaters make two kinds of speeches. First, each team presents *constructive speeches* to establish arguments the teams hope to win. Then, they attack the other team's arguments and solidify their team's position in *rebuttal speeches*. The two teams clash, or directly attack, each other's arguments to convince the judge or audience to vote for their side.

TOPICS AND PROPOSITIONS

Topics and propositions are related to each other but are slightly different in their scope. Topics are broad subjects while propositions, called *motions* or *resolutions* depending on the debate format, address the specific parts of an issue the speakers will debate. Topics are general, for example, voters' rights. In some formats, debaters will argue one broad topic per season. Obviously, debating something as broad as "voters' rights" would be very difficult, so a topic is narrowed down to a specific proposition—the aspect of the topic over which the two sides will clash in the debate. Propositions tend to follow common patterns such as banning or rescinding a ban; moral harms or moral goods (ethical or unethical); good or bad; benefits versus harms; or suggesting a particular action or policy be put in place or be removed. To take the example of voters' rights, propositions on this topic might look like "ban criminals from voting," or "lower the voting age to 14," or "restricting teenagers from voting is unethical."

ARGUMENTS

Debaters present their side of the debate in *cases* and *counter cases,* specific plans that each side proposes in which they suggest actions people should take; each side also explains how these plans should be implemented. These cases are supported by arguments, which in debate are not verbal fights between people but are proofs offered to support a case.

Offering arguments can be more complicated than it first sounds because an argument actually consists of many small parts—leaving out even one of these parts can turn a strong and important argument into a wimpy point or mere statement.[1] Every argument should contain five elements: a statement, a definition, reasoning, evidence, and impact.

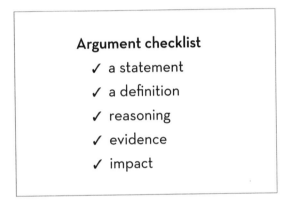

Argument checklist
✓ a statement
✓ a definition
✓ reasoning
✓ evidence
✓ impact

Statements

These sentences basically summarize what your argument will be about. It is like the heading at the beginning of section in a textbook that lets you know what to expect in the pages following.

When you start brainstorming on a new topic, first think of important statements on which you could build arguments, for example:

- ban smoking because smoking causes cancer
- oranges are better than apples because they are a good source of vitamin C
- plastic bags are wasteful because they do not biodegrade

None of these are arguments, but all are important starting points. These statements are the foundation of the arguments you will build.

---

1. This book provides you with pros and cons in each entry. Remember that these pros and cons are simply points and statements; they are the beginning of arguments that you will need to make.

Definitions

In debate, *definition* has a special meaning. It is not necessarily what you find in a dictionary. Instead, it tells the judge and the other team what you mean by a certain word or phrase. Definitions are very important because they expand on your statements and give a judge the context of what you are talking about. For the statement that plastic bags are wasteful, you might explain to the judge that you find anything that doesn't biodegrade wasteful because it just keeps piling up in landfills, thus wasting space and resources. Notice that this wasn't a dictionary definition of *wasteful*. Instead, you explained what you mean by *wasteful* in the context of this debate. Sometimes, your statements will need lots of definition, other times, they will need only a little.

Reasoning

Reasoning explains the logic or thought process behind an argument. When arguing that smoking should be banned because it causes cancer, for example, you might explain that even though cancer has many causes, smoking has been shown to greatly increase the risks of developing certain kinds of cancer. Further, you might explain that since we know that cancer can be deadly, the government should ban smoking because the government has the responsibility to protect people. You basically have to tell a judge why she should care about your argument.

Remember that you can't automatically assume a judge is concerned about the same issues you are. For example, you might make the argument that smoking leads to a lot of cigarette butts being tossed away carelessly; this refuse can be dangerous to animals like birds and squirrels, who might choke on a butt while scavenging for food. You might assume that the judge understands your reasoning—it is wrong to let any living creature die unnecessarily. But you cannot make this assumption! Maybe your judge is a city dweller who finds pigeons and squirrels to be an annoyance and so doesn't see this argument as having much merit. You must explain to the judge that causing the death of an innocent living creature is wrong, even if the judge considers the animal to be a pest, because causing suffering is ethically wrong and can desensitize us. Such desensitization may very well make us more prone to hurt other creatures.

Evidence

This can be statistics, historical or contemporary examples, or experts' opinions that you found during your research on your topic. It is very important to find multiple pieces of evidence for each argument your team plans to make in a debate. When the first person on your team presents an argument, she will use one piece of evidence to support it. The other team will then try to knock that argument down. When your team's turn to speak comes again, you will want to rebuild that argument—a great way to show that your argument really is superior is to present another piece of evidence to back it up.

Impact

Impact connects your argument to possible consequences. You want to show what the long-term and far-reaching effects will be. You can do this negatively by explaining all the bad things that could happen if the judge doesn't listen to you. You could explain that by not banning smoking, smokers will continue to smoke, which, in turn. leads to illness. These diseases drain money from our economy through absenteeism and by taxing the government to pay health care costs for those who get sick by a voluntary action. Basically, by not supporting you, the judge is supporting something that we know hurts human beings and the economy.

You could also explain your impact positively by showing all the good that could resullt if the judge listens to your side. For banning smoking, you could explain that fewer cases of cancer would result in less need for expensive medical treatments. As many smokers rely on government assistance to pay for health care, if fewer individuals smoked, fewer would develop cancer and require medical treatment—thus the government would have more money. You could explain to the judge all the useful projects this money could pay for rather than having to pay for treatment for a disease smokers could easily avoid. By explaining the benefits, you are demonstrating the positive effects of your argument.

All five parts are needed to make a single complete argument. Thus, a good debater can only fit three or four good arguments into one speech—you need time to explain all the elements. When practicing with your teammates, make sure you hit each item on the argument checklist. Practice this skill and be careful to make complete arguments and not just wimpy statements.

Causation versus correlation

When developing your arguments, be careful to distinguish between *causation* and *correlation*, especially when explaining your reasoning and impact. Both causation and correlation involve relationships between two or more events. *Causation* says that one event or action causes a subsequent event. A good example would be the relationship between smoking and lung disease. Smoking can cause lung cancer or emphysema. *Correlation* says that, while two things happen around the same time, one does not cause the other. For example, a school administrator is trying to find out what makes a student likely to be tardy. After a month of collecting data, the administrator has noticed a pattern: of all the students who were tardy, 97 percent of them wore sneakers. So, does wearing sneakers cause students to be late? Of course not! It just so happens that many students wear sneakers and many students are occasionally late for class. This is a correlation because, even though these two happen together, one does not cause the other.

When debating, link situations by causation when making your own arguments. You want to show that some action or policy actually results in other bad or good things happening. When knocking down an opponent's argument, you want to try to show that her arguments are based on correlations—even though two actions or results appear to be connected, one has not caused the other.

CLASH

Clash in debate requires that what you say in response to the other team must directly address what your opponent has said. For example, when debating the motion that the voting age should be lowered to 14, the proposition team says:

> The voting age should be lowered to 14 because by that age all students have completed the courses in U.S. history and government that will enable them to vote intelligently. Most voters will not take additional civics courses after this age, so there is no point in putting voting off until the age of 18.

To create clash, the opposition team must argue directly against this idea. But the team cannot simply argue against lowering the voting age in general. An example of a response that would *not* clash is:

> The voting age should not be lowered to 14 because, at the age of 14, teenagers are too immature to be allowed to make an important decision like who should govern the whole country.

While this is a valid statement that the team might want to bring into an argument later, it did not clash with the first team's argument because it did not address what the first team said. A response about the immaturity of 14-year-olds might score a point with the judge as a new argument, but it will lose points as rebuttal. To properly rebut the argument, the team would have to speak about 14-year-olds and civics education. Clash could look like this:

> The voting age should not be lowered to 14 because even if 14-year-olds have had government and history classes, such instruction is insufficient to make

an informed voter. While an 18-year-old might not have taken any extra government classes since middle school, she will still have had four years of additional experience in the world, observing the actions of politicians and the ramifications of policies. Time makes informed voters—14-year-olds just haven't had enough time, even if they have had enough civic education.

This statement not only says why the voting age shouldn't be lowered, it also speaks about why the proposition team's specific idea was wrong—not just why the motion itself is not a good idea. In a debate round, you and your team need to clash directly with every claim made by the other team. This is what makes good rebuttal.

The best way to ensure that you are prepared with vigorous rebuttals is to take good notes, or *flow* the debate. If you know what everyone has said, including the arguments of your team and the other team, then you will know what you have to clash with.

Debate Formats

Formal debate occurs in many different formats, each of which has its own proponents. The two most common in U.S. middle school debate are policy and American parliamentary. The two formats differ slightly from each other, but are united in requiring research on a topic, the creation of solid arguments, and the ability to directly clash with the opponent.

POLICY DEBATE

Policy debates involve two teams—the affirmative and the negative—each composed of two people. Each individual has specific responsibilities summarized in the table below:

SPEAKER	TIME	RESPONSIBILITY
First Affirmative Constructive Speech (1AC)	6 minutes	• lays out the details of the case • makes arguments and backs them up with detailed and carefully cited evidence • demonstrates that the affirmative case wins all stock issues (see below) • demonstrates the advantages of adopting the affirmative case • demonstrates that these advantages cannot possibly be achieved under the status quo
Negative Cross-Examination	2 minutes	• cross-examines the first speaker by calling into question the validity of his arguments and evidence and asking for clarification of anything vague
First Negative Constructive Speech (1NC)	6 minutes	• makes a counter case or proposes to uphold the status quo • makes arguments and backs them up with detailed and carefully cited evidence • demonstrates that the negative case wins all or some stock issues • demonstrates the disadvantages of the affirmative case
Affirmative Cross-Examination	2 minutes	• cross-examines the previous speaker by calling into question the validity of her arguments and evidence and asking for clarification of anything vague
Second Affirmative Constructive Speech (2AC)	6 minutes	• restates the case • offers new argumentation and additional evidence
Negative Cross-Examination	2 minutes	• cross-examines the previous speaker by calling into question the validity of his arguments and evidence and asking for clarification of anything vague
Second Negative Constructive Speech (2NC)	6 minutes	• restates the case • offers new argumentation and additional evidence

Affirmative Cross-Examination	2 minutes	• cross-examines the previous speaker by calling into question the validity of her arguments and evidence and asking for clarification of anything vague
First Negative Rebuttal	2 minutes	• refutes affirmative arguments • highlights weaknesses and disadvantages in the affirmative case • demonstrates that the negative has won some or all stock issues
First Affirmative Rebuttal	3 minutes	• refutes the negative case • highlights weaknesses and disadvantages in the negative case • demonstrates that the affirmative has won all stock issues
Second Negative Rebuttal	3 minutes	• refutes affirmative arguments • highlights weaknesses and disadvantages in the affirmative case • demonstrates that the negative has won some or all stock issues
Second Affirmative Rebuttal	3 minutes	• refutes the negative case • highlights weaknesses and disadvantages in the negative case • demonstrates that the affirmative has won all stock issues

In policy debate, you will debate the same topic for an entire school year; over the course of the debate season, you will debate both sides of the resolution. The topic might be something like "torture" and the resolution might be "Resolved: torture should be used in situations of national security." As the name *policy debate* suggests, the speakers propose the adoption of a specific plan or policy aimed at addressing a problem or controversy associated with the topic. The affirmative team then creates a plan—for example, detailing what is meant by torture, what "situations of national security" involves, who it would apply to, etc. The negative team then must show that the current policy forbidding torture should be maintained. This is defending the status quo (arguing to keep things as they are). Alternatively, the negative team can come up with a counter case where it suggests something different from the affirmative case and different from the status quo. An example of a counter case, or counter plan, might be to offer a pardon to suspects if they help gather intelligence in situations that are a threat to national security. The negative team would work to prove that offering a pardon to a captured suspect is preferable to and more effective than torture.

In policy debating, you and your teammates, with the help of your coach, will write out your constructive speeches before engaging in debate. The first affirmative speaker writes out her entire speech. The other speaker might write out some of his speech but must leave room to clash with the arguments of the other side. Often policy debaters will write lengthy speeches about their topic and practice reading these aloud in an effort to fit information into a short amount of time. Six minutes might seem like a lot at first, but after a few tournaments, the time will seem shorter and shorter! These speeches involve a considerable amount of specific knowledge and need detailed evidence, so policy debate involves much in-depth research. Speeches can be jam-packed with citations and statistics. As your team debates both sides in various tournaments, you will refine your case based on real experience that highlights the strengths and weaknesses of your original ideas.

Students in policy debate should flow both cases and use this information in cross-examination, where they call into question the validity of their opponents' sources and the weight, truthfulness, or impact of their arguments. The first affirmative speaker might have a "pre flow," since her speech would be written out word for word. All other speeches could be more spontaneous, depending on what arguments the opposing team introduces.

Policy debates revolve around standard points of controversy called *stock issues*: solvency, harms, inherency, topicality, and significance. The first three are the most important. *Solvency* involves each team showing that its proposed plans and ideas *solve* the problem being debated. *Harms* are self-explanatory: each side wants to demonstrate that adopting the other team's proposal will not solve the problem but will make it worse. *Inherency* is a trickier idea. It means that each team needs to prove what barriers are present that prevent change in the status quo. Such inherent barriers could include attitudes, conditions, or laws that allow the harms to continue. The affirmative team needs to prove that its plan can overcome the inherent barriers; the negative team proves either that the affirmative plan cannot overcome the barriers or that the barriers are incorrect. If the negative team argues a counter plan, it can show how its plan overcomes the barriers. *Topicality* determines whether the affirmative plan addresses the resolution. *Significance* asks debaters to prove how important the harms are and what might happen if the harms continue to be ignored.

The affirmative team should consistently defend *all* stock issues as they relate to the affirmative plan. Many policy debate judges hold that if only a few stock issues go to the negative side, then the negative side wins.

PARLIAMENTARY DEBATE

American parliamentary debate involves two teams of three speakers—with each speaker getting only one speech. Each speaker on a team has a specific role.

SPEAKER	TIME	RESPONSIBILITY
First Proposition	5 minutes	• defines the motion • lays out the details of the case • makes 3–5 arguments • accepts 2 or 3 points of interest or information (POIs)
First Opposition	5 minutes	• lays out the details of the counter case—this is optional with some motions • makes 3–5 arguments • refutes the first proposition's arguments • accepts 2 or 3 POIs
Second Proposition	5 minutes	• restates the case • rebuilds the first proposition's arguments with new evidence • adds 1 or 2 new arguments • refutes the first opposition's arguments • accepts 2 or 3 POIs
Second Opposition	5 minutes	• restates the counter case if there is one • rebuilds the first opposition's arguments with new evidence • adds 1 or 2 new arguments • refutes all the proposition's arguments • accepts 2 or 3 POIs
Third Opposition	3 minutes	• points out the most important arguments of the round • demonstrates why the opposition has won
Third Proposition	3 minutes	• rebuts the opposition's arguments • points out the most important arguments of the round • demonstrates why the proposition has won

As its name suggests, this form of debate comes from the styles of politicians arguing over issues in the British Parliament. In this format, the two teams (called *proposition* and *opposition* instead of *affirmative* and *negative*), debate a motion, often called a *resolution*.

Parliamentary debate tournaments differ from policy debate tournaments in that they require debaters to be familiar with five motions or resolutions for each tournament, instead of one for the whole year. A tournament has the same number of rounds as there are motions provided by the league; in each round, one motion will be assigned to all debaters, thus everyone debates the same motion simultaneously. In the next round, a different motion is assigned—by the end of the tournament, every team will have debated each motion once. On average, parliamentary debaters will debate as many as 30–40 different motions each season or school year, while policy debaters will debate only one.

In this format, debaters must be familiar with different topics, thus the research is less comprehensive than in policy debate. Policy debaters must do lots of research that is carefully cited from academic sources; parliamentary debaters need only look at newspapers and news magazines to find evidence to support their arguments. Unlike policy debate, parliamentary debate permits the use of anecdotal evidence—a little story, found either in your research or drawn from personal experience, that supports your arguments. Another big difference is that parliamentary debaters are not allowed to pre-write their speeches. Rather, they take notes in the form of bullet points or outlines during the preparation time before each round since they are usually not allowed to take additional materials into a debate with them. They expand on these new notes when they make their actual speech. Accordingly, parliamentary debate really tests your rhetorical abilities—the skill to speak eloquently while thinking on your feet. Because parliamentary debaters speak extemporaneously, the debaters flow everything that everyone says, including their partners. Noting what your partner says is important because she might introduce something new that you will need to build on or address later in your own speech.

Instead of cross-examining other speakers in a specific order, parliamentary debaters use POIs (point of interest or information) to interact with the other team. When debaters wish to address something said by an opponent, they will stand during their opponent's speech and offer a POI, which can take the form of a witty comment or specific question about the truth or importance of something the other team just said. Speakers don't have to accept all POIs, but they must respond to some to show they are prepared. Accepting too many may give the impression that you don't have enough to say and you need your opponent to help you fill your time. Accepting too few may give the impression that you are not confident that your material is strong enough to stand up to criticism. Debaters should always offer POIs during the other team's speeches to help forward their team's cause and show the judge they are listening actively.

Preparing to Debate

Regardless of the format of debate, all debaters need to complete several tasks when preparing for a tournament: develop their vocabulary; keep abreast of current affairs and research their topic; narrow topics and motions; and create cases and counter cases. Teams should also practice taking notes, as this skill, called *flowing,* is crucial—you must learn to write down only the most necessary information since a speaker in any format will speak quickly and say too much for you to write down everything.

VOCABULARY

Debaters need to have bigger vocabularies than the average middle school student. Expanding your vocabulary is simple: read! Extracurricular reading of fiction, nonfiction, and news sources will help you deepen your knowledge of language and help you to replace overused, vague, and unnecessary words, such as *like, stuff, things, good,* and *bad,* with better words.

CURRENT EVENTS

Debaters must be familiar with current events and popular news, so you should read newspapers and magazines (*New York Times* or *Time* magazine are good examples) that you can find in print or on the web; you might also follow reliable news blogs (CNN or BBC) online. You might also want to watch television news as you get your backpack together at night or eat breakfast in the morning. Just be careful to choose a trustworthy news source and try to pick one that does not support one political side over another. If you choose a partisan news source, for example, Fox News, balance it with a source such as MSNBC from the other end of the political spectrum.

RESEARCH

Since no team can be sure which side of a debate it will be given in a tournament, all debaters need to research and prepare both sides of a given topic or motion and create outlines or ideas for cases and counter cases well before the actual tournaments. Doing research is a must because it provides a context for the topic. Context will help you and your judge understand what is most important in a round, the same way you use context clues in English classes to understand new and difficult terms and ideas. Research will also give you ideas for arguments as you can see what experts have argued on the issue.

Research also provides the evidence you'll need to support your arguments. Make sure you find multiple pieces of evidence for each statement. Remember, these extra pieces of evidence become an asset in later speeches to either knock down an opponent's argument or back up your teammate. New tidbits of evidence are particularly useful in rebuilding a teammate's argument that was knocked down by the opposing team.

When conducting research, make sure you are using reliable sources. Doubtless your teachers and librarians have warned you that not everything found on the Internet is true or of equal value. Evaluate each website you use carefully to make sure you can trust its statements. When looking for websites to cite, pick trusted news sources such as the *New York Times*, NPR, or well-known information sites like *Encyclopedia Britannica*. When using other sites, first determine who is providing the information. If an author or a group is behind a website, a quick background investigation will help you determine if the website can be trusted. If you find that the author is a professor at a respected university who is an expert in her field, for example, then her information is probably useful. Avoid using sites that do not list an author or are maintained by those with no expertise.

To begin your research, look for websites that will give you an overview of the topic. You can find these by searching key words from your topic or motion. Opinion blogs, websites like ask.com, yahoo.com, about.com, and Wikipedia.org are all good places to start when trying to get a solid introduction to a new topic. Beware of using these websites for your more specific research, however. While good introductory sources, they are not academic websites with verifiable evidence, so they should not be used as proof or as citations during a policy debate—or a research paper or presentation in class! Wikipedia in particular is a site that is accurate about 90 percent of the time or more, but be careful as contributors can occasionally post incorrect information.

Be very cautious in using statistical evidence because it is both helpful and dangerous. An experienced debater will tell you that she can use a statistic on either side of a debate. Take, for example, an imaginary statistic that every day 1 million Americans eat all junk food and no vegetables or fruit. If you were debating a topic about obesity or mandatory health courses, you might see such a statistic. The question is: Which side of the debate will this help—the prop/affirmative or the opp/negative? The answer is both. It is all a matter of spin. One team might use this statistic and say that each day 1 million people engage in unhealthful eating. The other team might use the same statistic to say only 1 million people do this out of 300 million people who live in the United States—less than 1 percent of Americans, which is basically nothing! Just by looking at this statistic in a different way, two teams can use it on opposing sides of the debate. One lesson here is twofold: first, most statistics you find related to your motion or topic can be used regardless of which side you are assigned to argue at the tournament. Just take the same statistic and try looking at it in a different way—raw numbers or a percentage or fractions or as a comparison with something else. The other lesson is to be careful: do not base your whole case or very important arguments on a statistic because no matter how perfect it seems, any statistic can be turned against you by a skilled speaker.

NARROWING TOPICS AND MOTIONS

Regardless of whether your debate organization provides you with one or many motions, your first step when speaking in the debate as the first affirmative or first proposition is to narrow what has been given. Even motions like "lower the voting age to 14" can be made more specific in the introductory speech. Defining the motion is similar to establishing definitions in individual arguments, but here you are providing a definition for the whole debate. When talking about "lower the voting age to 14," for example, the first speaker might define "voting" as applying only to selecting the president or participating in federal and state elections. Or, to take an even sillier, yet important, example, we can look at organ donation. If the motion is that organ donations should be compulsory, the first speaker must explain that he is talking about donating body parts to those in medical need and not donating pipe organs to churches! It is up to the first speaker in any round to decide how terms are defined and she should use team practice time to work out these definitions with her team. In policy debates, your experience with a definition at one tournament might lead you to tweak that definition before the next one.

In defining elements of the topic, you are narrowing the debate. A motion like "ban sugary drinks in school" could be about many issues—by defining sugary drinks as any drink with sugar, including the natural sugar in fruit juice, and by defining schools as K–12 public schools, arguments about what to do about private schools and colleges, or exceptions for organic juice are no longer part of the debate. Narrowing topics is necessary: debates last anywhere from 30 minutes to around an hour—not enough time to say everything on any topic. Be careful though, not to narrow the topic so much that the other team has no arguments left to make—often teams that narrow a debate too much will automatically lose.

Many terms commonly used in motions require definitions tied to the particular debate. In cases that involve ethics or morality, the first speaker must define what is meant by *ethics* and *morals*. For example, you might choose to define a moral action as being anything a trusted figure might do in the same situation. You might choose to define ethical as anything that is helpful to the majority—thus, unethical would be something that hurts many and helps only a few.

In debates that discuss harms and benefits, the first speaker might want to say whether she means emotional, physical, political, or environmental harms and benefits. There are many other harms and benefits besides these that you might find relevant to a particular case. You might even think of new ones! In talking about harms and benefits, or even in debates about whether something is bad or good, remember to indicate who is harmed or who benefits.

Vague terms like *school* or *government* or *ban* and many others will also need more precise definitions. *School* can have many different meanings—from kindergarten to postgraduate schools, from public to private, from boarding to day schools, etc. *Government* could mean state or federal, local, or even the government of another country. *Ban* could be complete and total or partial with special exceptions. The initial task of the first speaker is always to give all necessary definitions to help narrow the topic. As you will never know if your team will be arguing the affirmative or the opposition, you must be prepared to do both.

CREATING A CASE

Creating a specific case involves stating a plan and telling everything we need to know about how it will be put into place, who it will affect, how much it will cost, how much time it will take, etc. A plan is necessary in all policy debates and many parliamentary debates as well. Creating a specific and actionable plan will provide a framework for developing arguments and will often help to stymie opposition arguments from the outset. You might want to think about major objections the opposing team might have and add elements to your plan to address some of these. Take the sample motion "lower the voting age to 14." The case might be:

> In this debate, I will advocate lowering the voting age to 14. For our purposes, voting will mean the ability to cast a ballot in all elections: federal, state, and local. All citizens of this country who are 14 years of age or older and meet certain requirements will be entitled to vote. To be eligible to vote in an election, citizens will have to complete a civics course that includes

information on general government processes and on issues that might be specific to a certain location, such as California's referendum process or the complicated local politics of New York City. Once a citizen has passed the exam with a score of 85 percent or higher, he or she will be allowed to register to vote. These classes will be given and the exam will be administered by the local DMV. In addition, the course will be required for any first-time voter regardless of age. Veteran voters can continue to vote. As all new voters, whether they are first-time voters at 14 or 94, will have to take this course, over time, all voters will be educated in civics.

As you can see, this specific plan contains definitions that help clarify the motion and gives a detailed action plan for implementation. By developing a detailed plan, the proposition can help to knock down potential arguments the other team might make about 14-year-olds not being educated enough before the other team even gets a chance to make that argument! By requiring voter education classes, the proposition shows that by approving their side of the debate, we eventually will have a more educated electorate. By saying that only citizens will be eligible to vote and by specifying who will take the test and who will administer it, the proposition team has limited the arguments the opposition can make.

CREATING COUNTER CASES

At times, the opposition, or negative, team will simply want to attack the proposition and argue for the status quo. At other times, however, you will want to make a counter case, proposing your own plan that is mutually exclusive of the proposition's plan. This will result in forcing the judge to choose one because no way exists for both plans to work. In the case of "lower the voting age to 14," the opposition could simply uphold keeping the voting age at 18. But the opposition could also argue the case for raising the voting age. A sample counter case for this motion might look like this:

> I will be arguing that we should not lower the voting age to 14. In fact, I will argue that we should increase the voting age to 21. We would allow those between 18 and 20 who are already registered voters to continue to vote, but all others wishing to vote must be 21 or older. Thus, within the next three years, all voters will be 21 or older.

By creating this counter case, the opposition has opened an avenue for a host of arguments that they couldn't make if the voting age stayed at 18. Now they can argue that all teenagers' brains are still maturing, that college-age students would often be voting in places where they only lived for a few months a year, or that requiring the age to be higher helps ensure that most voters will have completed high school and possibly some college, and, therefore, the DMV won't be required to spend money to educate voters. Creating a counter case can open up new avenues for arguing and can help to knock out arguments made by the proposition, or affirmative, team.

Things all good debaters should know

Debate requires you to be as informed as adults about important topics—sometimes even more so! Most of the time, everything you need to know for a debate you can find in your research. However, there are some concepts and subjects that come up frequently in debate rounds that you may not have learned in class yet. Because these things come up so frequently, you should learn them now to be prepared. This list below isn't exhaustive, but includes the most common ideas and subjects that come up in middle school debates.

Analyze your notes after tournaments and if you notice other subjects that keep recurring, make researching them part of your preparation work for your next debate.

GOVERNMENTAL AND ECONOMIC SYSTEMS

The various types of economic and governmental systems are frequently discussed in debates as they relate to many topics, particularly those that refer to domestic and international policies and legislations. Terms to know are the following:

Democracy: A Greek term that means government by the people. In direct democracies, like ancient Greece, policies are voted on directly by the people. In a representative democracy, such as the United States, the people elect representatives who act in the people's interest.

Dictatorship: One person or a group of people controls the government. The government exercises absolute power unrestricted by law, constitutions, or other political and social factors. In the twentieth century many dictatorships were totalitarian. That is, the central government regulated every aspect of the state and private behavior. Joseph Stalin's Soviet Union was such a state.

Monarchy: A hereditary leader, usually a king or queen, exercises power. In the seventeenth century several European nations, such as France, were absolute monarchies in which the king or queen ruled by divine right—God had given him or her the right to rule and the king or queen had the right to decide anything. Today, with the exception of some countries in the Middle East, monarchies are "limited." Political power is centered in the legislature. The ruling family serves as a symbol of the country's history. The monarch has little if any real power, and his or her main job is carrying out ceremonial functions.

Capitalism: An economic and social system in which the means of production, like factories, farms, and other businesses, are owned by private individuals or companies who operate in their own self-interest. There are many types of capitalist systems. In some systems, the state encourages competition and government rarely intervenes in the economy, preferring to let markets regulate themselves. In other capitalist systems, government will intervene to protect citizens through such measures as consumer laws and to ensure that the economy is functioning smoothly. For example, the U.S. government made a massive intervention in 2008–09 to prevent the American economy from collapsing.

Socialism: A political and economic system in which the state owns the means of production and distribution. Underlying socialism is the belief that capitalism has to be transformed so that the well-being of all is more important than the pursuit of individual self-interest. Socialism takes many forms, and the concept is constantly evolving. In some socialist systems, such as the former Soviet Union, the economy was planned by the state; in others, such as China, markets dictate what should be produced.

During the twentieth century two different systems of socialism emerged. Under Joseph Stalin in the Soviet Union and Adolf Hitler in Germany, for example, the government controlled all elements of society in order to create ruthless dictatorships. In much of Western Europe, socialism developed in the context of democracy that stressed the need for social justice and equality through the management of the economy. Government took on the main responsibility for providing for the social and economic security of citizens through pensions, free health care, unemployment insurance, and other benefits. By the end of the century many of these countries had begun privatizing and deregulating their industries while maintaining social benefits.

THE CONSTITUTION

The Constitution sets out the governing system of the United States. It is based on six principles:

1. *Popular sovereignty*: Under the Constitution all authority comes from the people, to whom the government is responsible.

2. *Separation of Powers*: The Framers wanted a strong central government. They feared that this could lead to tyranny, however, and so divided power among three branches of government. The legislative branch (Congress) creates the laws; the executive branch (the President and executive agencies) implements and enforces them; and the judicial branch (the courts) interprets them.

3. *Checks and balances*: The Framers, those individuals who drafted the Constitution, wanted to make sure that no branch was completely independent and so established a system of checks and balances so that each branch has some control over the other. For example, Congresses passes legislation, but the president has to power to veto it. Congress can pass the measure over the president's veto. The courts, in turn, can prevent implementation of a law by ruling it unconstitutional. Yet the courts cannot act independently to make this determination. They can review only questions of constitutionality that are brought before them in court cases.

4. *Federalism*: The Framers feared that a nation with just a national government could lead to tyranny because government would be far from the people. Therefore they established a federal system in which states ceded some powers to the federal government while reserving others. The distinction between federal and state powers is not clear cut and has been a major source of contention throughout American history. In fact, the dispute over the rights of the states was one of the causes of the Civil War.

5. *Supremacy of National Law*: To make sure that a federal system would work, the Framers established the principle that state laws could not violate the Constitution. If a national law conflicts with a state law, the national law prevails.

6. *Civilian Control of Government*: The military is subordinate to civilian government. The president is commander-in-chief of the armed forces, while Congress has the power to declare war.

The Constitution is a short document, reflecting the Framers' desire for limited government. It sets out only the general structure of government, not how the government should operate. Framers thought the latter would evolve over time to reflect the needs of the people.

The Constitution is divided into three parts:

Preamble: Sets out the principle that government is a compact among the people, who are sovereign. It also sets out the goals of the document.

Body: The body consists of seven sections that establish the various branches of government, explain the relationship between the states and the federal government, describe how the constitution will be amended, and establish the supremacy of national law over the states.

Amendments: These are the changes that have been made to the Constitution over the past 200 years. Few have been made because the amendment process is difficult. To amend the Constitution, Congress must pass the proposed amendment by two-thirds vote of both houses and then three-fourths of the states must approve it. Amendments deal with a wide variety of concerns, from the direct election establishing the income tax, to congressional pay raises, but a large portion of them are designed to protect and extend basic liberties. These protections are set out in the first ten Amendments, known as the Bill of Rights.

The Bill of Rights

First Amendment: Guarantees freedom of religion, speech, press, assembly, and petition

Second Amendment: Guarantees the right to bear arms

Third Amendment: Prohibits quartering solders in homes in peacetime

Fourth Amendment: Prohibits unreasonable search and seizure

Fifth Amendment: Guarantees due process of law; bans double jeopardy; protects against self-incrimination

Sixth Amendment: Guarantees rights to speedy, public trial and right to counsel in criminal cases

Seventh Amendment: Guarantees jury trial in civil cases

Eighth Amendment: Forbids cruel and unusual punishment, or excessive bail

Ninth Amendment: Stipulates that the rights of the people are not confined to those enumerated in the Constitution

Tenth Amendment: Stipulates that the powers not expressly delegated to the federal government or prohibited to the states are reserved to the states and people

---

Other Amendments have extended rights. The Thirteenth Amendment abolished slavery. The Fourteenth Amendment guarantees people equal protection under the laws and has been used to make most of the Bill of Rights applicable to the states. The Fifteenth Amendment gave black men the right to vote by prohibiting the government from denying a citizen the right to vote based on his race, color, or "previous condition of servitude" (a reference to slavery). The Nineteenth Amendment granted women the vote.

MORAL/ETHICAL THEORIES

When dealing with motions about whether or not certain policies or actions are moral or ethical, you need to know basic ethical theories so you can offer a good definition of what it means to be ethical or unethical in the context of the topic. Philosophers have debated ethics since the time of the ancient Greeks, so over the course of history, many theories have developed. Five are most commonly useful in middle school debate. Below are very simple statements of each.

Virtue Ethics: The roots of this theory lie with ancient Greek philosophers Plato and Aristotle. This philosophy emphasizes the character of the individual rather than the consequences of his or her action. It says that what is moral or ethical is what an honorable person would do in the same situation.

Hedonism: This philosophy deals with what is good or bad to pursue. It says that what is good is what gives pleasure and avoids pain. Some hedonists contend that what is good gives the greatest quantity of pleasure; others stress the quality of the pleasure. Because of the popular use of the word *hedonism*, many people wrongly think that hedonists emphasize sensual pleasure.

Deontology: The word deontology means "duty ethics." This theory determines rightness or wrongness from adherence to moral laws, such as the Ten Commandments, and equates right or wrong action with obedience or disobedience to these laws. Murder, for example, is always wrong. Helping the suffering is always right. Deontologists would say that a "little white lie" is wrong because one must always tell the truth, even if it hurts someone's feelings.

Utilitarianism: This theory is associated with the British philosophers Jeremy Bentham and John Stuart Mill. It emphasizes right and wrong actions. Utilitarianism gets its name from the belief that what was morally justifiable could be determined by applying the principle of "utility," which they defined as that which tends to produce pleasure, good, or happiness or prevents evil and unhappiness. These philosophers believed that society and politics should be based on the principle of the greatest happiness for the greatest number of people. An action is morally right if it provides as much good (utility) for the people affected as an alternative.

Consequentialism: This theory maintains that the consequences of one's actions are the basis on which to judge right or wrong. Think of the common saying "the ends justify the means."

When debating topics about ethics, you can choose either to consolidate all you arguments under one of these theories or to use several theories in one case by tying each argument to the theory that fits best with it. Remember when referring to moral theories that they are not all mutually exclusive. Some utilitarians are hedonists, while consequentialism is a very broad category that encompasses many schools that focus on the consequences of the act rather than goals or the virtue of the actor.

Debate Topics

Adoptions, International

Motion   **International adoptions do more harm than good**

Introduction   Many couples who cannot conceive biological children opt to adopt from foreign countries. They do so for several reasons. Some choose an international adoption because fewer restrictions are placed on who can adopt than in domestic adoptions. Other families want to help children who would have fewer chances in life because of the lack of resources in the country where they were born. Opponents of international adoption point to the variety of risks that arise in less-regulated situations. Some countries do not allow their youngest citizens to be adopted by outsiders because they fear for the child's safety and want to maintain their culture through a new generation.

Debating the Motion   Teams should research the countries that release the most infants and children for adoption and why they do so. Also interesting would be to look at statistics about the kinds of families who adopt, as harms or benefits might arise from the characteristics of adopting families. Finally, both teams should look for scandals or scams related to foreign adoptions.

Proposition: The proposition may want to research which countries do not allow foreign adoptions and look particularly at their reasons. Also look into general harms such as lack of medical information about the child or health and psychological problems attributable to lack of early care. The proposition must also clarify the term *harm*—what kinds of harms do they see—and who or what is being harmed—the children, families in general, other children in the adopting family, relations between countries, etc.

Opposition: The opposition has the option of either defending international adoptions as neutral or beneficial. In the case of neutrality, demonstrating that international adoptions are no more or less risky than the practice of adoption in general will derail the proposition's case. If the team decides to defend international adoption as beneficial, frame the benefits to clash with what has been set out by the proposition. For example, if the proposition is only talking about harms to international relations, talking only about benefits to individual children won't be considered clash unless the opposition links the two by saying that the benefits to the children outweigh the harms to relationships between the U.S. and other countries. Finally, the opposition could always argue a combination of the neutral and beneficial standpoints.

The relative ease of international adoption deters parents from adopting needy children in the United States. Other countries have fewer regulations and are less protective of the rights of the birth mother, making international adoption much easier. However, plenty of children in this country need stable homes and loving care—foreign adoptions prevent these children from being welcomed into good families. We permit foreign adoptions at the expense of our own children, which does more harm than good to our country.

International adoptions create a venue for human trafficking. Unscrupulous persons know wealthy Americans are desperate to adopt and forcibly take children from their parents or convince parents to sell their child. Recent abuses include adoptions in China (officials forced couples to put children up for adoption if they could not afford fines for violating family planning regulations), Samoa (parents were not informed that the adoption was permanent), and Vietnam (more than 250 babies were sold). The harms of taking children from loving families, as well as the ethical problems of selling human beings, outweigh any good.

Foreign adoptions are not adequately regulated. Because foreign adoptions are less regulated than those in the United States, parents often find out later that the child is not the age they thought she was or that the child has severe physical or psychological problems. Conversely, parents who ought not to be able to adopt manage to. American parents often see international adoption as the

International adoption is not the cause of adoption difficulties in the United States—it is the effect. The U.S. has many legal restrictions on domestic adoption, so some parents may not qualify and some may not want to go through the complicated process. Most children available for adoption in the United States are older, and most people looking to adopt want an infant. It is better that at least some children are adopted than that none are.

Adoptive parents should take precautions to make sure their adoption is legitimate, avoiding this harm. Parents should work with reputable adoption agencies, research the policies of the country they adopt from, and make sure they can investigate the orphanage or agency they adopt from to ensure it is legitimate. The U.S. government should, and does, advise potential adoptive parents on the safest ways to adopt. All of these safeguards are currently available. Although some abuse is inevitable, the benefit to the vast majority of children who receive loving homes that they otherwise would not have had does outweigh the tragedies of a few.

Such serious harms could occur anywhere—they are not confined to international adoptions. Domestic adoptions can go awry, and biological parents neglect their children when they decide they cannot cope with parenthood. While these parents' actions are in no way excusable, we would not conclude from this that domestic adoptions or childbearing do more harm than good. Rather easy route and consequently face problems greater than they are able to handle.

International adoptions make children objects—turning them into goods that can be purchased. Parents often pay great sums—disguised as "donations"—to adopt from overseas and often pay additional fees to expedite the process. In essence, the child is being bought; the dehumanization of such a process is harmful in and of itself.

A child who is removed from her birth country in an adoption loses her cultural birthright. Despite the adoptive parents' best intentions, this removal severs a child from the culture he was born into and prevents him from being able to truly identify with it. Aside from the fact that loss of culture is a harm in and of itself, such severing can lead to other harms—including children struggling with self-identity as they grow older.

than discredit all international adoptions, the U.S., other countries, adoption agencies, and adopting parents should be vigilant to ensure the protection of the child and the prospective family.

Adoptions cost money whether they are domestic or foreign. Adoption is a complicated process—to conduct it safely, an agency must exist to ensure no one is exploited and legal assistance is necessary; orphanages in Third World countries cannot afford to lose money with adoptions. It is no more degrading to pay for the expenses of an adoption than it would be to pay the expenses of prenatal care; however people choose to have children, they will have to spend money.

Responsible adoptive parents should be able to educate their children about the culture they were born into. All children struggle with self-identity; rather than leave orphans uncared for so that they may conform to the culture into which they were born, parents should help their child appreciate both their country of birth and of residence. Immigrants leave their homelands without major crises; a person's life should not have to revolve around the connection to the geographic region of birth.

OTHER MOTIONS:
 Foreign adoptions should be banned
 Foreign adoptions do more good than harm

RELATED MOTIONS:
 Adoption does more harm than good
 Adopting families should be required to adopt domestically

WEB LINKS:

- Adopt.com. "Pros and Cons." <http://international.adoption.com/foreign/pros-cons-of-international-adoption.html>. Site reviewing the pros and cons of international adoption.

- Newsweek. "The Case for International Adoption." <http://www.newsweek.com/2010/03/01/the-case-for-international-adoption.html\>. One person's experience with international adoption.

- U.S. Department of State, Office of Children's Issues. "Intercountry Adoption." <http://adoption.state.gov>. Statistics and background information on international adoptions.

Airline Passengers, Pay by Weight

Motion Airline passengers should pay according to their weight

Introduction The heyday of airlines seems to have passed as many travelers these days will never take a flight with complimentary snacks or pillows and blankets. Most airlines now charge for checking baggage, and some are talking about charging to use the bathroom! Some have suggested that airlines should go further and require larger passengers to pay extra or even to purchase two seats. Airline workers and some frequent fliers support this move, citing the inconvenience to those seated next to a large neighbor. Others cry out that this is discrimination and should not be allowed.

Debating the Motion Since this topic is very current, both teams should investigate the issues surrounding how airlines handle obese passengers.

Proposition: The proposition should be prepared to discuss a specific policy, including outlining how much passengers would have to pay and how such charges would be determined, as well as any exceptions they might recommend. The proposition can also focus on the rights of paying passengers to be comfortable and the benefits of such a policy to average, non-obese passengers.

Opposition: The opposition should discuss issues of discrimination—are people of certain sizes treated differently? It can also consider the logical consistency of the proposition's plan—should every pound cost extra cash or would the extra charges only kick in at a certain level of obesity?

PROS

Passengers who cannot comfortably buckle their seatbelts should be required to pay an additional fee because their extra weight will actually cost the airline more money to transport them. The heavier a plane is, the more fuel it consumes. Just as additional charges are imposed on the passenger who brings heavy bags, bringing extra weight on

CONS

It is wrong to punish people for something they may be unable to control. We support charging extra for heavy baggage because the passenger has chosen to pack extra or heavier items. However, many people are heavy despite efforts to diet or exercise, and it is unfair to penalize them. Furthermore, taking this argument to its logical conclusion would mean

PROS	CONS

your person will cost the airline—thus, a heavy passenger should have to pay more.

Charging larger passengers extra fees allows airlines to treat all passengers better. If obese people were forced to pay for two seats rather than one, then surrounding passengers would no longer be crowded and uncomfortable, as they might be when a large person is spilling over into their space.

Charging obese people extra could help fight the growing problem of obesity in the United States. Obesity has become a public health problem. While airlines are not obligated to contribute to the fight against it, it is a nice side benefit that charging extra could motivate individuals—particularly frequent fliers—to lose weight in order to save money. In addition, media coverage could bring more awareness about the issue.

This is not an issue of discrimination but rather of practicality. If someone takes up more than one seat, then he should pay for more than one seat. Forcing overweight people to pay for the price of two tickets is not a social comment on their appearance, but rather a realistic measure that requires people who take up more space to buy more space.

charging every passenger a different amount, since everyone weighs a slightly different amount—an idea that is clearly ridiculous.

If airlines are truly concerned about comfort, they should just make larger seats. The size of airplane seats is ridiculously small—even average-sized passengers complain about the lack of leg room and uncomfortably narrow width. The way to make flights less grueling is to provide adequate space.

It is unlikely that the higher fees would realistically affect levels of obesity. Most individuals do not fly regularly, so an occasional extra fee is unlikely to be a significant deterrent. Furthermore, obese people might simply look victimized, thus increasing sympathy for the overweight, rather than encouraging them to do more to fight the problem of unhealthy lifestyles.

To charge people according to their size is discriminatory. People should never be treated differently because of their personal appearance or stigmatized because of the way they look. This is especially true when we consider that obesity is an especially significant problem among people from low-income backgrounds—the plan would discriminate on more than one level. A "fat penalty" goes against basic human decency, as well as individuals' rights to be treated equally.

OTHER MOTIONS:
Passengers should pay by the pound
Overweight passengers should be required to buy two seats

RELATED MOTIONS:
It is unethical to charge passengers according to their size

WEB LINKS:
- Council on Size and Weight Discrimination. "Airline Seating." <http://www.cswd.org/docs/airlineseating.html>. Arguments opposed to the tax.
- News.com.au. "Call for Airlines to Charge Passenger 'Fat Tax'." <http://www.news.com.au/call-for-airlines-to-charge-passenger-fat-tax/story-0-1111114846588>. Article with arguments on both sides of the issue.
- Stocks, Jenny. "Budget Airline Considers 'Fat Tax' for Overweight Passengers." <http://www.dailymail.co.uk/travel/article-1172536/Ryanair-considers-fat-tax-overweight-passengers.html>. Article with arguments on both sides of the issue.

Animal Testing

Motion   **Medical testing on animals is acceptable**

Introduction   Animal experimentation goes back to the ancient Greeks, who dissected animals to better understand anatomy. Louis Pasteur used animal testing extensively in his research into smallpox, cholera, and anthrax. Over the course of the twentieth century, animal testing has become more controversial as the public has become more conscious of a responsibility to other living creatures. However, as medical advances lead to more medications with more unknown side effects, animal testing has increased. Most notably, after the Thalidomide tragedy in the early 1960s, where thousands of babies were born with severe physical defects attributable to the drug, the U.S. Congress passed strict legislation requiring extensive animal testing before releasing certain drugs.

Debating the Motion   Both teams will want to provide clear definitions: What is meant by *acceptable*? What is meant by *medical testing*? What species will be used? What limits would exist on testing and what conditions must the animals be kept in? Note that the motion does not require either team to defend animal testing as a good. Rather, the motion speaks about acceptability.

Proposition: The proposition must explain clearly what kind of drugs and procedures are worth animal testing, what kinds of animals will be used, and, most important, what does the nebulous term *acceptable* mean? This term is interesting because it allows the proposition to agree that animal testing is not an act to be undertaken lightly, but if it can be shown to be necessary or be shown that humans carry more moral weight than animals, then testing that ultimately saves human lives is acceptable.

Opposition: The opposition team must argue that animal testing is not acceptable and that the option of neutrality is not available. This can be argued both from an animal rights' perspective as well as that of the potential dangers that arise to humans from animal testing.

PROS

Animal testing is necessary to make sure that products are safe for humans. Developing medicines tend to have a lot of problems—we could never find enough human volunteers

CONS

Human subjects are capable of understanding the risks of a new medicine and have the ability to consent to testing. Before medicines are tested on humans, the human test subjects to conduct enough tests. Although medications must eventually be tested on humans, we can identify most problems by testing first on animals. Testing medicine on people before identifying these problems puts them at risk for no reason, and a process that minimizes risks to humans must be acceptable.

We have a greater duty to humans than to animals. Realistically, we cannot fully protect our own species without using other animals. Thus, we can sacrifice the lives of laboratory animals to help humans.

Animal testing benefits other animals as well. Losing a key species in an ecosystem poses a risk for all surrounding organisms. Currently, several species are suffering from incurable diseases—for example, the Tasmanian devil is being wiped out by a form of cancer. Medical research, involving animal testing, can help us determine how to cure these diseases. This result helps sustain the environment and the animals themselves, rendering this practice acceptable.

Humans have a relatively long life span. To study effects of a substance over a human's lifetime could take more than 80 years. Other animals develop faster, allowing us to identify long-term effects in relatively little time. This procedure prevents use of treatments that seem helpful but do harm in the long run. This makes testing on animals with shorter life spans necessary and thus acceptable.

are given a thorough briefing on the tests and the risks involved. Animals, on the other hand, do not understand their situation; if they did, they would refuse. It is immoral, and thus never acceptable, to take advantage of their helplessness.

As the more sentient beings, our moral duty is to protect those who cannot protect themselves. Thus, we have laws to protect the young, the old, and the infirm—we must likewise protect animals. Humans are already the most successful animals; we now need to help other creatures.

We wouldn't kill one person to save another and we should not do so with animals either. All creatures have intrinsic worth; actively choosing to disregard that worth is inexcusable and unacceptable. Besides, most testing does not focus on saving animals like the Tasmanian devil, and most species are unlikely to benefit from testing aimed only at helping humans.

Just as animals have radically different life spans, a variety of genetic differences limit their usefulness in medical research. There have been numerous cases where a substance seemed effective in animals and then had adverse effects in humans. Medicine eventually has to be tested on people, and that takes a long time—we must accept that. Using animals to "get closer" is simply wasting their lives and not helping humans, rendering it an unacceptable practice.

PROS

Humans are superior to other animals. The concept of human worth—that people have intrinsic value merely by being *human,* by having consciousness, is fundamental to any society. Proving moral superiority scientifically is impossible, but we assume it to be true. Thus, it is better to risk animals' lives than those of humans, which makes testing on animals instead of humans acceptable.

CONS

We have no reason to believe humans are worth more than other animals. We do not consider smart, successful, or athletic people to be morally superior to others. People are not better for their consciousness—if they were, we could experiment on infants and severely mentally disabled persons without a problem. We cannot prove that one being is worth more than others, so it is not acceptable to experiment on a creature without its informed consent.

OTHER MOTIONS:

It is unethical to test on animals

Testing on animals does more harm than good

RELATED MOTIONS:

Animals deserve the same moral consideration as humans

WEB LINKS:

- Markkula Center for Applied Ethics. "Of Cures and Creatures Great and Small." <http://www.scu.edu/ethics/publications/iie/v1n3/cures.html>. Summary of arguments on both sides of the issue.

- The Primate Diaries. "Animal Testing Statistics and Perspectives." <http://scienceblogs.com/primatediaries/2010/03/animal_testing_statistics.php>. British article opposed to testing.

Art Subsidies, Government

Motion **End government subsidies for the arts**

Introduction While we recognize that the arts play an important and even necessary role in life and thus should be saved, archived, preserved, created, and celebrated, many wonder whether it is the role of government to help fund them.

Debating the Motion Both teams should research the history of art sponsorship by the government and the level of funding currently allocated for art subsidies. They should also investigate what kinds of projects get funded and what kinds get rejected, as well as who the major recipients of government money are and how government grants compare with major art institutions' overall operating budgets.

Proposition: *Arts* is a very broad term, so the proposition must clearly define it. In this case, looking at how the government defines art, particularly for the purpose of giving grants, will allow the proposition to give a narrower yet arguable definition.

Opposition: The opposition might want to run a counter case wherein they propose not only to keep government art subsidies but actually increase them. A number of artists and art institutions have publicly declared the need for more government funding; looking into the specific needs and values of these programs can provide arguments and evidence for a strong counter case.

PROS

Government funds are an infinitesimal part of the operating budgets of major arts institutions. Most funds come from endowments or private donors. The percentage of government money in budgets is so small, in fact, that most institutions won't even miss it. If government funds are so unnecessary, government should not waste money where it isn't needed when so many other important programs struggle to make ends meet.

CONS

This may be true for major venues, but is certainly not so for small independent galleries and theaters. These are just as necessary as large, famous institutions because every artist needs a place to start before his art can be seen at the Museum of Modern Art or her music heard at Carnegie Hall. The absence of government funding will hurt young artists and will affect even major institutions in the long run.

Art is undeniably a very important part of human society and history, but you cannot eat it. As long as people are struggling to make ends meet, governments must give priority to programs involving housing, food, and health. These necessities must take precedence over art subsidies.

Government subsidies discourage charitable donations to arts institutions. If people believe that the government should and will cover the costs of art institutions, they consider their own contributions to be unnecessary. In the long run, the arts will suffer since private donations actually constitute a much larger portion of the funds needed to operate arts programs in this country. Government subsidies discourage small donors in particular because they think their gift is unimportant compared with a large government grant, yet many small donations together make a big difference.

The struggle for government subsidies discourages innovative art. Government funding stifles creativity; it creates pressure for artists to engage in projects that the government considers worth funding. Would a government bureaucracy have given Picasso, with his Cubist figures, funding when he was beginning his career? Government funding will create substandard work that contributes less to our society.

The process of giving government money is inherently politicized. When the government is involved, what is considered art is not based on artistic merit but on a political agenda. For example, many New Yorkers expressed outrage that the city government funded the Brooklyn Museum of Art's exhibit "Sensation," which included a painting of a black

We will always have poverty. We cannot ignore all that makes our culture rich, such as the arts, simply because society is imperfect. The arts are necessary for the advancement of our society because they open people's minds and encourage us to think creatively, which helps further innovation.

Private and government funding are not mutually exclusive; they should work in concert and not against each other. Arts institutions must make clear how their budgets work and where their money comes from so that patrons can understand that every little bit helps, even a student's donation of $10 or a family's contribution of $100.

The government does not impose restrictions on the art it funds. Government subsidies are given to a variety of artists and venues. Art is judged on its own merit—the more authentic it is, the more likely it will speak to someone and receive funding. Furthermore, this problem is not unique to government grants. As long as art is funded by anyone, there will be pressure to satisfy wealthy patrons.

This is the case whether artists seek funding from a public or a private source. Every artist must make strategic choices to garner necessary support. Most of history's greatest artists worked for patrons who had to be flattered. Without government aid, artists will have to seek money from private patrons, who can exploit artists.

Madonna covered in elephant dung. The government should not fund offensive art, yet all artists should have a venue to express themselves. Thus, the government cannot fund the arts in a fair manner.

The government cannot support all art, but this does not mean it cannot support any art. The government rewards taxpayers who give to charity, encourages parents to act responsibly, and engages in many social campaigns meant to better society. The government does not step outside its bounds by funding the arts any more than it does by having an art classroom in public elementary schools.

OTHER MOTIONS:

Art subsidies do more good than harm

The government should not support the private tastes of some citizens

Arts programs need government funding

Society has a responsibility to fund the arts

RELATED MOTIONS:

The government should support the private tastes of some citizens

WEB LINKS:

- Fulsom, Burton. "Is Your County Losing in Arts Subsidies?" <http://www.mackinac.org/97>. Article arguing against government funding of the arts.

- PBS. "Funding the Arts." <http://www.pbs.org/newshour/bb/entertainment/jan-june97/arts_3-10.html>. PBS interview with representatives on both sides of the issue.

- Sunset Caucus. "Eliminate the National Endowment for the Arts (NEA) Subsidy." <http://rsc.tomprice.house.gov/UploadedFiles/Waste_Action_Alert--03_04_10_NEA.pdf>. Article arguing that government funding of the arts through the NEA is wasteful.

Cell Phones in Schools

Motion   **Cell phones should not be permitted in schools**

Introduction   As technology advances and becomes more readily available, the reality that it can provide as many distractions as conveniences becomes ever more apparent. More and more individuals rely on cell phones as their primary form of communication, and so schools have had to cope with an influx of mobile phones into classrooms and hallways. Rules on cell phone use differ, with some schools allowing students to keep their phones throughout the day while some ban them entirely from school premises. The many potential harms and distractions posed by cell phones are apparent; however, some schools are easing restrictions in light of the potential benefits. For many students who enjoy their phones and their multitude of functions, this topic hits close to home.

Debating the Motion   Both teams should look for statistics on how cell phone possession and usage affect academic performance and social interactions in schools, as well as how many students have phones and what their primary usage is. Since many schools already have bans in place, teams should look into the particulars of current policies as well as their efficacy.

Proposition: This topic is very broad in scope. The proposition needs to begin by creating a specific plan. This would entail determining whether the ban would be absolute or partial, deciding what circumstances might pose exceptions, and whether having a phone set on vibrate or having a phone with Internet capabilities should affect authorities' decisions. Of course, any time the word *school* comes up, the proposition must define specifically the kinds of schools they mean: Do they want to narrow the scope in terms of age, public or private, urban or rural?

Opposition: The opposition also has a number of options for this topic. Depending on how the motion is narrowed by the proposition, the opposition can either argue broadly against any kind of ban or more specifically against a total ban with special exceptions. A counter case detailing exactly how students should be allowed to have and use phones in schools is also a possibility in opposing a blanket ban.

PROS

Cell phones should be banned from K–12 schools because having them in the building presents a possible distraction. School is for learning; the school environment is designed to minimize distractions so that students can focus on their work. Cell phones could distract and detract from work in a number of ways: students could decide to play games or text or they could be distracted by incoming calls from family and friends.

While text and instant messaging can be fun, they can also be used by bullies. We all know that bullying is a serious problem in schools and that cyber-bullying is on the rise to the extent that some students have taken their own lives to escape it. Bullies relish the use of cell phones because it gives them anonymity when harassing their victim. By blocking their number from appearing, bullies can text offensive messages or post inappropriate images and the victim will only see that it comes from "number blocked" or "caller unknown." Without a means of detection, bullies can go unpunished.

CONS

In and of themselves, cell phones do not present a distraction. We cannot ignore the many benefits that a cell phone might offer in a school environment—as a tool for communication during an emergency or as a calculator during teacher-designated moments, for example. Therefore, schools should impose restrictions on the use of the phones rather than banning them altogether. By requiring phones to be off during the day or kept in lockers, students could still have access to them at appropriate times such as for personal use during lunch and study hall or before and after school to call to their families. Students could also have access to their phones during an emergency such as an unexpected school closing. In these cases, students could turn their phones on or retrieve them from their lockers.

Bullying is a problem regardless of whether or not cell phones are allowed in schools. Schools must create a safe environment for all students; school administrators need to understand that technology can offer both an avenue for bullying and a tool for combating it. Schools should teach victims how they can fight back against a cyber-bully and how to avoid cyber-bullying (give your number only to those you trust; ask your service provider to investigate harassing calls; block threatening callers and texters). In fact, cell phones could be used to combat bullying by calling a teacher for help or to access a school hotline or textline to anonymously report bullying and ask for help.

PROS

Cell phones can be used to cheat on assignments and exams. All cell phones have calculators that could be used to determine answers during exams where calculators are not allowed, such as most state tests for children in middle school grades and younger. Also, as more and more features are added to cell phones, they could be used to cheat in a variety of ways. Students could text each other answers, photograph the exam to show others what to expect, or even access the Internet to find answers to test questions. A student could even have access to an entire book or its annotated summary on a phone during a literature exam!

Many cell phones now come with Internet access—allowing such unrestricted access in school could lead to students browsing for inappropriate content or inappropriate websites. While schools have installed filters on their computers to protect students from websites with violent or sexual content, schools cannot control access to Internet sites that a student could receive on her phone.

If contact needs to be made with families, the school should be responsible. Schools can use one-call alert systems and email messages to communicate with parents in emergencies; students who need to check in on arrival can use office or classroom phones. Students and parents without cell phones manage with these tools, so everyone else can, too. The means of ready communication are already in place, no need to add cell phones.

CONS

Students can cheat in a number of ways not involving cell phones. Just as teachers and other school staff must be vigilant about old-fashioned methods of cheating such as hidden notes or answers copied onto the back of a hand, they need to be vigilant in watching test takers to make sure that phones do not appear. A student cannot use his phone to cheat without getting it out to look at it, and a teacher would notice this action the same way she might notice a student taking out hidden notes. Consider—students use notes to cheat on tests, but we don't ban note taking in school! Accordingly, we shouldn't ban cell phones, either.

Just because some students may view inappropriate content is no reason to impose a blanket ban on phones. Benefits of phones greatly outweigh their potential for harm, thus, schools should work to create rules to protect students from violent or sexual content. Such rules could include requiring phones to be off during the day or left in lockers. Schools could also require students to disable their Internet access upon arriving at school.

Cell phones are an important additional means of communication and should not be banned in schools. Students can check in with parents as they arrive and leave each day; in case of emergency, cell phones are the most readily available way for students to get in touch with parents or guardians.

Allowing students to use cell phones in some circumstances would open the door to students using them at inappropriate times or during activities when their attention needs to be focused on the task at hand. Students might also take advantage of situations where they are allowed to use their phones for a specific assignment to utilize their phones for texting or web browsing. Permitting the use of cell phones could also serve to stigmatize those who don't have a cell phone—a student would surely stick out using a clunky graphing calculator or bulky desktop to do math or surf the web if her friends and fellow students are using sleek phones.

Cell phones should not be banned because they can also be used as a tool during class when directed by the teacher. Since most students have cell phones and cell phones have increasingly complex tools built in, schools could save money by purchasing fewer calculators or fewer copies of books and allowing students to take advantage of such functions or to access such material on their phones instead. Indeed, many phones now function as mini-computers; schools could save a great deal of money and better incorporate technology into their curricula by utilizing the cell phone tools that students already have.

OTHER MOTIONS:

Cell phones should be banned in all schools K–12

The use of cell phones should be banned in schools except in an emergency

Cell phones should be prohibited in all middle and high schools

Cell phones should be banned from college classrooms

RELATED MOTIONS:

Cell phones for children do more harm than good

Cell phones are detrimental to a child's education

WEB LINKS:

- Bullying Statistics. "Text Bullying." <http://www.bullyingstatistics.org/content/text-bullying.html>. Discusses the impact of text bullying.

- CBS News. "School Cell Phone Ban Causes Uproar." <http://www.cbsnews.com/stories/2006/05/12/national/main1616330.shtml>. Report on reaction to cell phone ban in New York City schools.

- Cell Phones in Learning. "New Statistics on Teen Cell Phone Use." <http://www.cellphonesinlearning.com/2008/09/new-statistics-on-teen-cell-phone-use.html>. This site includes statistics about teen phone use and suggests ways in which to incorporate cell phones as learning tools in curricula.

Cell Phones while Driving

Motion **Use of cell phones while driving should be banned**

Introduction In the short span of a decade, cell phones have drastically increased in popularity and common use. However, cell phones have brought some new problems. One of the chief controversies related to cell phones is the issue of using them while driving. Studies suggest that driving while talking is as dangerous as driving drunk—many countries have banned talking on the phone while driving. The United States currently varies in regulations among the states.

Debating the Motion Because all manner of bans currently exist, teams should research the rules in other countries as well as in various states. They should also research the ample statistics associated with the issue.

Proposition: The word *use* is very vague, so the proposition should begin by stating exactly what will be banned. Does this ban allow hands-free talking with headsets and voice controls or no cell phones in use in the car at all? Does it apply only to drivers or to passengers as well? The team also must state whether the ban would be total or if exceptions would be made.

Opposition: If the proposition does not carefully define what it means to *use* a cell phone, the opposition should exploit this. Cell phones serve many functions from phone to web browser, to GPS device or sound system. Should all these uses be banned?

PROS

Holding a cell phone while driving is dangerous because one hand is not on the wheel for an extended period. In the case of an emergency where shifting or steering is unexpectedly necessary, having one hand unavailable will slow the driver's reaction time and increase the chance of an accident.

CONS

This argument is not unique to cell phones. Eating or putting on make-up also cause drivers to take a hand off the wheel, but we do not ban these actions. Some drivers cannot drive safely while talking on the phone; these drivers should not use their cell phones while driving. Drivers who can, however, should be allowed to do so.

All cell phones can cause distractions, so talking on phones in moving cars should be totally banned. Dropped calls, answering incoming calls, or conversations with alarming and unexpected information can distract a driver from the road. The driver cannot control all distractions, and some cannot reasonably be avoided, but the use of cell phones while driving is unnecessary.

There will always be distractions. Literally anything—other passengers, commotion outside, shocking news on the radio—might distract a driver. Rather than ban cell phones, we should focus on driver education that instructs drivers on handling interruptions while driving.

Smart phones have a variety of functions that increase the possibility of distraction. More and more drivers engage in activities like texting or web surfing while on the road. Drivers may not intend to drive recklessly but find themselves doing so when making plans on the phone. It is safer to simply ban all cell phone use while driving.

We can ban drivers from texting or surfing the web while driving. These activities clearly take their eyes off the road. However, the fact that a phone has multiple functions does not make it inherently dangerous. These reckless activities should be punishable, but drivers should be able to talk on the phone as it is not an excessive distraction.

Teens are more likely to use phones in cars. Teens are already the highest-risk drivers; a cell phone ban would decrease reckless driving proportionately more among the most dangerous group.

To get a license, teens must complete driver education. Since driver education has become widespread, drunk driving has decreased significantly. These courses should also focus on eliminating distractions when driving and emphasize the dangers of cell phones. This reduces the danger without the heavy-handedness of a ban.

Most other countries regulate the use of phones while driving; the United States should do the same. If other countries can implement this safety law with no devastating consequences, the U.S. can, too.

"Everyone else does it" is not a reason to do something. Everyone else uses the metric system, but we don't. The United States values each state's autonomy so that each group of people is governed as it sees fit; this issue should be left to state governments.

There is no significant disadvantage to a ban, so even if it only helps a little bit, it is worth it. Americans have been driving for about a century, while cell phones have only been used for a decade or two. People do not need to use the phone while driving, and it is a

Unnecessary federal bans increase government power and diminish respect for individuals. As noted above, state-by-state autonomy is very important in our country. Furthermore, cell phones have become an important part of our lives. A century ago, many Americans

PROS	CONS
proven distraction. If some lives are saved by the ban, then it is worth it.	did not have automobiles, but we would not argue that people can easily give them up. Sometimes, a driver needs to contact someone using his cell phone, and he should be able to do so.

OTHER MOTIONS:

Handheld devices should be forbidden while driving

Cell phones in cars are necessary

RELATED MOTIONS:

The presence of cell phones in cars does more good than harm

GPS devices in cars should be banned

WEB LINKS:

• Cellular-News "Countries that Ban Cell Phones While Driving." <http://www.cellular-news.com/car_bans/>. List of countries banning the use of cell phones while driving.

• CNNMoney.com. "Cell Phone Driving Bans Don't Work." <http://money.cnn.com/2010/01/29/autos/cell_phone_law_results/>. Review of a study revealing that cell phone bans have no effect on crash rates.

• Glassbrenner, Donna, and Tony Jianqiang Ye. "Driver Cell Phone Use in 2006." <http://www-nrd.nhtsa.dot.gov/Pubs/810790.PDF>. Statistics on driver cell phone use.

• Ogg, Erica. "Cell Phones as Dangerous as Drunk Driving." <http://news.cnet.com/8301-10784_3-6090342-7.html>. Article on the dangers of using cell phones while driving.

Charter Schools

Motion   **Charter schools should be disbanded in favor of school vouchers**

Introduction   Charter schools are one of the most controversial issues in education. Charter schools are public schools that receive public money but have been freed from some of the regulations that govern other public schools in order to try to improve the standard of public education. They were designed to enable experimentation and creativity to achieve more student success and allow for earlier subject concentration and specialization. Students are not assigned to these schools; they attend charter schools by choice. Many opponents favor spending charter money on a school voucher system. They insist that good schools already exist and that vouchers will make these available to all. Supporters argue that the charter school movement is the only reform that is showing success with struggling students.

Debating the Motion   Both teams need to research charter schools and school vouchers. Because rules and regulations about charter schools and vouchers vary, the teams should become familiar with local and state policies as well as those in other areas. Teams might also research statistics on the efficacy of vouchers and compare those to statistics on charter schools.

Proposition: The proposition would do well to present an action plan that includes information about who would be eligible for vouchers, what the vouchers could be used for, and a timeline and plan for closing charter schools to minimize impact on students and families. The plan might include proposals like free information sessions for parents or a five-year time frame in which to implement the plan, etc.

Opposition: Much information is available that supports charter schools, so arguing that charter schools are superior to all other education alternatives would be easy. By showing that charter schools are the best of all options, the opposition can demonstrate that no other program makes sense—which necessarily counters the proposition statement that vouchers are superior. However, as is almost always the case, the opposition has other options in framing their case. They could also argue against the voucher program. If the opposition could show that the voucher program is the least desirable of all possible education alternatives, then demonstrating the value of charter schools would be unnecessary.

PROS

Most people agree that U.S. public schools need reform, but charter schools are not the answer. They are an experiment that has failed. Poorly performing charter schools have been forced to close, money for the schools has been misused, and, most important, they have not shown long-term success. School vouchers would permit low-income families to send their children to successful private institutions that they now cannot afford.

Charter schools offer parents only a limited choice—another version of public school. Vouchers allow parents to make the best choice for their children. They can choose a local public school or they can choose private or parochial schools if they feel these would be better for their children.

Charter schools require significant state and local funding. Because these schools often are start-up institutions, their costs are enormous. They have to search for talent, build basics like libraries, purchase furniture, and obtain facilities. If we reallocated all the money currently going to charter schools, we would have more than enough funds for vouchers.

CONS

True, our public schools are struggling, but struggling or not, we cannot abandon public education. We cannot afford to send every child to a private school nor would the private schools accept them all. Charter schools currently are the best option for improving public education. Charter schools bring innovative programs and individuals to the field of education, which can only help in the long run. Charter schools often have extended days and certainly offer rigorous programs—all of which benefit students in many ways. They also offer post-high school counseling programs that follow the student through college and beyond, offering them assistance in getting part-time and summer jobs during the college years, help in preparing for exams like the LSAT and MCAT, and guidance around getting into graduate school. Most public schools, on the other hand, at most help high school juniors and seniors apply to colleges—students are on their own from graduation on. Charter schools are an example to other public schools and an equalizer for students who cannot afford private schools.

Since most charter schools do not restrict who can attend, parents can choose the school that best serves their children. Charter school legislation has resulted in a wide variety of choices. These range from the size of a school to the length of a school day to the curriculum used to the kinds of trips and other extracurricular activities offered.

Charter schools actually cost less than vouchers because they often get significant support from private donors and institutions. In contrast, vouchers are paid for totally from public funds. If we support charter schools, we can improve education standards without imposing more taxes.

Vouchers are the best tool for improving neighborhood public schools because they offer competition. When parents have a workable alternative, they will choose the school that they believe will best educate their children. Such competition will force public schools to innovate and to improve their level of instruction. Unfortunately, public schools, traditional or charter, are all too often bound by bureaucratic regulations and requirements that make innovation difficult. Faced with the need to offer a superior experience or have no or few students, public schools may well rise to the challenge. If so, then all the students will be winners; wherever they attend class, they will get a good education.

Charter schools are the best tool for improving the neighborhood public school because they offer much-needed competition. Because they are also public schools and must work within similar constraints, any innovations implemented in charter schools are more likely to be applicable in a public school than those developed in private schools. Charter schools also attract new and young talent to the field of education. These teachers and administrators will ultimately be able to bring fresh ideas and processes to the sphere of public education. Charter schools are the best way to provide the innovation that will help improve the average public school.

OTHER MOTIONS:

School vouchers trump charter schools

Charter schools are the best way to improve public education

RELATED MOTIONS:

School vouchers make education equal for all students

Parents have the right to choose the best education for their children

WEB LINKS:

- AFL-CIO. "Charter Schools and School Vouchers." <http://www.aflcio.org/issues/education/vouchers.cfm>. Article outlining the arguments in opposition to charter schools.

- Brookings. "Vouchers and Charter Schools: the Latest Evidence." <http://www.brookings.edu/events/2000/0224education.aspx>. Transcript of a panel discussion of charter schools by education experts.

Cigarettes, Ban

Motion **Cigarettes should be illegal**

Introduction Since the 1960s, society has become increasingly aware of the health effects of tobacco products. Many states have placed high taxes on cigarettes, while the federal government regulates when, where, and how cigarette companies may advertise. According to the National Institutes of Health, 23 percent of American men and 18 percent of American women still smoke cigarettes, despite increasing regulation. Given the severe health and social consequences of smoking, some insist that cigarettes and other tobacco products be banned. Others argue that a ban violates autonomy. Historians note that the failure of Prohibition indicates that a ban would be largely unsuccessful and potentially dangerous.

Debating the Motion Teams can research two lines of inquiry in preparing for this topic. The first is the general impact of tobacco products on society. This includes the cost of health care, the cost of cigarettes, and even the money that tobacco companies bring to certain communities. The second would be to look at the legal ramifications of such a move. Both teams should research whether such a ban could be passed and enforced under our legal system. Remember also that no one is required to argue that cigarettes are good or bad, only whether they should be made illegal or not.

Proposition: The proposition team might want to find some precedents to help them lay out a detailed plan for the ban.

Opposition: The opposition might research other bans that have failed, like Prohibition and the ban on marijuana.

PROS

The federal government already bans other dangerous drugs. Marijuana is illegal in the United States—many argue that cigarettes are worse than marijuana as they are addictive. Drugs are banned because they have a negative effect on society—addicts are less

CONS

America's war on drugs has been largely unsuccessful. America imprisons a higher percentage of its population than any other country. According to the Bureau of Justice Statistics, approximately 20 percent of those in prison are incarcerated for drug-related productive, prone to commit crimes to get money for drugs, die younger, and their children are more likely to become addicts. Although cigarettes are certainly much less destructive than cocaine or heroin, they nevertheless have a negative effect on society and individuals and thus should be banned.

The government has a vested interest in keeping its citizens alive. The Centers for Disease Control (CDC) estimates that on average, a smoker's life expectancy is 13 to 14 years less than a nonsmoker. The Supreme Court has ruled that states can ban euthanasia because a state has a fair interest in preserving life. Although the Court has not approved a ban on cigarettes, tobacco products are essentially a form of suicide; tobacco companies are giving people a product that slowly kills them.

Cigarettes cost society money. The CDC estimates that cigarette smoking annually costs the United States $97 billion in lost productivity and $96 billion in health care expenses—$10 billion of which is related to secondhand smoke. Smokers tend to be low-income individuals, so much of their health expenses are paid for by Medicaid. The rest of society should not have to foot the bill for a smoker's decision to engage in self-destructive behavior.

A ban is really the only option the government has left. The U.S. government has launched awareness campaigns and limited tobacco companies' advertising possibilities as much

offenses. Unscrupulous individuals make a business of drug smuggling; the high stakes of the trade increase gang activity, and civilians are often the victims of gang/drug violence and shootings. These problems arguably make the benefit of getting extremely dangerous drugs off the streets obvious, but cigarette addicts do not cause the same social problems that drug addicts do; banning cigarettes would create the problems of a black market for no good reason.

The government cannot ban everything that carries a risk. Under this logic, the government would ban all unhealthy foods, most kinds of alcohol, and require people to exercise daily. Americans are entitled to a certain degree of autonomy; people have smoked cigarettes for more than one hundred years without the collapse of society. A ban on cigarettes is unnecessary and simply violates a person's right to control her own life.

The CDC's estimates are twisted to reach a desired end. First, it does not take the amount of taxes paid on packs of cigarettes into consideration. It also does not consider the money saved on health care, pensions, and Social Security payments by smokers' early deaths. Duke University economist W. Kip Viscusi estimates that, when all the expenses incurred by aging citizens are considered, society saves 83 cents for every pack of cigarettes sold.

People thought the Eighteenth Amendment would rid society of alcohol. Prohibition, however, was largely unsuccessful. If people are aware that smoking is bad for them and are as is constitutionally permissible. Many states have placed taxes on cigarettes that more than double the cost. The government has exhausted its soft-power options for getting people to quit smoking. While these measures have helped, they haven't stopped the problem entirely—a ban would rid our society of smoking altogether.

willing to pay large amounts of money to smoke anyway, we can conclude that most likely cigarettes will still be smoked even if they are banned; a black market is more dangerous than smoking to both smokers and nonsmokers. Furthermore, the proposition implies that previous measures have not worked, whereas the Public Health Service statistics suggest otherwise. In 1964, 50 percent of American men and 46 percent of American women smoked; in 2008, the National Center for Health Statistics reports that those numbers were 23 percent and 20 percent, respectively. In an ideal world, no one would smoke. In reality, it is better to try to convince people not to smoke than to try to ban them from it.

OTHER MOTIONS:

Ban smoking in all public places

Substance bans do not work

RELATED MOTIONS:

Smokers have the right to smoke where they want

Ban all tobacco products

WEB LINKS:

- Haig, Scott. "Fixing Health Care Cheaply, Chapter 1: Butt Out." <http://www.time.com/time/health/article/0,8599,1889469,00.html>. Article advocating a ban on tobacco.

- Quit Smoking Hub. "2010 Smoking Statistics—US and Worldwide." <http://www.quitsmokinghub.com/blog/2010/02/2010-smoking-statistics-us-and-worldwide/>. Statistical resource.

- SmokingLobby. <http://www.smokinglobby.com/>. Online smokers' rights forum.

Cloning

Motion **Cloning should be legal**

Introduction Cloning is a topic that stirs deep emotions. Scientists agree that cloning an entire human seems like a very distant possibility that will not happen in our lifetimes, but they do have the technology to clone other living organisms right now, ranging from sheep to perhaps parts of humans. Whenever we embark on the exploration of technology as futuristic sounding as this, it always brings up the question: Just because we can, does that mean we should?

Debating the Motion This debate involves two elements: the scientific and the moral/ethical. Both teams should research what cloning entails and its potential applications; they should also review the literature on the ethical aspects of cloning. Finally, both teams need to research recent legislative proposals calling for a ban or restrictions on cloning.

Proposition: For the proposition, a major focus of this topic is the benefits that could potentially arise from cloning. The team might also want to look into the benefits of other controversial procedures to help justify making cloning legal.

Opposition: The opposition has two options. The first would be to argue for making cloning illegal. Talking about the dangers of cloning and the moral slippery slope will speak to this particular case. On the other hand, the opposition might want to argue that cloning is an area of science in which the government should not be involved.

PROS	CONS
Cloning could be a reproductive option for infertile couples. Currently, such families have to turn to adoption or surrogacy. While these are acceptable options for some couples, for others they are undesirable—many feel strongly about having biological connection to their children, while surrogacy can lead to legal disputes over custody. Cloning would result in children that are genetically	*Allowing parents to have children via cloning creates too much of a risk of unethical conduct.* If a couple cannot have children, sufficient options—adoption or surrogacy—are already available. Allowing people to reproduce via cloning presents legitimate dangers. Irresponsible adults may choose to clone themselves to try to live forever or for the sole purpose of providing transplant

identical to a parent. This can have long-term benefits—cloned children can be a source of bone marrow, blood, or stem cells for their parent if needed.

Cloning technology could be used to develop organs for medical procedures. Currently, many more people are waiting for organs than are organs available. One of the major goals of research cloning would be to produce organs so that people could receive needed transplants without requiring someone else to donate an organ or lose his life.

The best way to control the outcomes of research cloning is to legalize it. By outlawing it, we would drive this research underground where the danger truly lies. "Mad scientists" are far more dangerous if they are hidden from the eyes of responsible scientists and ethicists. By legalizing research cloning, we can regulate it and ensure the research is done responsibly and ethically.

The research done via cloning could be adapted to create individualized therapies for debilitating diseases like Alzheimer's or Parkinson's that currently ravage our society and are without cures or effective treatments. These degenerative diseases could be addressed by using cloning to rebuild the organs and bodily systems that need fixing.

material for family members. The ethical pitfalls are too grave to allow research cloning to exist.

Even if organ cloning could save some lives, it would certainly destroy others—the lives of the embryos used in such processes. Most of the research being done on this front requires the use of embryonic stem cells, thus human embryos are destroyed just so we can use their cells. It is morally unacceptable to use human embryos as a means to an end.

Cloning requires advanced tools and technology and will not go underground anyway. Doing it without proper support is not like making bathtub gin during Prohibition—your average Joe cannot cook up a cloning lab in his basement. Therefore, we need not worry about driving this technology underground. Rather, the best way to prevent science fiction from becoming reality is to ban it from the get-go.

Using science to push humans to live longer goes against nature. Degenerative diseases have become more and more common as our population has aged and reached new heights in life expectancy. We find that as people push into their 80s and further, bodies start to break down. What this tells us is not that we need some space-age technology to turn an 80-year-old back into a 20-year-old, but rather that human bodies have limits even science cannot overcome. People die at a certain age because bodies were made to last only so long.

OTHER MOTIONS:

Human cloning should be legal

Ban cloning

Ban human cloning

RELATED MOTIONS:

Cloning is unethical

Stem cell research should be government-funded

Stem cell research is unethical

WEB LINKS:

- Bionet. "Human Cloning: The Risks." <http://www.bionetonline.org/english/content/sc_cont5.htm>. Arguments against cloning.

- CNN. "Ethics of Human Cloning." <http://archives.cnn.com/2001/COMMUNITY/08/07/caplan.cnna/>. Interview with a medical ethicist on the subject.

- HumanCloning.org. "The Benefits of Human Cloning." <http://www.humancloning.org/benefits.php>. List of arguments in support of human cloning.

Contraceptives in Schools

Motion   **Schools should provide free contraceptives**

Introduction   Schools provide students with many materials—from pencils to laptops to bandages and icepacks. Should schools extend their help by providing kids with contraceptives? Even though we might not want to admit it, kids are experimenting with sex at ever-younger ages. Schools already care for students in a variety of ways, so some argue that providing students with free contraceptives should be added to schools' responsibilities. Others believe that providing condoms to children is completely out of line and encourages inappropriate behavior.

Debating the Motion   Both teams should research information about teen and preteen rates of sexual activity, sexually transmitted diseases, and pregnancy. Some schools already provide condoms to their students, so both teams should also research these schools' policies and their effect.

Proposition: The proposition needs to define the kinds of schools it proposes should adopt contraceptive-distribution policies, focusing especially on the age of the students. This topic definitely requires the proposition to lay out a detailed program: the kind of contraceptives; who will be in charge of distributing them, and what, if any, counseling or consent would be required.

Opposition: The opposition has two courses of argumentation to pursue and can choose to pursue only one or use a combination of both. The first, more general stance, is that schools should not offer contraceptives at all. The second would be to attack specific aspects of the proposition's case, such as age range or system of distribution.

PROS

While schools need to teach academic skills, they also need to prepare students for life in general. Schools teach children skills ranging from cooking to driving—giving them the tools for safer sex is a natural extension of their mandate to instruct.

CONS

While lessons in life are important, schools are not the only source of information and instruction. A school might offer drivers' education, but it certainly doesn't give every student in the driving class a car. Likewise, a school can teach what to do to prevent pregnancy and sexually transmitted diseases, but it is in no way responsible for providing contraceptives.

Schools already provide necessary equipment to students—basketballs, writing paper, textbooks, for example; they can provide contraceptives as well. Some larger schools also provide health services. Students can get check-ups, glasses, even braces in some places because schools recognize that some parents cannot provide these needed services and devices. If a student is engaging in sex, birth control is just as necessary. The school is the perfect place and institution to provide it.

Fewer and fewer schools provide health care, and those health services they do provide are the ones parents cannot provide. Parents can provide basic contraceptives if they see fit.

Schools are the logical place for a student to look for information about making sex safer. Many children are uncomfortable talking to their parents about sex; some parents would refuse to provide contraceptives to their children. With or without their parents' consent, however, many students will engage in sexual activity. What a student cannot talk to his parents about, he may discuss with a favorite teacher, counselor, or peer educator at school.

By stepping in where they shouldn't, schools are actually making the communication problem worse. If a teen knows she can talk to a counselor at school, she is less likely to talk with her parents. Students with poor relationships with their families are more likely to engage in risky sexual activity.

By providing contraceptives, schools are recognizing the reality that students will have sex, whether parents and other adults like it or not. Schools are also recognizing their responsibility to keep students as safe as possible. Schools can say "don't bully," yet know that bullying will still happen, so they have programs to address the problem. Likewise, schools can encourage abstinence and responsible behavior, but need to plan for the realities of life.

Providing contraceptives is not making sex "safer." While some teens may be having sex, making condoms and other forms of birth control easily available will encourage more students to engage in sexual behavior. Without a doubt, these kids are more at risk for pregnancy and contracting a sexually transmitted disease. There is a difference between recognizing reality by providing sex education courses and encouraging kids to have sex before they are adults by giving them condoms.

Teen pregnancy and sexually transmitted diseases interfere with schools' mission of educating children. They are enormous distractions and cause repeated absences. If, by giving out condoms and providing information about

If a school is worried about distractions, handing out condoms and encouraging sexual behavior are the worst possible actions. For hormone-crazed teenagers, nothing is more distracting than contact with their gender

PROS	CONS
birth control, a school can reduce absenteeism and address other issues that distract from education, then a school is acting as it should and is working toward fulfilling its mission.	of choice; by handing out contraceptives, schools encourage this contact and definitely increase distraction. Distributing condoms and birth control is not the job of the school nor does such distribution help the school fulfill its mission because birth control does not contribute to a school's ability to educate children.

OTHER MOTIONS:

Schools should hand out condoms

Schools should provide free contraceptives

RELATED MOTIONS:

Students have a right to contraceptives without parental consent

States should not require parental consent for students seeking sexual and reproductive health care

WEB LINKS:

- Associated Press. "Most OK with Birth Control at School, Poll Finds." <http://www.msnbc.msn.com/id/21577133/>. Results of poll on the subject. The article also contains a link to a middle school in Portland, Maine, that started providing contraceptives.

- Bloomberg Businessweek. "The Debate Room: Schools Should Give Kids Free Contaceptives." <http://www.businessweek.com/debateroom/archives/2009/07/schools_should.html>. Article addressing both sides of the issue.

- Washington Post. "The Debate: Contraceptives in Schools." <http://voices.washingtonpost.com/parenting/2007/11/the_debate_contraceptives_in_s.html>. Article providing background on the issue.

Copenhagen Accord

Motion   **The Copenhagen Accord does not go far enough**

Introduction   In 2009, the Copenhagen Accord was created to address changing standards in environmental science and the imminent expiration of the Kyoto Protocol, which was the first international agreement that addressed climate change. Many have been highly critical of this Accord, which was meant to take us even further toward protecting our planet. Critics decry the fact that the Accord is nonbinding and does not set concrete goals, allowing countries to set their own within a certain time frame. Proponents counter that the Accord extends the terms of the expiring Kyoto Protocol and reaffirms the commitment of developed countries to aid developing nations in addressing climate change. As the effects of climate change become more and more apparent, we can all agree that environmental standards are needed. The question is: Does the Accord go far enough to accomplish such needed change?

Debating the Motion   Obviously, both teams should be thoroughly versed in the Kyoto Protocol and the Copenhagen Accord. Research on the success of the Protocol and on the continuing evolution of the Accord would also be helpful. Because the phrase "go far enough" is rather vague, though common in debate, both sides need to attempt to clarify what this means.

Proposition: The proposition should explain what alterations would be required for the Accord to go further. This might include requiring a binding agreement, setting blanket goals for all countries or goals specific to a country's current emissions. In terms of "going far enough," the team needs to explain what they think an international agreement should do and, more basically, what is needed to stop and then reverse climate change as soon as possible.

Opposition: How the team defines "far enough" will have a lot to do with what options are available to counter the proposition's case. The opposition might want to explain why the Accord may have gone as far as it can, bearing in mind that even though the Accord may not be sufficient to completely reverse climate change, that doesn't mean that the Accord is insufficient. The opposition might want to speak about the Accord as a necessary part of a larger campaign to save the environment. If this is the case, the opposition might want to present a counter case in which they speak about what is required to stop climate change and why the Accord is a necessary part of achieving environmental goals.

PROS

Unlike the Kyoto Protocol, the Copenhagen Accord is nonbinding and thus is more likely to fail. Rather than being an actual plan of action, the agreement has been reduced to the level of making suggestions that the signing countries will have an incentive to abandon as soon as their financial interests lead them in another direction. This is putting financial considerations in direct competition with the greater good of the environment; sadly, history shows that finance usually wins and the environment suffers. The Accord needs to be binding international law if it is to ensure that its provisions are actually implemented.

The Copenhagen Accord is flawed in that it includes a continuation of the Kyoto Protocol as part of its stipulations. That agreement was ineffectual and basically ignored. The Kyoto Protocol accomplished little for the environment, and a program whose only binding element is a continuation of it can expect to be just as ineffectual.

The Copenhagen Accord is nothing but a general list of the damaging effects of climate change and vague goals to address them. Without stating any means to achieve the goals, it cannot be an effective plan for reversing environmental damage. The Accord needs to include real steps and enforceable caps on emissions, for example, as well as require fuel economy in vehicles and the gradual move away from fossil fuels, if we are to have any real hope of

CONS

No international authority is in place that can really force sovereign nations to act in specific ways. Placing binding requirements on any nation is impossible—many nations, for example, ignore "binding" U.N. human rights covenants, because no international police agency or real mechanism of enforcement is in place. It also makes no sense to impose binding regulations on developing nations that might find meeting all standards and regulations to be impossible. At the very least, the Copenhagen Accord provides useful suggestions and a yardstick so that citizens can see how in keeping with the Accord their governments are.

Perfect or not, Kyoto was the world's first major step toward recognizing the extensive damage humanity had done to the planet. It was a first attempt at working together to improve the atmosphere, the oceans, and the land. Its initial goal of halting environmental damage was the first step toward beginning to repair that damage. As the Kyoto Protocol was scheduled to expire in 2012, the Copenhagen Accord did well to extend it so the nations of the world can continue to work together, and, at the very least, ensure that environmental issues are discussed and debated.

The flexibility of the Copenhagen Accord is a benefit, not a flaw. General goals are a necessary first step in developing a comprehensive approach to a problem; they shape the directions of our research and future plans that will be needed to save our environment. It was a logical first step. In addition, the Copenhagen Accord did something better than setting a concrete goal that countries may or may not have been willing or able to

PROS	CONS
saving the environment. And, what is still unclear is the source of any funding—much talk about "alternative sources" has been heard but no definite or clear budget has been proposed.	meet. It established a schedule for countries to determine their own goals within what is reasonable for them. Flexibility is necessary; nations must have time to do research so they can make informed decisions about what they can realistically do to achieve emission caps. There is no point in setting a goal that no one can reach.
Climate change is a global concern because it affects all of us, yet the Copenhagen Accord was dictated by only five countries. The U.S., China, India, Brazil, and South Africa were the only nations involved in drafting the Accord. We need a global effort to reverse the damage we have done to the environment; thus, setting goals and establishing standards should be the responsibility of every nation. Also, "engagement" (see the opposition's argument) has little substantial meaning—there is a difference between demonstrating agreement and actually making pledges to reduce emissions or donate funds.	*The countries that were in major control of the Copenhagen Accord are the countries with the financial means, the expertise, and the most power and influence to make an environmental plan happen.* These countries are among those with the highest emissions—their willingness to begin to change is essential to getting the rest of the world on board. In addition, even if these big polluters are the only ones to make a real effort, that will still go a long way toward reducing the effects of climate change. Indeed, according to the U.S. Climate Action Network, countries representing almost 87 percent of global emission have or are likely to consider and implement the Accord.

OTHER MOTIONS:

The Copenhagen Accord will do more harm than good

RELATED MOTIONS:

The Kyoto Protocol was insufficient

Abolish international protocols in favor of self-regulation

WEB LINKS:

• Broder, John M. "U.S. Official Says Talks on Emissions Show Promise." <http://www.nytimes.com/2010/01/15/science/earth/15climate.html>. Chief U.S. climate change negotiator outlines possible benefits of Copenhagen talks.

- Climate Action. <http://blog.usclimatenetwork.org/climate-negotiations/copenhagen-accord-weekly-roundup-bonn-edition/>. Provides up-to-date information and resources on the Copenhagen Accord.

- Greenpeace. "Was the Copenhagen Accord an abject failure or a smashing success?" <http://members.greenpeace.org/blog/greenpeaceusa_blog/2010/02/03/was_the_copenhagen_accord_an_abject_fail>. Argues that Copenhagen does not deserve to be seen as either a great success or a terrible failure.

- Pew Center on Global Climate Change. "Summary: Copenhagen Climate Summit." <http://www.pewclimate.org/international/copenhagen-climate-summit-summary>. Gives a summary of the Copenhagen Climate Summit and reviews the Summit and the Accord.

Death Penalty

Motion   **The United States should ban the death penalty**

Introduction   Few issues involving crime and punishment create as much controversy as the death penalty. The United States is the only developed Western nation that permits capital punishment. Policies differ among the states: 35 have the death penalty, 15 do not. Many consider capital punishment to be the only adequate sentence for the worst crimes. Conversely, other countries condemn the United States for what they consider a barbaric and antiquated practice.

Debating the Motion   Both teams need to become familiar with the history of the death penalty in the United States, including Supreme Court rulings on the issue. They should also research what states and nations permit it. Finally, they need to research statistics on the application of the death penalty and find studies of its effectiveness as a deterrent.

Proposition: The proposition should also research cases in which individuals sentenced to death have later been found innocent.

Opposition: Remember that the opposition team need not defend the death penalty as a good, they simply need to assert that it need not be banned. Given the wide variety of death penalty policies in the country, the opposition might want to run a counter case in which they propose a specific plan for standardizing death penalty sentences across the nation.

PROS

Innocent people have been executed. The death penalty is irreversible. In light of the growing numbers of false convictions, we should be extremely reluctant to pronounce death on someone who may turn out to be innocent. Obviously, having a criminal justice system means accepting some danger of convicting the wrong person, but prisoners can be released if vindicated. There is no need to administer a punishment that can never be undone.

CONS

Fair trials are essential, but fear that a guilty verdict is given to an innocent should not stop us from punishing convicted criminals. Anyone who is convicted of a crime should be proved guilty beyond reasonable doubt. Once this is done, we should not fear executing a criminal who committed truly heinous acts of violence.

The death penalty is hypocritical. Killing is considered immoral; yet we kill when we execute people. The message, "killing is so atrocious, we are going to take away your life for doing it," is powerful. But "killing is so morally depraved, we would not do it to even the worst people" sends an even stronger social message. Furthermore, the U.S. prison system is secure enough so that there is no real danger of a maximum-security prisoner escaping.

A person who murders another forgoes his human rights because he has taken away the most basic human right of the person he kills. By using capital punishment as a response to murder, society is affirming the value that is placed on the right to life of the innocent person. More innocent people have been killed by released murderers than innocent individuals executed. Moreover, the state's highest duty is to protect its citizens. When faced with a truly heinous crime, the only way the state can protect its citizens is to put that criminal to death.

Capital punishment is administered unfairly. Minorities are more likely to receive the death penalty than whites. Studies of race and the death penalty have shown that there is a pattern of discrimination. Blacks who kill whites are far more likely to receive the death penalty than whites who kill blacks.

Where discrimination occurs, it should be corrected. Defendants on death row should and do receive special representation and are considered with special diligence by the courts to ensure that they receive a fair trial. A correlation between race and the death penalty exists, but a causal relationship has not been proven.

Administering capital punishment is a lengthy and expensive process. The trial and appeals generally last about 25 years, and all the expenses add up. For example, a 2008 ACLU paper, "The Hidden Death Tax," revealed that executing all of the people then on death row in California would cost the state an estimated $4 billion more than if they had been sentenced to life in prison. What does it say about our society that we are willing to spend more money to kill, rather than imprison, criminals?

The cost of saving lives cannot be measured in money alone. Despite the cost, the death penalty is the only way to stop some criminals, as no jail is truly escape-proof. Four billion dollars is a worthwhile cost to pay if it stops a murderer from destroying more families.

The Eighth Amendment protects prisoners from cruel and unusual punishment. Capital punishment exerts unnecessary force and harshness for the sheer purpose of inflicting additional suffering. There are four purposes

The Supreme Court has found that the death penalty does not constitute cruel and unusual punishment. Furthermore, the Fifth Amendment states that "no person shall . . . be deprived of life . . . without due process of law."

of punishment; if a punishment does not sufficiently serve these purposes, it is excessive and unconstitutional. These are: (1) rehabilitation—which is impossible under the death penalty; (2) incapacitation—the death penalty is not necessary to keep criminals off the street, jail is sufficient; (3) deterrence—the death penalty has not been proven to be a deterrent; and (4) retribution—though the death penalty serves this purpose, the Eighth Amendment implies that we cannot administer a punishment purely because a person deserves it. This would lead us to torture tormentors and rape rapists; these punishments are universally viewed as barbaric.

We damage our international reputation by using the death penalty. All of our peer countries condemn the death penalty. Do we really want to be lumped with countries like China or Iran, which condemns women to death by stoning for adultery?

Keeping the death penalty makes working with other countries on matters of justice difficult. Countries will not permit the U.S. to extradite people who face the death penalty. This would prevent us from prosecuting criminals who committed crimes in and against the United States and thus deprive victims of justice.

This clearly implies that, with due process, a person *can* be deprived of life. Citizens forfeit their rights when their actions cause injury or death to others. Although the death penalty prevents rehabilitation, it is the most assured method of incapacitation. We can logically conclude that people are less likely to commit a crime if they can be sentenced to death—capital punishment serves to emphasize just how heinous the worst crimes are. Last, we do not torture criminals, and so the death penalty is the only retribution for those who commit truly unspeakable crimes.

The United States needs to do what is right for its citizens, regardless of what other nations think. Our legal system permits capital punishment; we should not bow to pressure to change it merely because only some of our allies think it is wrong. The United States must make independent decisions and this is one of them.

We have procedures in place to handle these situations. In the rare cases where this happens, we can continue to operate as we have in the past by making good-faith guarantees that if other countries agree to work with us, we will not execute an individual they agree to send here. This is the status quo and it works. Otherwise, these cases are too rare to be a reason why we would ban the death penalty altogether.

OTHER MOTIONS:
The death penalty does more good than harm

RELATED MOTIONS:
  Capital punishment is unconstitutional
  Capital punishment is unethical

WEB LINKS:

- Death Penalty Information Center. "Facts about the Death Penalty." <http://www.deathpenaltyinfo.org/documents/FactSheet.pdf>. Statistics and facts on all aspects of the death penalty.

- Liptak, Adam. "Does Death Penalty Save Lives? A New Debate." <http://www.nytimes.com/2007/11/18/us/18deter.html>. News story about studies showing the death penalty deters crime.

- National Coalition to Abolish the Death Penalty. "Death Penalty Overview: Ten Reasons Why Capital Punishment Is Flawed Public Policy." <http://www.ncadp.org/index.cfm?content=5>. Summary of reasons for opposing capital punishment.

- University of Alaska Anchorage Justice Center. "History of the Death Penalty & Recent Developments." <http://justice.uaa.alaska.edu/death/history.html>. Brief history of the death penalty in the U.S., with statistics.

Defense Spending, Cut

Motion   **Redirect defense spending toward social services**

Introduction   The United States has a huge defense budget; in 2011, it will be more than $700 billion. Some say that this is way too much and that in economically troubled times defense spending should be cut to provide funds for social services, while others argue that such spending is necessary to defend Americans and preserve our international reputation as a world power.

Debating the Motion   This motion is very vague, so the teams need to define it more narrowly. What, for example, is meant by *social services*? Good research into what is paid for by defense funding and what is covered by social services funding is a must. Research into how much money the U.S. spends on defense in comparison with other countries will be helpful, as would a comparison of how much the U.S. allocates to defense versus social services.

Proposition: The proposition should lay out a plan in which they talk about which kinds of social services will receive the money and how much money will be redirected from defense spending. The team might also want to talk about which areas of the defense budget it would cut.

Opposition: The opposition has many options in this case: it can argue against a redirection of defense funds; propose an alternative case in which social services receive money from other sources; or cut the defense budget without reallocating the money. Because the team has so many options, they need to focus on one; combining too many could lead to a wishy-washy and confused overall counter case.

PROS

Education is a better way to promote peace than military spending. Peace cannot be imposed with military might. Rather, the best way to ensure a peaceful world is through education that teaches tolerance and appreciation for diversity. With sufficient tolerance, the source of animosity between people would be removed as would the cause for violence and aggression.

CONS

This is a wonderfully utopian view, but we cannot control the content of education in other countries. Even if U.S. school kids are taught to promote peace and tolerance, children in other countries may be taught the opposite, or not taught at all, thus putting our lives at risk. We need a strong army to keep us safe from those who want to harm us.

The U.S. lags behind other countries in terms of caring for its citizens' welfare. True, the U.S. spends more on its military than any other country in the world, but we are far behind on other measures—for example, life expectancy and academic test scores. An easy way to improve our education and welfare would be to divert some of that defense money to bolster struggling domestic programs.

It is unfair to taxpayers to use so much of their money for causes that do not directly benefit them or that they do not support. For example, $700 billion of taxpayers' money went toward military spending in Iraq, despite the fact that many did not support the war and that it was not generally agreed that Iraq posed a serious security threat to the United States. Of course, there will never be a government policy that everyone agrees with. However, at least some objective sense that the policy is helping citizens should be present.

Quite simply, the U.S. does not need to spend so much on defense—it can have an army that is just as strong but with a lower budget. The Pentagon is full of unnecessary bureaucracy, with very little personal accountability for hiring, expenditures, etc. We should reform the Pentagon's structure and put the money we save to more constructive use.

The status of the U.S. as the world's most powerful nation allows us to maintain our freedom and level of consumption. We believe in our citizens' rights to pursue their own happiness—for them to do so, they need to be kept safe and free. A strong military protects U.S. citizens, and their rights, from countries and nongovernmental actors who want to harm them. Besides, federal spending on programs such as Social Security, Medicare, and Medicaid (more than $1 trillion!) currently far outpaces spending on defense.

If citizens do not like government policy, they can vote in new elected officials, but there is no reason why lots of defense spending is inherently bad. Citizens voted for the politicians responsible for creating the budget—so the budget as it currently stands theoretically represents the majority's will. If taxpayers vote for change, there should be change, but defense spending is as legitimate a cause as any other.

Reducing bureaucracy is a good idea, but why should any money saved be directed into social services? Many argue that the government is spending far too much and needs to cut back. If we can find a way to reduce costs, why not actually save money and reduce the national debt rather than obsess over finding an alternate use for the funds?

OTHER MOTIONS:

The government should increase the defense budget

The United States should adopt a policy of isolationism

RELATED MOTIONS:
The U.S. should cut its defense budget
The U.S. should raise taxes to fund social programs

WEB LINKS:
- Johnson, Wm. Robert. "U.S. Expenditures for Defense and Education, 1940–2009." <http://www.johnstonsarchive.net/policy/edgraph.html>. Graph and table of comparative figures.
- Shah, Anup. "World Military Spending." <http://www.globalissues.org/article/75/world-military-spending>. Background statistics on U.S. military spending.

Die with Dignity, Right to

Motion **Terminally ill patients have the right to assisted suicide**

Introduction Assisted suicide is currently being discussed and debated in many countries. The central question is: If a terminally ill person decides that he or she wishes to end his or her life, is it acceptable for others, primarily doctors, to assist them? For many years assisted suicide was illegal in all U.S. states, but in the past decades organizations such as Compassion & Choices and physicians such as Jack Kevorkian have campaigned for a change in the law. They argue that terminally ill patients should not have to suffer needlessly and should be able to die with dignity. In 1997, Oregon became the first state to legalize physician-assisted suicide. In 2001, the Netherlands became the first country to legalize euthanasia and physician-assisted suicide. Most developed countries recognize the fundamental right to life, yet some believe that implicit in that right is the right of an individual to choose when he or she dies. Others maintain that no one has the right to take a life, not even his or her own.

Debating the Motion Both teams should research how existing assisted-suicide laws have worked and if permitting assisted suicide has resulted in unforeseen problems. A large number of groups, from churches to organizations like Compassion & Choices, have taken strong stands on the subject; researching these would provide arguments on both sides of the issue.

Proposition: The proposition should carefully define what is meant by a *terminal illness* and under what circumstances individuals would have the right to end their own lives. The proposition would also want to address whether consent and aid from a doctor is required or whether it would simply be legal for people to purposely end their own life. Experienced debaters ready to present an inclusive and actionable case might also include a plan to protect those who help others to commit suicide from legal penalty.

Opposition: Nearly all U.S. states as well as many countries do not allow assisted suicide despite moves to make it legal, thus, looking into the reasoning behind such position will also help provide arguments.

PROS

Of course nonvoluntary euthanasia, or murder, should not be allowed, but all that means is that we should regulate physician-assisted suicide as closely as we can. Perhaps the procedure should only be available in certain circumstances and after examination by multiple medical professionals, but potential flaws in implementation should not cause us to abandon altogether the concept of the right to die. Indeed, individuals could ultimately be better protected in a society that allowed assisted suicide because desperate patients would not have an incentive to kill themselves "illegally" in ways that might cause undue pain.

The right to control our own bodies is an essential part of the right to privacy. Privacy has been recognized as a right by the Supreme Court in such cases as *Roe v. Wade* and includes the right to control our bodies. An individual's body is perhaps her most personal "possession"—no one can tell us how to treat it. For example, we can decide to have—or not have—all manner of surgeries and other medical procedures. Assisted suicide, or the right to say when we will die, is a natural extension of such freedoms.

Allowing patients to choose when to die in the course of a terminal illness simply acknowledges the inevitable. The very definition of terminal illness is a disease or condition that will inevitably kill the sufferer. The individual is going to die no matter what, so we are not causing a death that would not come

CONS

Allowing physician-assisted suicide is one of the first steps on the slippery slope to killing individuals who want to remain alive. Once doctors have the ability to "assist" patients in committing suicide, negligent or ill-intentioned physicians or even doctors who are simply unclear on what their patients want may kill their patients without their consent. Indeed, the Remmelink Report of 1991, an analysis of euthanasia practice in the Netherlands, found thousands of instances of "nonvoluntary euthanasia" and instances where patients were either killed or denied life-prolonging treatment without their having voiced an explicit request.

The right to control over a person's body is limited all the time to protect society. For example, the government regulates substances one can or cannot eat or inhale and has, at times, made certain vaccinations mandatory when diseases posed a threat to the community. If the government has a rational basis for believing that allowing assisted suicide will harm society—for example, that it threatens the state interest in preservation of life—it has a right to regulate, or ban, the procedure. Indeed, almost every state and Western democracy ban assisted suicide, showing that it is most definitely not recognized as a right—absolute or otherwise—in present-day society.

It is dangerous and cruel to allow individuals to throw their lives away when they may live longer than expected. The term *terminal illness* can encompass a broad range of conditions and is not necessarily a sentence of death in the near future. Some illnesses thought to be terminal turn out not to be, soon anyway. We are simply giving this individual the right to die with more dignity and less pain.

Allowing a person to die peacefully and painlessly is better for him and his family in the long run. Watching a family member suffer and linger is enormously traumatic. Families would be less traumatized if they could have a concrete and predictable time frame in which to say their good-byes and then be content in the knowledge that their relative didn't suffer. This would allow surviving family members to heal and move on more quickly.

By forcing the terminally ill to suffer, lingering in pain, we increase the likelihood that they make the choice to die when their illness has led to extreme agony and thus they are not able to think clearly. But, by making assisted suicide legal, when a patient is first diagnosed—before pain or medication clouds judgment or before relatives with suspect motives can make decisions—the individual patient can direct a course of treatment that could include dying peacefully once the disease had progressed past a certain threshold or all treatment would be futile.

CONS

and patients often live longer than expected. People may make decisions based on incorrect predictions—decisions that they would certainly end up regretting if they were one of the lucky individuals who surpassed the predictions. Just look at Dr. Kevorkian: he managed to get himself paroled from jail in 2009 by claiming that his death from hepatitis C was imminent in 2007, and he is still alive today!

In fact, the notion that patients may choose to commit suicide to help their families is one of the chief arguments against assisted suicide. For example, in *Washington v. Glucksberg*, the Supreme Court raised the concern that individuals might feel pressured into committing suicide for financial reasons (expensive medical bills, etc.). This is exactly the type of loaded situation that individuals should not be put in.

The very condition of being diagnosed with terminal illness can cause patients to lose hope and make desperate decisions. Pain or medication can affect both the mind and judgment; doctors would simply not be able to know if the patient made this all-important decision with a sound mind or was influenced by impatient and cheap relatives, the effects of medication, or to escape pain.

OTHER MOTIONS:

Patients have the right to die with dignity

Physicians should not assist in the suicide of terminally ill patients

RELATED MOTIONS:

Those who assist terminally ill patients to commit suicide should not be punished

Physician-assisted suicide is contrary to the Hippocratic Oath

WEB LINKS:

- Annals of Internal Medicine. "The Debate over Physician-Assisted Suicide: Empirical Data and Convergent Views." <http://www.annals.org/content/128/7/552.full>. Paper reviewing the issue and proposing a common ground between supporters and opponents.

- Assisted Suicide. "Tread Carefully When You Help to Die." <http://www.assistedsuicide.org/suicide_laws.html>. Review of assisted-suicide laws around the world.

- BBC. "Euthanasia." <http://www.bbc.co.uk/religion/religions/christianity/christianethics/euthanasia_1.shtml>. Outline of a Christian view of assisted suicide.

Draft, Military

Motion   **Reinstate the draft**

Introduction   The draft has been used many times throughout U.S. history—while we currently have no active draft, the Selective Service still keeps a record of eligible citizens. As the U.S. Army finds itself increasingly stretched with engagements on many fronts, a fully voluntary military seems less able to meet our military needs. In recent years, some politicians have proposed reinstating the draft. They argue that it is necessary, not just for numbers, but for equity.

Debating the Motion   Both teams need to research the history of the draft as well as the current Selective Service rules. By looking at the draft protests of the 1960s, teams may be able to garner information to create their arguments.

Proposition: The proposition should begin with a plan that includes a time frame for reinstating the draft as well as guidelines for who can be drafted and what exceptions exist that would exempt individuals from the draft.

Opposition: The opposition could argue against the draft in general but also has the option to take exception with particular aspects of the proposition's case—for example, who is and is not eligible for the draft.

PROS

Conflicts in Iraq, Afghanistan, and Pakistan have strained U.S. military resources. This strain has occurred despite incentives to join a voluntary army. The most efficient way to sustain a strong army is through a draft.

A draft would equalize the military, reducing the cliché of "a rich man's war, but a poor man's fight." Voluntary recruitment targets low-income and minority Americans. The less educated and the economically disadvantaged can be more easily manipulated into

CONS

Currently, we have no major push to draft men to sustain troop numbers. This is true even though we are increasing forces in Afghanistan. Military commanders say a volunteer army is a stronger, better fighting force.

First, no one is forcing minority/low-income Americans to join up, and second, even with a draft the wealthy and privileged could find loopholes. Filling the military only with individuals who want to be there is a good strategy! And, it's untrue to say that the joining—they are often more desperate for money and less aware that military propaganda may be romanticized or even untrue. Introducing the draft would force individuals from all backgrounds to share the burden of serving, and force middle- and upper-class Americans to face the consequences of the policies they support or allow. Why should Congress be allowed to vote to send low-income men and women into combat, while keeping their own children at home?

Military experience builds character, physical fitness, and life skills such as self-discipline and teamwork. The military provides training in a large number of areas, ranging from working with computers to assisting physicians or fixing helicopters. Drafting young people will provide them with the skills they need in the civilian world.

Everyone has a duty to serve their country. Those who choose not to serve are free-riders on others' bravery, just as those who evade taxes are cheating the system.

volunteer force is made up disproportionately of minorities—in fact, blacks are only slightly overrepresented, and Hispanics are actually underrepresented. Second, even if the draft were implemented, it's likely that many middle- or upper-class Americans could find ways out—for example, through less-than-honest medical deferments.

Several other avenues are available for building these skills, and nonmilitary service is a great alternative. Granted, the military provides good training, but, as past experience with the draft suggests, not all military skills are transferable to civilian life; for example, a soldier trained as an infantryman, as were many draftees in the past, cannot take those skills to the civilian world. Some training instills traits such as heightened aggression that can even be maladaptive, creating difficulties for veterans in everyday society.

Americans can serve their country in many ways—spending a few years teaching in an inner-city school, for example, or by community service. We should stop thinking that only those in uniform serve or that defense means taking up arms. In the twenty-first century, when our greatest threat comes not from hostile nations but from Islamic extremists, those Americans building schools in Afghanistan to educate girls and keep boys out of radical madrassas are defending their country just as strongly as the soldiers stationed there.

Reinstating the draft will end wars faster. Drafting citizens from all parts of the population ensures that everyone is concerned with troop safety. Thus, the entire electorate will demand that troops are used only in conflicts where they are necessary—such reluctance will save American lives.

A frantic public will only hurt our national security in the long run. A voluntary military has individuals more willing to take risks to protect the country. Prematurely bringing troops home creates a security risk because unstable governments are unable to keep down insurgent groups.

The draft is constitutional. The Supreme Court ruled in *Butler v. Perry (1916)* that the Thirteenth Amendment does not apply to "duties owed to the government." Furthermore, article 1, section 8 of the Constitution states that Congress has the power "to raise and support Armies." This implies the power to conduct a draft.

The draft is unconstitutional. The Thirteenth Amendment prohibits involuntary servitude. Forced military service is, by definition, involuntary servitude.

OTHER MOTIONS:

The draft does more good than harm

Drafts are unethical

RELATED MOTIONS:

The draft is necessary to ensure equity in the military

WEB LINKS:

- CNN. "Rangel Introduces Bill to Reinstate Draft." <http://www.cnn.com/2003/ALLPOLITICS/01/07/rangel.draft/>. Article presenting one representative's reasons for reinstating the draft.

- Paul, Rand. "A Draft Violates Individual Liberty." <http://www.debate-central. org/2006/research/a-draft-violates-individual-liberty>. Argument against the draft from a libertarian perspective.

- WRAL.com. "Springer Journal: A Military Draft?" <http://www.wral.com/news/local/story/108956/>. Article favoring a volunteer army.

Dress Codes in Schools

Motion **Public schools should not implement dress codes**

Introduction Many private schools have regulations about apparel, with a number of schools requiring uniforms. However, the issue of whether to regulate dress is somewhat different in public schools, since students are mandated to attend if they do not want to pay for a private education. Many public schools have implemented dress codes and are increasingly recommending uniforms, and many students and student-advocacy groups have fought them—arguing that they restrict freedom of expression and suppress individuality. Some students and parents have supported dress codes, however, arguing that they contribute to a safer, more orderly classroom and that they reduce peer pressure to dress in a certain way.

Debating the Motion Both teams should research sample dress codes to see what is typically covered as well as court cases on this issue.

Proposition: The proposition should begin by defining *public schools* as the ramifications of a dress code will differ greatly between kindergartners and students at a public high school. The proposition might also wish to narrow the topic by specifying the kinds of clothing a school should not include in a dress code. The alternative is to argue against dress codes of any kind for any and all age groups.

Opposition: Because of the wording of this topic, the opposition should make a case that public schools should have dress codes. With this motion, the opposition would want to create a sample dress code to defend as a counter case, making sure that it is flexible enough to be used no matter how the proposition might narrow the age range of the students in public schools.

PROS

Dress codes in schools are unconstitutional because they violate the students' right to expression. Many individuals, including students, like to express their views and feelings through the clothing they wear. As the Supreme Court

CONS

While students do have the right to express themselves, this right is not without limits. Tinker v. Des Moines goes on to explain that schools can ban conduct that "interfere[s] with the requirements of appropriate discipline in the wrote in the 1969 case *Tinker v. Des Moines*, students do not "shed their constitutional rights to freedom of speech or expression at the schoolhouse gate." Consequently, students are entitled to express themselves as they like, with the protection of the First Amendment, within schools.

Buying specific apparel to adhere to a dress code or having to buy a mandated uniform will cost more money, thus discriminating against lower-income students. If students must conform to certain standards, they may need to purchase additional clothes. This is a financial burden that many families cannot afford, particularly if they are just above the income cutoff for aid.

Dress codes do not attack the root of the problem of gang violence. Not letting students wear gang colors in schools does not eliminate membership in gangs outside of schools. Students usually know who is in what gang without needing to identify members by apparel; rivalries are based on allegiance and tradition, not simply on colors. The study presented by the opposition demonstrates correlation, not causation—we have no reason to believe that school dress codes would significantly reduce tensions. Furthermore, myriad other ways are available to prevent weapons or intruders from coming into the building—for example, security checks and ID scanners.

operation of the school." In other words, if a school believes that a uniform dress code allows for an environment more supportive of education, it can mandate such code. A school could not stop students from expressing political views, but it could, for example, ban inappropriate clothes—such actions would not be unconstitutional.

Lower-income students actually benefit from dress codes since funding is usually available to cover the costs; in addition, money is saved because students do not feel pressured to buy expensive clothes. Public schools must be free, so schools necessarily find ways to ensure that all students are able to afford to buy the necessary clothes, for example, by providing vouchers. Furthermore, when students can wear whatever they like, it is often very clear who the wealthiest students are—they have the fanciest and most expensive clothing. With a mandatory dress code, low-income students need not feel out of place because everyone is dressed alike.

Dress codes or uniforms can make schools safer. Dress codes prevent students from wearing gang colors or symbols to school. In schools where gang-related violence is a problem, removing controversial symbols and colors can help reduce tensions. Dress codes can also mandate that students expose the belt line on pants, helping to ensure that guns are not brought into school. Finally, school uniforms can help security guards tell who goes to the school and who doesn't, thus improving their ability to keep out intruders. In fact, a 2000 survey reported by the New York Police Department found that crime decreased by 14.7 percent after the introduction of a uniform policy.

PROS	CONS
Appreciating diversity and difference is also an important function of schools. Students are supposed to learn more than facts and figures when they enter the school building—they are also supposed to learn how to appreciate differences and become tolerant of various ways of life. Students need to know how to focus and learn in an environment where people do *not* look the same, thus allowing students to wear what they please prepares all for the diversity of the real world.	*Dress codes allow students to focus their energy on school, not on what others are wearing.* First, with a dress code in place, students will be less distracted by classmates wearing provocative or inappropriate outfits. Second, when students know exactly what they are wearing to school each day, they can focus on homework and studying, rather than on choosing outfits or worrying about what their classmates will wear.
Dress codes suppress students' individuality. Many young people enjoy expressing their views and identities through the clothes they wear. Adolescence is the time when many people begin to feel the need to form a unique identity—physical appearance is one way to do so. It is unfair to deny young people the right to discover themselves during this pivotal time in their lives.	*Students do not need to rely on clothes to make their voices heard.* No one is suggesting censoring student speech, so students would still have the means to express themselves. Furthermore, students should learn to create an identity based on meaningful choices and characteristics, not on superficial traits such as hair color or shoe type.
Dress codes will increase lateness and absenteeism. Many schools with dress codes have penalties for coming to school out of uniform or with parts of the uniform missing. So, if a student is out of clean uniform shirts or cannot find her uniform belt, she will either be late because she was looking for the missing item or she might even skip school altogether to avoid a penalty. The lack of flexibility actually encourages a student to be absent just because of an article of clothing.	*Dress codes will increase punctuality among students.* Deciding what to wear can take a sizeable amount of time in the morning, especially when students are at an age where dress is socially important. Having a dress code removes this distraction, thus ensuring that more students will eat breakfast and get to school on time.

OTHER MOTIONS:

Ban uniforms in public schools

Uniforms in schools do more harm than good

RELATED MOTIONS:
  Uniforms are unconstitutional

WEB LINKS:
- First Amendment Center. "Clothing, Dress Codes & Uniforms." <http://www.firstamendmentcenter.org/speech/studentexpression/topic.aspx?topic=clothing_dress_codes_uniforms>. Discusses dress codes from a constitutional perspective.
- Fresno Pacific University. "Pros and Cons of School Dress Codes." <http://www.fresno.edu/scholars_speak/key_and_wilder/>. Discusses pros and cons of dress codes, with a special emphasis on the impact of dress codes on school safety.
- The Public School Parent's Network. "Dress Codes." <http://www.psparents.net/Dress_Codes.htm>. Directed at parents, this article outlines the major arguments for and against dress codes in schools.

Drilling for Oil in Parks and Preserves

Motion **Drilling for oil in protected parks and reserves is justified**

Introduction As the cost of fuel rises and tensions in oil-producing regions do the same, the United States is searching for local sources of fuel. The nation has untapped sources of fossil fuels lying under the land in some national parks and wildlife reserves. The question of whether to drill for oil in these areas has sparked heated debate. Many argue that nothing can be more valuable than the country's legacy of protected wildlands. Others argue that if we can make our own position more secure through the local production of oil, no wildlife reserve is more important than the security of the nation.

Debating the Motion First, both teams should research those parks and preserves with oil and natural gas reserves that are at issue. In addition to information about foreign oil, teams should look briefly into the history of wildlife reserves and national parks. It would be beneficial to ascertain how invasive such drilling would be and what the yield would be in comparison with operations everywhere.

Proposition: Remember the word *justified* in the motion indicates that the proposition does not necessarily have to argue that drilling in parks is a positive, but rather that, in the face of all other things, it is permissible. Setting out a potential plan and citing the circumstances under which drilling would occur would explain why drilling is justified.

Opposition: The opposition can argue that drilling in a national park is never justified or that it is unnecessary. Finally, the team could argue against specific elements of the proposition's plan, reasoning that the harms of the plan outweigh any possible benefits.

PROS

Drilling for oil or natural gas anywhere is justifiable if it helps reduce our dependence on foreign oil. Relying on outside sources, no matter how secure we believe them to be, as our main providers of energy puts us at great risk. Whether as a result of diplomatic problems or a natural disaster, we could

CONS

We don't need to drill in national parks; we have other sources of energy. In addition to the much more environmentally friendly alternatives like solar and wind power, we have large supplies of coal and the increasingly reliable technologies behind nuclear power that can help meet our energy needs.

easily get cut off from critical fuel, leading to an economic catastrophe. By producing our own fuel, we are making the entire nation safer—thus, drilling in national parks is justifiable, if not ideal.

Drilling in national parks will help consumers. Whether for powering a home, a car, or a heating system in winter, fuel is a major expenditure for almost every American. Oil is expensive, all the more so because of the cost of importing it from distant lands. By producing our own, we can greatly reduce costs for the average person. Such savings justify drilling in park land.

While national parks are a luxury we may enjoy and a heritage we may desire to keep, fuel is a necessity of everyday life. When weighing a luxury against a need, we find that we cannot afford to preserve land at the expense of what is a necessity for so many. This makes drilling unfortunate but justifiable.

At the end of the day, national parks are government lands, and citizens, through their government, can do what they see fit with them. Although in the past the federal government may have thought it beneficial to set aside and preserve this land for public recreation, when necessary, the government can use this land for a different purpose. If the resources from this land will provide the previously mentioned benefits to the security of the nation and the financial well-being of its citizens, then drilling is justifiable.

If we have other choices, we cannot justify destroying national parks.

Extracting this oil will cost a great deal of money, so Americans will not seeing savings anytime soon. Possibly such savings will never come about if alternative energy sources are perfected in the next few decades. In the meantime, Americans can enjoy the benefits the national parks and wildlife reserves. Destroying this heritage is completely unjustified.

Parks are necessary for something more important than powering a gas-guzzling SUV—they are necessary for personal health and the health of the environment that affects us all. In the long run, clean air and clean water are far more necessary than satisfying immediate energy needs to fuel our extravagant energy-using lifestyle. We won't always need oil or natural gas as we develop and adopt better energy technologies, but we will always need clean air, clean water, and the balanced environment that national parks help to create and maintain.

Government land or not, designations should not be removed just to respond to public concerns. The whole purpose of setting aside land for national parks is precisely to protect something important to our national heritage from being destroyed for momentary gain—which is exactly what drilling for fossil fuels would be.

Drilling will help local economies. Many of these untapped oil resources are found in relatively remote places where jobs can be scarce. New drilling operations will provide jobs—both directly for the drilling and also in related fields, for example, building, engineering, and maintenance. Drilling will bring a great economic boost to areas that badly need it.

In the long run, drilling will hurt local economies. Drilling in national parks will actually take money away from those areas. Currently, communities around parks rely on a profitable tourism industry. In damaging the parks, tourism will die and local economies will be destroyed.

OTHER MOTIONS:

Drilling for oil or gas in national parks would do more good than harm

Drilling for fuel in national parks is never justified

RELATED MOTIONS:

The government should drill for gas in the Finger Lakes

Drilling for oil in Alaska is justified

WEB LINKS:

• Arctic Power-Arctic National Wildlife Refuge. <http://www.anwr.org/>. Site presenting arguments in support of drilling.

• Cleveland, Cutler J., and Robert K. Kaufmann. "Why the Bush Oil Policy Will Fail." <http://www.hubbertpeak.com/cleveland/bushpolicy.htm>. Article arguing against the Bush administration promoting drilling in the Arctic National Wildlife Refuge.

• Lavell, Marianne. "Arctic Drilling Wouldn't Cool High Oil Prices." <http://politics.usnews.com/news/national/articles/2008/05/23/arctic-drilling-wouldnt-cool-high-oil-prices.html>. Article arguing that drilling will not affect gas prices.

• MSNBC. "Panel: Alaska Drilling has Pros, Cons." <http://www.msnbc.msn.com/id/3339907/>. Site presenting arguments on both sides of the controversy.

Driving Age

Motion   **Increase the driving age**

Introduction   In the United States, the voting age is 18; the drinking age is 21. To join the military, a young man or woman must be 18. Most states don't allow individuals to rent cars until they are 25. In the array of age-related privileges, however, the first to arrive is the ability to get a driver's license; in some states, teenagers can take a written and road test at the tender age of 15. Why are we are so quick to allow children to move tons of machinery around when we don't trust them to help us pick our elected officials? Cars can be deadly when used improperly! Citing the higher incidence of accidents among teenage drivers, many argue that the United States should adopt a nationwide standard, higher driving age. For kids yearning for the freedom of the open road, it would be a real blow to lose this first rite of passage into adulthood.

Debating the Motion   Driving age differs from state to state, so both teams should find information about the current range in ages. Both teams should also research issues particular to teen drivers such as increased accident rates and texting while driving. Many states have minimum requirements for getting a license, including graduated systems and mandatory safety courses, so both teams should utilize systems currently in place to both argue for new regulations and defend the adequacy of the current regulations.

Proposition: The proposition team should lay out an explicit plan for raising the minimum driving age and would do well to include not only a new age but additional license requirements, such as additional safety courses or graduated privileges.

Opposition: The opposition team has the option of upholding the status quo or even standardizing the age of driving at 16 across the country. A bold team might even try the challenge of running a counter case wherein they argue to lower the age limit even further! Arguments such as better eyesight, increased agility, and even experience from ever-more-realistic gaming systems might point to why younger drivers are better.

PROS

Teenagers below the age of 18 are not developmentally mature enough to drive safely. Their brains are still changing. In particular, the parts of the brain that govern self-control and risk-taking behaviors take the longest to fully develop. Yet, these are the centers that are most necessary for making the myriad decisions involved in driving safely. Without a fully mature brain, teens might decide to drive in dangerous circumstances or become too readily distracted. Thus, we should not allow teenagers to drive because their brains simply aren't ready yet.

At the very least, the driving age should be raised to match to the age of legal majority, the age at which the law views the person as capable of managing his or her own affairs and legally responsible for his or her actions. That's 18 in most places or, better yet, the driving age should match the drinking age of 21. The right to vote or buy beer is granted at ages at which most people are mature enough to handle the responsibility. Getting a driver's license should wait until the age of legal majority—when most people are mature enough to accept and undertake certain responsibilities.

Those who learn to drive when they have a better appreciation of the risks—that is, when they are older—will be better drivers. They are more likely to be cautious, less likely to engage in risky driving behaviors, and also more likely to be defensive drivers—which driver safety instructors say is key to keeping everyone on the road safe. Kids who learn while they are carefree will be more likely to be risky and offensive drivers, which will increase the danger they pose on the road.

CONS

These are precisely some of the reasons why teenagers should learn to drive at around the age of 16 and 17. If we wait longer, then teens will be learning to drive while they are in college, and the lack of supervision would put them at greater risk. Learning to drive while still in high school allows kids to do so while surrounded by their families—especially their parents, who will give firm support and guidance and make sure they have adequate instruction.

The ages at which majority is granted in other aspects of life have changed over time to reflect practical reality. For example, the voting age was lowered during the Vietnam War because society realized that if young men could be drafted at age 18 they should be able to choose the leaders who sent them to war. The driving age makes sense where it is: 16 and 17 are the first years where teens need to be places (an after-school job, for instance) independent of their parents. Thus, it makes sense for them to learn then rather than waiting until they are out of high school.

This statement is a sweeping generalization that is not true in all cases. Some who learn to drive when they are older may still be poor drivers. Granted, some teenage drivers are flighty and inattentive, but others are very responsible. We should not penalize those teens because some of their peers act irresponsibly, especially when irresponsible drivers come from all age groups.

PROS

For the already scattered teenage brain, the distractions offered by modern cars create the perfect storm for an accident. Today's cars zoom along at inhuman speeds while having a million distractions—from cell phones to stereos to power window controls. Forcing people to grow up before learning to drive will minimize the effects of these distractions.

Accident rates are highest among teens. Teens are more likely to be in and cause accidents than any other drivers. Thus, we can make driving safer for everyone by taking teenage drivers off the road and not allowing individuals to drive until they have gained the wisdom and self-control that only come with age.

The solution to that problem is not with the driving age but with mass transit. This is a wake-up call to this country that we need to invest in public transportation! If better bus and train service were available, we would not have to worry about teenage drivers everywhere causing accidents and near-accidents.

CONS

Distractions exist for everyone these days. Texting while driving used to be pretty much exclusive to teens—today, even grandmothers are hammering away at the keyboard on their smart phones. What is actually needed is not an increase in the driving age but assurance that every driver is taught how to handle distractions, including training for new drivers and refresher courses for older ones.

Perhaps the high number of accidents is related to inexperience rather than age. If we cut out teenage drivers, we won't cut the rate of accidents. We will, instead, just increase the average age of new drivers and consequently the age of the group most likely to cause accidents. New drivers will still be new (and inexperienced) no matter what age we require them to reach before granting a license.

Teenagers need to drive to function in modern American society. The U.S. is a nation of drivers. With many places having little or no public transportation, driving is necessary. This need first becomes truly evident in early high school. Teens need to get around, not just for important social reasons that will shape their abilities to interact in the real world, but also to get to jobs, attend college prep courses, and participate in other after-school activities.

OTHER MOTIONS:
  The driving age should be raised to 21
  Teenagers should be banned from driving

RELATED MOTIONS:
  Lower the driving age

WEB LINKS:

- heraldonline. "Don't Raise Driving Age." <http://www.heraldonline. com/2008/09/14/815230/dont-raise-driving-age.html> <http://www.edmondsun. com/homepage/x519233262/Teens-Keep-driving-age-16?keyword=leadpicturestory>. Article opposing raising the driving age on practical grounds.

- National Highway Traffic Safety Administration. <http://www.nhtsa.gov/>. Summary of government efforts to deal with the problems associated with teen drivers.

- USA Today. "Report Makes a Case for Raising Driving Age." <http://www.usatoday. com/news/nation/2008-09-09-teen-drivers_N.htm>. Review of a report from the Insurance Institute for Highway Safety.

Drug Testing in Schools

Motion **Schools should be allowed to conduct random drug tests**

Introduction Professional athletes and workers in some jobs are required to undergo random drug testing; today, many schools have followed suit, requiring students to submit to such tests as well. Adults voluntarily take jobs that require drug tests, however, students have no choice but to attend school, thus many wonder whether random drug testing in schools is appropriate. Proponents say it is part of a school's mandate to educate and protect its students. Opponents argue that testing violates student privacy.

Debating the Motion Both teams should research the wide variety of existing programs—what drugs are tested, how the program is implemented—as well as their impact on students and on the rate of drug use. They should also investigate the legal decisions surrounding the topic.

Proposition: The proposition must present a detailed plan that explains what will be tested; how the tests will be conducted; under what circumstances; who will be tested; and what the consequences might be for a positive test.

Opposition: The opposition has several choices in attacking the case. The most general strategy is to show that no benefits accrue and many possible harms arise from random-testing programs. The other choice is to attack elements of the proposition's plan. The opposition might also focus on the problems with implementation or possible abuse arising from the proposition's plan.

PROS	CONS
Since a school's main mission is to educate and protect children, the catastrophic effect of drugs outweighs a student's right to privacy. Drugs are dangerous not only to the user, but also to children who may be influenced by peers (some high school addicts push drugs on younger students to make money to support their own habit). This can cause a shift in school culture and an attitude that drug use is normal, even "cool." By testing students	*Random drug tests are unnecessary and unwarranted.* A schoolwide trend would be apparent through decreased class attendance, poor academic results, etc.—mandatory drug testing is not necessary. If administrators and teachers do have reasonable cause to suspect drug use, they may search a student, but the fact that drugs are dangerous is not sufficient to warrant random drug tests. Box cutters are dangerous too, but we would

for drugs, a school is able to address a student's drug abuse before it becomes a serious problem. Early intervention could also stop the spread of drugs throughout a school.

Schools act in loco parentis, taking on the role of parent to care for and instruct children during school hours. Schools can mandate that students receive vaccines, receive sex education/are aware of HIV/AIDS, and teach students values like tolerance and cooperation. Schools have a vested interest in making sure students are healthy, well-behaved, and on their way to success; drug use gets in the way of these goals. Thus, schools, like parents, are entitled to force children to comply with drug tests.

Legal precedent exits that supports drug testing measures. The Supreme Court ruled in *Board of Education v. Earls* (2002) that schools can require students in competitive extracurricular activities to comply with random drug tests because this furthers an important school interest in preventing drug use among its students. For the same reason, schools should be able to perform random drug tests. Students generally have reduced rights; no one can censor a newspaper for inappropriate material, yet the Supreme Court has held that schools may do so with school newspapers. Schools have a specific mission—safety and education. Because drug use hampers a school's ability to keep students safe and interferes with the learning environment, school officials may infringe on students' privacy to conduct drug tests.

Any rule can be abused, but rules are still necessary. School officials can establish set procedures to make sure that students are really searched randomly or for a legitimate

certainly consider daily strip searches to find box cutters extremely intrusive into a student's privacy.

Schools act like parents in certain respects, but that role is limited. Schools must receive parental permission to take children on field trips, to give medical assistance, to use photographs of children, etc. Parental permission is not implied by school attendance. If a school wants to test a student for drugs, school officials can approach the parents for help or permission.

The decision in Board of Education v. Earls *is based partly on the concept that when students become involved in extracurricular activities, they are not entitled to the same level of privacy.* As Justice Breyer emphasizes in his concurrence, students can refrain from playing sports to avoid a drug test; they cannot refuse to go to school. Current precedent, based on *New Jersey v. T.L.O.* (1985), dictates that schools may search students, but only with reasonable suspicion of wrongdoing. In *United School District v. Redding* (2009), the Court found that a school's strip search of a 13-year-old girl suspected of drug possession was unreasonable and violated her rights. Unless a school has reason to believe a student is using drugs, forcing students to comply with drug tests is a violation of their constitutional rights.

Programs that give absolute discretion to the school are ripe for abuse. If school officials can search students without probable cause, they can use searches to harass, intimidate, or "get purpose, rather than as punishment or harassment. Furthermore, such searches would not intimidate a student who is not using drugs, as she has nothing to fear.

Students can abuse over-the-counter medications. Students sometimes take cold medicine for its (low) alcohol content, and many students abuse prescription medication. We cannot assume that all medication that is legal and readily available is safe. Furthermore, if students are using these medications in a normal and legal manner, they need not be penalized. A drug test is merely a red flag that something is probably wrong; it is not an immediate conviction.

back at" a student. Furthermore, random searches are unlikely to be random; schools inevitably will profile students, resulting in discrimination.

Many drug policies go too far, extending to the use of legal drugs. Students have been punished for having over-the-counter pain medications, which they use for normal purposes. Unfair punishment has long-term effects on the student: other students may mock her, the ordeal can cause stress and anxiety, and the "offense" will affect the student's chance at scholarships and college admission. Making students fear repercussions for using legal medication in appropriate doses forces them to choose between their health and their academic reputations.

OTHER MOTIONS:

Drug testing in schools does more harm than good

RELATED MOTIONS:

Student athletes should be subject to random drug testing

Schools have the right to search students for drugs without a warrant

WEB LINKS:

- CNN Health. "Parents Be Warned: Your Children May Be Robotripping." <http://pagingdrgupta.blogs.cnn.com/2010/07/08/parents-be-warned-your-kids-may-be-robo-tripping/?hpt=T2>. New studies show students are getting high on OTC cold medications.

- Ezine @rticles. "School Drug Testing—Pros & Cons of Student Drug Testing at Schools." <http://ezinearticles.com/?School-Drug-Testing---Pros-and-Cons-of-Student-Drug-Testing-at-Schools&id=306774>. Offers pros and cons on the topic.

- National Drug Strategy Network. "Students Suspended for Carrying Midol®, Advil®." <http://www.ndsn.org/nov96/midol.html>. Two cases where students were punished for using the recommended doses of OTC pain medication.

- Office of National Drug Control Policy. "What You Need to Know About Drug Testing in Schools." <http://www.ncjrs.gov/ondcppubs/publications/pdf/drug_testing.pdf>. Overview of the issue of drug testing in schools.

Electoral College

Motion **Abolish the Electoral College**

Introduction The Electoral College is an indirect method of electing the president. Citizens vote for the presidential candidate they prefer, but they actually are voting for electors, who later formally vote for president. Although electors are allowed to vote for either candidate, they are expected to vote as the people have indicated by their ballots. To win the presidency, a candidate must received 270 Electoral College votes (out of a possible 538). The process: after presidential elections, electors in each state cast their votes—all the electoral votes go to the candidate who won the state ("winner takes all"; exceptions are Maine and Nebraska, where electors follow the voters percentages in indicating their vote). Periodically, this system becomes controversial when a presidential candidate wins the popular vote but does not win the Electoral College vote—in 2000, Al Gore won the popular vote but George W. Bush won the Electoral College vote and became president. At such times, some voters call for the abolition of the Electoral College.

Debating the Motion Both teams need to research the history of the Electoral College, particularly the controversies it has engendered; they also should be familiar with how the College operates and why it was established. The issue of abandoning the Electoral College has often been raised following close elections, so both teams should find arguments surrounding such elections.

Proposition: The proposition would benefit from offering an alternative; the team should research electoral systems in other democracies to help construct a case.

Opposition: The opposition has the option of either arguing to keep the Electoral College as is or to argue for modification. A very well-researched team might want to propose a counter case that would include laying out specific changes in the operation of the College.

PROS	CONS
The Electoral College is an indirect form of democracy; the people do not actually get to pick their own leaders. The Founders established the Electoral College because they feared the people might not always make a wise choice	*The United States was established as a republic to protect us from direct democracy.* The Electoral College prevents candidates from winning on a plurality (no one gets more than half the votes). A plurality victory can put

of president. They thought that because of poor communications many voters would not really know the candidates. In addition, they thought that the most popular candidate might not be the best president. They believed that setting up the Electoral College would assure that the best men with cool heads would choose the president. Over time, communication has vastly improved, and we have rejected the idea that the people are incompetent to decide. Just as the Constitution was amended to protect minorities and women, so should it be amended to get rid of the Electoral College.

In a democracy, the candidate who was actually chosen by the people should win the election. Because of the Electoral College, occasionally the candidate who won the popular vote lost the election, as happened in 2000. Democracy is government by the majority; the person who gets the majority of votes, even if it is by a single ballot, should become president.

In most states, the members of the Electoral College can vote for whomever they please. Only 24 states penalize "faithless electors" (electors who do not vote as they say they will); only Michigan will actually change a faithless elector's vote. To date, electors have changed their votes on 158 occasions. This leaves us in the dangerous position wherein electors can capriciously overturn any semblance of true representation and democracy.

The Electoral College gives small states undue power. The Electoral College is set up so that smaller states have more votes in relation to actual population than do larger states. The United States was different when it was first

someone in office who appeals to some but is disliked by most. Also, the Electoral College is part of our history and is provided for by the Twelfth Amendment. To abolish it, part of the Constitution would need to change. Because of the relative sanctity of the Constitution, we should not pass and ratify amendments unless they are absolutely necessary.

In the rare situations where the popular vote and the electoral votes do not coincide, the victor has always received a vast number of votes. Accordingly, regardless of which candidate is chosen, the people's will has not been totally ignored nor is the eventual president unsupported.

Faithless electors have never changed an election. Of the 158 incidents mentioned, 71 were because the original candidate died, and 2 were abstentions, not changes in votes; only 85 electors in the history of our nation have actually changed their votes. For more than 200 years, the vast majority of electors have proven worthy of our trust. It is the responsibility of the people to pick an elector who will represent their interests.

The Electoral College protects small states. A few large, highly populated states should not be able to control what happens to the entire country; smaller states have a right to have their interests seriously considered as well.

formed; the Founders envisioned a group of states that were mostly independent of one another. Today, the United States is more united and political interests are not as starkly divided by state. Thus, a system that "protects" small states is unnecessary and simply disenfranchises people living in states with large populations.

Our nation rests on the principle that all people are equal, and that one person should get one vote. However, because the winner in a state gets all the votes for that state, the Electoral College gives citizens in swing states more power. Candidates ignore states like New York, Texas, and California, even though together they can claim more than 25 percent of the country's population, because the majority in these states always votes the same way. Candidates focus on states like Pennsylvania, Ohio, and Florida because these states may swing the election. This violates the principle that we are all equal in our ability to choose our government's leaders.

Voter turnout is notoriously low in our country, in part because the Electoral College discourages voting. States are given electors based on population statistics, not how many citizens vote. The Electoral College system also discourages local political minorities from voting because their votes have no effect on the election. For example, a Republican in New York City or a Democrat in Texas cannot influence the election because New York City will vote Democratic, Texas will vote Republican, and the winner will take all of the state's electoral votes. This lack of control creates apathy.

The Electoral College was created as part of a compromise that ensured that smaller states would not be at the mercy of larger ones because of a simple population differential. The bicameral system of our legislature guaranteed equal representation in the Senate for all, and the allocation of electoral votes stems from this system guaranteeing a voice to even very small states. Because the Electoral College is part of a compromise, it does not lead to unfairness—the House of Representatives, for example, gives greater voice to larger states.

Voter turnout is not strongly influenced by the Electoral College. The recent decrease in voter turnout is largely because the number of noncitizen residents and disenfranchised felons has increased; these individuals do not vote because they are not allowed to. Furthermore, the 2008 election saw an increase in voter turnout even though the Electoral College did not change. People decide to vote depending on whether they care about the election, not based on the Electoral College.

OTHER MOTIONS:

The Electoral College does more harm than good

The U.S. needs a new electoral system for presidential elections

RELATED MOTIONS:

The Electoral College is outdated

The Electoral College is necessary

WEB LINKS:

- Exploring Constitutional Conflicts. "The Electoral College." <http://www.law.umkc.edu/faculty/projects/ftrials/conlaw/electoralcoll.htm>. Background and arguments on both sides of the issue.

- NPR. "Debating the Merits of the Electoral College." <http://www.npr.org/templates/story/story.php?storyId=4127863>. Interview on the subject.

- Raasch, Chuck. "Electoral College Debate Intensifies." <http://www.usatoday.com/news/politicselections/nation/president/2004-09-24-electoral-college_x.htm>. Overview of the debate in the context of the 2004 election.

Environmental Standards, Differing

Motion **Developing nations should be held to different and lower environmental standards**

Introduction One of the major concessions made in current international environmental protocols is holding developing nations to lower standards of environmental responsibility. These provisions are controversial. Now that developed countries are amply aware of the damage done to the planet by uncontrolled pollution as they were developing, they hesitate to allow other nations to pollute the planet as they develop. Some say, however, that imposing the same environmental standards on all countries is unrealistic and that developing nations need different and lower standards.

Debating the Motion Both teams will need to research the Kyoto Protocol and the Copenhagen Accord to see how these agreements address the issue. Information about the emissions, waste production, etc., of the major developing nations such as China, India, and Brazil would also be helpful to both teams.

Proposition: This topic is one in which the proposition must provide many definitions and clarifications about what is a rather indistinct motion. What is meant by *developing nation*? What do we mean by *environmental standards*? How will standards for developing nations differ from those for developed countries? The team must introduce a plan to support the motion—looking at current proposals will give a good framework to help the proposition create its case.

Opposition: The opposition has the option of arguing that no exemptions on environmental standards should be allowed for anyone, period. This line will take a lot of research into the current effects of climate change, both in terms of economics and impact on humans. The opposition could also propose a counter case of tougher blanket environmental standards for everyone, including First World countries.

PROS

Lower environmental standards for poor nations are important for international security. Nations with large numbers of uneducated

CONS

Spewing pollutants also creates a risk for the world. Who knows how long a struggling country will take to achieve economic and poor citizens pose a security risk to themselves and to more developed nations. By imposing lower standards on these nations, we can encourage development and, therefore, stability within their borders. This increases the security of the entire world.

The United States and other developed countries were allowed to advance without restrictions on their emissions—this is what permitted them to progress the way they did. They went through industrialization phases that set the foundation for development and now that they are developed they are able to start worrying about the environment. Other countries should be allowed the same developmental stages that the U.S. was.

Implementing high environmental standards is very expensive. We can see in the U.S. how regulations can add to the cost of doing business. Developing nations, most of which have limited financial resources, cannot meet these standards. Developing nations must be allowed, as the U.S. was, to do what is necessary to develop.

Creating new technologies or paths to development that bypass the environmental damage of an industrial revolution requires lots of education and ingenuity. However, we know that many developing countries lack an educated population. Most citizens of developing nations have no access to training in sciences, engineering, economics, etc., thus, they are unable to help their countries move forward into newer and greener technologies.

prosperity and political stability? In the meantime, it might engender emissions that will pose a global risk to the environment. The proposition wants us to ignore this immediately evident harm to worry about a potential problem. We cannot do this.

When the United States was developing, the world was unaware of the harm industrialization could do to the environment. Now that the world is aware of how human actions affect the well-being of the planet, currently developing countries have the opportunity to modernize in a rational way that does the least harm.

By establishing so-called green methods of industry and development, developing nations are actually saving themselves money in the long run. First, in working to create new technologies, they can make themselves internationally competitive as providers of commodities, manufactured goods, and new ideas. Second, by committing to using cleaner technologies, they will save themselves the costs of clean-up in the future when they are more stable.

Just because a poorer country lacks a widely educated populace doesn't preclude the presence of an educated elite. The truth is that even Third World countries have some people with the financial means to educate their children. Many times this educated elite, who have often gone to universities in the United States, Europe, and China, hold high posts in government—putting them in a perfect position to establish responsible environmental standards and practices in their countries.

PROS

Developing countries have more pressing worries than emissions standards. While many developing countries probably want to regulate emissions, governments have to focus on meeting basic needs and developing their economies. Until these are met, these countries need to be held to lower environmental standards. While environmental concerns are important, especially in the long run, immediate concerns take precedence.

CONS

While we recognize the need to address immediate concerns, countries need to do so in a way that will not compromise their future. So that when they have developed economically, the country and, indeed, the world are still places where people can thrive. If a country worries about the immediate need for development at the expense of water and land quality, it is going to suffer down the road.

OTHER MOTIONS:

Developing nations should not have to meet emissions standards

All countries should be held to the same environmental standards

RELATED MOTIONS:

The Copenhagen Accord does more harm than good for poor countries

First World countries have a moral obligation to help developing nations stay green

WEB LINKS:

- Bell, Ruth Greenspan, and Clifford Russell. "Environmental Policies for Developing Nations." <http://www.issues.org/18.3/greenspan.html>. Article discussing the problems developing nations have in implementing environmental policies.

- Xin, Zhou. "Environment vs. Growth Debate Heats Up in China." <http://www.reuters.com/article/idUSPEK30490820070803>. Article providing an overview of the debate in China.

Factory Farming, Banning

Ban factory farming

Factory farming is the large-scale, industrial production of livestock and poultry designed to produce the highest output at the lowest cost. The practice began in the 1920s after the discovery of vitamins A and D and vitamin supplements, which allowed large numbers of animals to be raised indoors without sunlight. Proponents of the practice point to its economic benefits, while opponents say it has led to cruelty and environmental destruction.

Teams should familiarize themselves with what constitutes factory farming and if viable alternatives are available. Both teams should look at the laws that currently govern factory farming, as well as proposed changes to factory farms that have arisen in Europe and the United States. Comparisons of cost and productivity between factory farms and their competitors are necessary.

Proposition: The proposition must define *factory farming* and offer a plan that includes a timeline for its discontinuance. The plan should also indicate how the proposition intends to replace the loss of food production from the discontinued farms.

Opposition: The opposition can take two different approaches—a moral defense of factory farming or a more practical case outlining the difficulties of implementing a ban. A careful look at the economics of factory farming could be helpful—aside from knowing the money that is saved by this method of food production, understanding the employment and other economic benefits a factory farm can bring to a region will provide powerful tools for argument. The opposition should also be sure to point out if the proposition is being overly sentimental and maintain a logical position about the importance of meeting human needs before farm animals' needs.

PROS

Factory farming should be banned because it promotes the unethical treatment of animals. Animals are often forced to exist in cramped and dangerous spaces, without room to move or the chance to see the light

CONS

Animals are not as aware as humans; cramped living spaces do not have the same effect on a chicken as they have on a human. Animals are generally considered to be less conscious and have less capacity for complex feelings than of day. Babies are torn from their mothers, and bodily modifications in the name of safety are common, for example, debeaking and clipping the wings of fowl. Animals can feel pain just like humans, making this treatment unjust.

America does not need to eat as much meat as it does. There are many alternatives to eating lots of factory-farmed meat, such as eating smaller amounts of organic meat or not eating any meat at all. Indeed, eliminating factory farms could encourage Americans to pursue these alternative diets by making meat less readily available and more expensive.

Factory farming is unsafe. Animals are often fed antibiotics, which end up in the food we eat, possibly contributing to the development of drug-resistant organisms. And, the cramped conditions necessary for factory farming can give rise to epidemics. When animals are in such close quarters, diseases and infections spread far more quickly and can mutate to become dangerous to humans. For example, many scientists have linked swine flu to factory farms, such as Smithfield Foods in Mexico.

Factory farming harms the environment. The amount of waste produced by factory farms is huge—U.S farm animals produce 130 times more waste than U.S. residents, according to Vegan Outreach. Danger comes also from soil and water contamination caused by waste leakage, which contains pesticides and medications. Indeed, agricultural runoff has killed millions of fish. In addition,

humans. Certainly we should not go out of our way to abuse animals, but human needs should come first.

Banning factory farms would hurt ordinary Americans, as organic farms would be unable to provide for the nation's dietary needs. According to the Organic Farming Research Foundation, only about 2 percent of America's food supply comes from organic farms, and many Americans do not have access to the products (or if they do, they are too expensive). If someone lives in a town where the only meat supply is factory-farmed, it is unfair to take that away.

Factory farming allows for more regulation of food. When just a few farms are producing most of the meat, it is easier for the government to impose production standards and quality controls. If meat were to come from different locations, it would be much more difficult to monitor health conditions, and it would be more likely that harmful products would enter the market.

Factory farming uses less land, thus reducing the environmental impact. The sad truth is that most farming is bad for the environment—meat farming creates a large carbon footprint and plant farming often occurs at the expense of natural forests. Given that we know that farming will be environmentally unfriendly, it is better to keep it in the smallest area possible, which factory farming greenhouse gases are released not only by the animals but also by the machinery used in factory farming—in fact, the livestock industry is responsible for 18 percent of greenhouse gas emissions.

does. The alternative is to destroy whole ecosystems to make space for more grazing land for cattle and other domesticated animals.

Does factory farming actually help the economy? The answer is not clear. First, because factory farming is done in concentrated locations, food must be transported long distances, at costs that rise as the price of gas goes up. In addition, because diseases can arise from factory farming as explained above, money is needed to treat pandemics such as swine flu. Also, factory farming takes away jobs from small farmers and businesses, and often uses machinery instead of employing humans.

Factory farming is good for the economy. It uses less land but produces more meat, thus meat is produced at a lower cost, and Americans can buy more of it. Furthermore, factory farms are large enterprises and can provide much-needed jobs to struggling communities.

OTHER MOTIONS:

Factory farming is unethical

Factory farming does more good than harm

RELATED MOTIONS:

Eating meat is unethical

All farming should be organic

WEB LINKS:

- DeQuassie, Karen. "The Myth of Factory Farms." <http://animalagalliance.org/images/ag_insert/manurematters_may03_page18.pdf>. Article in support of factory farming, arguing that the very phrase is biased.

- Farmsanctuary. "Factory Farming." <http://www.farmsanctuary.org/issues/factoryfarming/environment/>. Anti–factory farming website.

- The Humane Society of the United States. "Factory Farming." <http://www.humanesociety.org/issues/all_issues.html>. In-depth analysis of the issue from an organization opposed to factory farming.

Farm Subsidies

Motion **The government should reduce farm subsidies**

Introduction U.S. agriculture has changed since the introduction of farming subsidies to help struggling families during the Depression. Initially, subsidies were designed to help small family farms, but now U.S. agriculture is dominated by agribusiness—huge agricultural corporations that control not only farming but also distribution, marketing, and retail sales of agricultural products. In light of this change, many have questioned the need for agricultural subsidies. Subsidy proponents argue that because farms provide one of our most vital needs—food—and because farming success remains dependant on unpredictable weather conditions, we should continue to provide subsidies. Opponents argue that subsidies benefit large corporations, block foreign competition, and encourage the production of useless products, unnecessarily large amounts of corn, for example.

Debating the Motion Teams should research the history of farming and farm subsidies as well as the current subsidy program. Research into current changes in farming such as the recent push toward local and organic farms will also be helpful.

Proposition: The proposition could argue either that all subsidies should be reduced or that some, such as those to agribusiness, should be lowered. The team needs to present a plan outlining how much this reduction will be, the time frame involved, and, if they want to limit only certain subsidies, what types of farms will have their subsidies reduced.

Opposition: The opposition's case will change depending on the proposition's case. Generally speaking, the opposition might want to argue to keep farm subsidies as they are or even to increase them for certain subsets of the farming industry, for example, those that engage in greener and organic farming practices.

PROS

Large agricultural enterprises are far better equipped to deal with natural disasters than small farms. While in the past one bad year would spell the ruin of the family farm, this is no longer the case. According to the

CONS

Agricultural subsidies will always be necessary because crop yields can vary from year to year. The nature of Mother Nature is to have good years and bad—sometimes the year is bad with frost killing young plants,

Department of Agriculture, as of 1997, just 2 percent of U.S. farms produced more than 50 percent of U.S. agricultural goods, suggesting that most goods come from huge agricultural centers. These megafarms are able to use advanced technology and farming techniques to weather tough times.

In fact, the markets for nonsubsidized products have grown far more than the markets for subsidized products. For example, according to the U.S. Department of Agriculture, cash receipts for nonsubsidized products like nuts and fruits grew by 186 percent from 1980 to 2005, while receipts for the most subsidized crops, for instance, corn and sugarcane, rose just 14 percent. Because the current subsidies target just a few areas and do not necessarily target those products that consumers most want, decreasing subsidies would not necessarily drive Americans to buy foreign products.

Subsidies cost a lot in tax money and distort the market system. First, the U.S. Department of Agriculture reported that as of 2007, they cost taxpayers almost $20 billion a year, yet

rain flooding them out, or sun scorching them before they can be harvested. One bad year could put many farms out of business, which could compromise our food sources by sending prices skyward. Bad weather in other parts of the world can even lead to shortages here—in which case subsidies would be necessary to allow farms to engage in larger operations than they usually do, for example, to supply extra cotton in the face of the shortage that arose from freak weather in 2010.

By subsidizing agricultural products, we reduce the need to import food from elsewhere and possibly encourage countries to reduce their tariffs. Agricultural goods entering the U.S. are subject to an average tariff of about 12 percent, while American agricultural goods entering other countries are subject to average tariffs more than five times that figure. The government should support local food production so that people buy fewer foreign products, which might force other countries to reduce their tariffs to get our business. Such action will ultimately result in more, and cheaper, goods for everyone and is more environmentally sound as it reduces the need to use fossil fuels to transport produce and other foodstuffs thousands of miles. Besides, the need for crops can change: while some countries are plagued with too much corn, for example, others face a shortage as they use it increasingly as an alternative fuel in the form of ethanol.

Subsidies lower food prices. Even in this wealthy country, many Americans are quite poor and struggle to put food on the table. When production is subsidized, farmers do go to only a few agricultural products. Indeed, in countries like New Zealand, which has mostly dismantled its subsidy program, citizens have not experienced disruptions and are no worse off. Second, when farmers are forced to compete in the market, they will be more efficient, which will lower the cost of production and thus push down prices.

Subsidies encourage waste and overproduction. Many farmers are given money whether or not they actually need it, which is a waste of money. Farmers then grow more crops or raise more animals than can be sold, saved, or exported, leading to waste. Such overproduction is also bad for the environment, as land is deforested and used for food production.

Agribusinesses in the United States are enormous and aim to make a profit; thus as farming needs change, so will the practices of these businesses. Accordingly, subsidies will still be unnecessary. The concept of supply and demand is the cornerstone of our capitalist economy. If different crops become more or less in demand, large businesses will adjust their supply. While this may have been difficult in days past—where small farmers wouldn't have had the knowledge and equipment to adapt—this is no longer the case. Agribusiness conglomerates have access to almost unlimited capital and the latest farming technology.

not need to charge as much for their products to cover their costs. Reducing subsidies would make it harder for Americans, and even people in other countries who rely on American exports, to get enough to eat.

What is better? Too much or too little? An adequate food supply is essential for the health of the nation, so it is worth ensuring. Besides, if farms actually produce too much, then we should look into ways to provide this food to areas in the world where it is needed rather than ask farmers to produce less when there are still people who are hungry. Furthermore, farmers know how to take care of the land—according to the Department of Agriculture, from 1982 to 2001, the average erosion rate for an acre of farmland dropped by about 34 percent.

Even if subsidies seem superfluous now, they are only going to become more and more necessary. As the population explodes, we will certainly be facing global food shortages. Our crops will be necessary to feed our own population and to help others. As a food crunch hits, other countries will be less likely to export to us as they save their agricultural production for internal use, the way India slowed cotton exports in 2010 when a shortage didn't leave enough to both export and satisfy domestic demand. Additionally, some crops that seem abundant now will become more necessary as we discover new uses for them, for example, some may be used to replace fossil fuels.

OTHER MOTIONS:

End agricultural subsidies

Agricultural subsidies do more harm than good

RELATED MOTIONS:

Increase farm subsidies for organic production

WEB LINKS:

- Council on Foreign Relations. "Should the U.S. Cut Its Farm Subsidies?" <http://www.cfr.org/publication/13147/should_the_united_states_cut_its_farm_subsidies.html>. An in-depth debate on the issue between two experts.

- Environmental Working Group. Farm Subsidy Database. <http://farm.ewg.org/farm/>. Information on farm subsidies from an organization opposed to them.

- Powell, Benjamin. "It's Time to End Farm Subsidies." <http://www.independent.org/newsroom/article.asp?id=1477>. Argues against maintaining current levels of farm subsidies.

Fashion Models, Size Zero

Motion **Size zero fashion models should be banned**

Introduction Eras in modeling often have names that proclaim the unhealthy slenderness of the women who wear the clothes, for example, the "gamines" of the 1950s, the "waifs" of the 1960s, and the "heroin chic" of the 1980s and 1990s. Designers prefer tall, extremely slender models because their bodies do not distract from the clothing. Opponents say the models are unhealthy and what the models do to remain slender is dangerous. The extremely thin bodies of most models send the wrong signals to women—who often try to achieve the same size. Ordinary young women engage in practices that eventually lead to full-blown eating disorders. A backlash is now growing—with some major fashion venues refusing to work with models with BMIs (body mass indexes) that are too low for their height. Health watchdogs praise this move; opponents say it is discriminatory—some women are naturally very slender.

Debating the Motion Several major fashion houses as well as fashion industry heads have said they will not employ models whose BMI is below the healthy minimum. Both teams can start their research by investigating the reasons for that decision. Research into the history of fashion modeling might also reveal clues about why the industry decided that only very thin women were best for modeling clothes. Many examples exist of models who both suffer from eating disorders and, more rarely, are naturally slender despite eating reasonably. Finding examples of such cases will be necessary to back up the arguments that both teams create.

Proposition: The proposition might want to include a plan for this ban that would state any alternatives or circumstances in which exceptions to the rule of no size zero would be allowed.

Opposition: The opposition does not need to argue for the use of very thin models; they could opt for arguing that private employers have the right to choose their employees. Additionally, they might focus on the difference between "causation" and "correlation." Does the fashion industry actually cause eating disorders or does there just happen to be a connection between skinny people and modeling?

PROS

Using size zerow models sends the wrong message, particularly to young women: skinny=beautiful. This concept is dangerous; it can lead to low self-esteem or even eating disorders. The potential damage to both models and other women is not worth having significantly underweight models.

The current pressure for models to be size zero promotes eating disorders among them. Further, the emphasis on being just skin and bones encourages models to develop an unhealthy relationship with food. Eating disorders can result in life-altering illnesses and even death.

The opposition's suggestion is very unlikely. Models are generally required to be taller than average. To be a size zero while also being nearly six feet tall (or taller) indicates that a model is certainly too skinny and thus unhealthy.

CONS

Saying that low self-esteem or eating disorders are caused by skinny models is simplistic. The underlying causes of eating disorders are complex. Eliminating thin models will not solve the problem; the obsession with being thin can be found outside the fashion industry, for example, in the entertainment industry. Actors have a far broader impact than runway models. Only when actors can be as successful at size ten as they are at zero should we consider banning size zero models.

Being thin is a necessary part of a model's job. No football team is criticized for telling linebackers to beef up! Many naturally thin women try modeling because this is the only industry where they won't be criticized for being very tall and very thin. If women are not naturally a size zero, the fashion industry should not hire them. Instead of banning models who are healthy and naturally thin, the industry should develop guidelines for hiring. These guidelines should prevent the hiring of anyone who does not naturally have the body shape and weight that the industry wants.

Nature gave each of us a body type—some of us may be a natural size zero. It's important to remember that BMIs aren't everything: they aren't accurate for non-average body types like women with boyish figures, very short people, or even most Latino people, just to name a few. An average woman who naturally doesn't have curves might be healthy at size zero, while a petite woman might easily be a healthy size zero. Are we going to ban them from modeling because their body is naturally a healthy size zero?

Using size zero models doesn't make good business sense since the average woman is closer to size 12. What would make more sense is for fashion houses to use models whose bodies more closely resemble those of the women who will actually wear the clothes. Using average-size models will also encourage designers to design clothes that look good on the average woman. If the average woman can easily find clothes that are fashionable and that fit, they will purchase more. Fashion industry profits will go up!

The need for a "blank slate" to show clothes does not necessitate a size zero model! Surely designers could find models without distracting features who are a healthy size. Additionally, it makes very little sense for designers to show clothes in this manner: if a dress only looks good on a six-foot-tall, 100 pound person—who in real life would buy it?

Designers should consider what is best for society and not use very thin models. Designers have a great deal of influence on how women view themselves. Therefore, designers have a moral responsibility not to encourage unhealthy behavior. They must choose the greater good over their own preferences.

The main point is: Who are you trying to sell to? Certain companies design for and try to sell their products to average or even larger people—they often employ bigger models. But many high fashion houses sell their products to celebrities or the wealthy. These individuals tend to be, for the most part, much skinnier. Thus, it makes sense for high fashion designers to show their clothes on bodies that resemble the people they are trying to sell to.

Designers prefer size zero models for a reason. Designers aim to sell clothes, not people. When patrons are leaving a fashion show, the designer wants them to remember the clothes and not the person wearing them. Models with straight bodies that lack distinctive curves or features are the closest designers can get to a mannequin, thus the need for slender models.

Designers should be able to choose the models who display their clothes. Just like moviemakers can pick the location the actors work in or the artist can choose what to create, designers should have the right to show their clothes as they see fit. If their choice is a size zero model, it is their choice.

OTHER MOTIONS:
Models with unhealthy BMIs should be banned
Designers should be free to choose whomever they wish to show their clothing line

RELATED MOTIONS:
The fashion industry has a moral obligation to set a healthy example

WEB LINKS:

- BBC News. <http://news.bbc.co.uk/2/hi/europe/5341202.stm>. Article on Madrid Fashion Week's ban on very thin models.

- Derbyshire, David. <http://www.telegraph.co.uk/news/uknews/1540595/Fashion-leaders-refuse-to-ban-size-zero-models.html>. Article discussing the British Fashion Council's decision to resist a ban on ultrathin models.

- Disordered Eating. <http://www.disordered-eating.co.uk/eating-disorders-news/milan-bans-thin-models.html>. Article on the Milan fashion industry's code of conduct, which bans ultrathin models.

Federal Student Aid

Motion | **The government should increase federal student aid**

Introduction | Across the United States, students have protested increases in tuition at both private and public universities. Soaring costs now keep a college education out of range for poor and even middle-class families. In the 1970s, government Pell Grants were sufficient to cover the entire cost of tuition at a state college, with enough left over to pay for room and board. These days, annual tuition has soared to almost $20,000 a year for a public college, while the same grant still provides only a few thousand dollars. Many believe that the government needs to increase the aid it provides to students, while others say it is not the government's responsibility to fund a college education.

Debating the Motion | Both teams should familiarize themselves with the various types of federal aid as well as the trends in the amounts allocated for federal grants and subsidized loans. They should also research the cost of colleges and trends in private aid for students. Finally, they should investigate the plight of middle-class families, many of whom cannot afford college and are ineligible for all types of federal assistance.

Proposition: Because the words *increase* and *aid* are vague, the proposition needs to define them. Is the proposition recommending an increase in grants, loans, or both? The team should also offer a plan specifying the dollar amount or percentage of increase and a time frame for implementation. They also need to consider the kinds of students who would be eligible for aid for specific expenses.

Opposition: The opposition has a number of options in countering the proposition's case. The first is to argue that it is not the government's responsibility to pay for anyone's college education. The opposition might also argue that it is the responsibility of universities to help their students pay for an education. The opposition can also argue that college is a luxury, and that families either need to save to send their children to college or recognize that college is not an option for their children. Finally, the opposition can run a counter case, for example, one in which they suggest that Congress pass a law making private borrowing for college easier without putting the financial burden on the government.

PROS

The government has a responsibility to provide access to higher education for those who are not wealthy. In today's service-driven economy, college is crucial for almost any career. The government has also consistently recognized the importance of making college accessible by establishing publicly funded universities and giving government grants and government loans. Tough economic times make paying for college increasingly difficult; therefore, the government should increase the amount of aid it offers.

The lack of government aid forces universities to choose candidates based on their ability to pay. This is unfair because in forcing students to come up with rapidly increasing tuitions, universities may end up scaring off some of their best applicants. Who knows if tuition concerns might thoroughly discourage or force a university not to admit the next Einstein or Obama?

Failure to increase student aid unfairly targets the poor. The government already has legislation in place to ensure the equal treatment in education of people of all colors, races, and classes. Offering more federal aid would be an extension of this, guaranteeing that individuals would not be judged on their financial means, which is often the deal breaker in college admissions today.

CONS

The government certainly is not responsible for sending everyone to college. The creation of the Pell Grants and the Higher Education Act of 1965 happened in the midst of the Cold War and the space race, when the United States needed to dominate in science and other fields to counter the Soviet Union. This legislation was passed as a matter of national security. The Cold War is long over and that necessity has passed. No one has a right to higher education. Basic education—like learning to read—is a prerequisite for individuals to use their abilities and successfully navigate modern-day society, but governments need do no more than equip their citizens with the basic tools. At a certain point, individuals must do what it takes to get an education.

If the ridiculous increases in tuition are keeping potential geniuses from college, then the universities themselves must rethink their spending habits. The government is not obliged to cover a university's financial mismanagement. Universities spend ridiculous amounts of money on public relations campaigns and fancy sports centers—they simply need to budget better.

Private universities are exactly that—private. Of course they should not discriminate, but they are not obliged to offer their services to those who cannot afford them. Just as private employers may try to hire employees willing to take the lowest salary, so can universities look at financial status when evaluating candidates. It is up to families to make a long-term plan to pay for their children's college education—whether that means cutting back on spending, taking out private loans, or finding the funds somewhere else.

PROS

Investing in education is good for the U.S. economy. To remain a global power, we need an educated population. Today, we are falling behind other countries in math and science; we need to be able to compete with rapidly developing nations like China and India. Spending more on education is the government's key tool in maintaining U.S. global dominance. Individuals with college degrees also make—and thus probably spend and pay taxes on—more than those lacking a degree. According to the U.S. Census Bureau, in 2007, the average salary of someone with a four-year degree was twice as much as the average salary of someone with just a high school degree.

CONS

The aid itself costs the government—and the taxpayers—tens of billions of dollars, without guarantee of returns. Many with college degrees have been laid off in recent years or are having trouble finding work to begin with. As a college degree decreases in value, it is no longer a guarantee of a good job and higher earning potential. In fact, as the world economy changes, skills necessary for careers in fields like technology are not necessarily learned in colleges, which often focus on the liberal arts.

OTHER MOTIONS:

The U.S. should increase the Pell Grant

The government should increase spending on college financial aid

RELATED MOTIONS:

Higher education is a right for all citizens

Federal aid should only be used for public schools

Government loans should be abandoned in favor of grants for any needy student

WEB LINKS:

- ChessInc. <http://www.chessconsulting.org/financialaid/history.htm> A history of financial aid.

- Financial Aid Finder. "New Federal Grants for American College Students." <http://www.financialaidfinder.com/new-federal-grants-for-american-college-students.html>. Latest information on new government aid for students.

- Kroll, Andy. "Shut Out: How the Cost of Education Is Dividing Our Country." <http://www.commondreams.org/view/2009/04/03-3>. Overview of the crisis of college affordability.

Felon Disenfranchisement

Motion **Restore voting rights of ex-felons**

Introduction According to The Sentencing Project, over 5 million U.S. citizens are ineligible to vote because of their criminal pasts. Most states impose limitations on the voting rights of convicted felons; many do not permit incarcerated felons to vote, but some continue the voting ban for a period of years even after the felon has completed his sentence. With the growth of the prison population in the United States, these laws are affecting increasing numbers. Momentum has grown for change, with reformers arguing that prohibiting an individual from voting is an inappropriate punishment in a democracy. Supporters of the ban assert that convicted criminals have forfeited that right.

Debating the Motion Both teams need to research state laws on disenfranchisement; provisions vary significantly. In addition, they should research statistics on who and how many people are affected as well as the arguments of legal advocates on both sides of the issue.

Proposition: The proposition should create a clear plan outlining whether they want to end the ban on disenfranchisement completely, which would mean those in prison could vote, or whether they would end it at some point after felons had served their time. The team can use whatever state policy seems best to them as a framework for their own plan or they can create a new plan altogether.

Opposition: The opposition could propose a blanket counter case wherein felons lose their rights to vote period. The other option would be to argue against the specifics of the proposition's plan.

PROS

Not allowing former felons to vote punishes those who have already done jail time and paid for their crimes The concept of sending people to prison boils down to something very simple: if you do the crime, you are going to do the time. Essential to this idea is that once an offender has finished his prison term, he has paid for his crime and should no longer be treated differently from other citizens.

CONS

No reason for punishment to consist only of prison time. Felons commit the most serious of crimes, and so they should receive the most serious punishment. Criminals are often banned from obtaining licenses for certain occupations or from going near certain areas (for example, sex offenders in school zones)—many punishments extend past prison time and this is not inherently unjust.

PROS

Disenfranchisement does not deter others from committing crimes and may even encourage former felons to continue disobeying the law. When releasing criminals, one of the biggest risks is recidivism (or reoffending). By disenfranchising felons, we deny them the ability to fully reintegrate into society and to exercise their political rights. Making former felons second-class citizens may discourage them from obeying laws, since they have had no part in making them and are not seen as full or respected members of society. Furthermore, disenfranchisement is unlikely to deter others—if someone is irrational enough to be undeterred by the possibility of many years in jail, adding disenfranchisement to the punishment is unlikely to change his behavior.

Felon disenfranchisement unfairly targets poor and minority communities, since felons disproportionately come from such backgrounds. A cycle is created wherein felons cannot vote to bring attention to their communities, so these communities get, at best, inadequate social services, which leads to more poverty and crime—and more felons who cannot vote. Indeed, The Sentencing Project reports that 13 percent of black men in America cannot vote because of felon disenfranchisement laws.

Denying people the right to vote is unconstitutional. Because disenfranchisement carries out a punishment for an unspecified length of time and hurts a citizen long after he has served his sentence, it constitutes a cruel and unusual punishment. This is especially so if someone's rights are rescinded for life based on one offense, for example, a single instance of a nonviolent crime.

CONS

In fact, disenfranchising felons sends them, and others, a very clear message that what they did was wrong. Disenfranchised felons are constantly reminded that they will be punished for committing crimes. Furthermore, disenfranchisement may deter others from doing wrong, since most people do not want to lose the right to vote. The harsher the punishment, the more likely rational individuals are to want to avoid it. Stopping the felon from reoffending is important, but so is discouraging other individuals from committing crimes.

If particular racial and economic groups are overrepresented in our prisons, the solution is not to reduce the punishment—it is to attack the root of the problem and fight poverty and inequality. If we recognize that certain neighborhoods have higher levels of crime, then we need to invest in these neighborhoods by increasing education, social services, etc. Such grassroots work can stop individuals from committing crimes in the first place. There is no need to interfere with justice. Furthermore, disenfranchising one subset of society does not stop the majority of people in these communities from being heard.

The state already reserves the right to impose indefinite punishments such as life sentences in prison. For those lucky enough to get out, losing the right to vote is not cruel or unusual. It does not physically harm the person in any way, so it cannot be considered cruel.

PROS

Disenfranchisement is especially unjust for those individuals who have committed less serious crimes. Even if we concede that some felonies are so serious that we would not want to have people who committed them picking our president, we have to recognize that felonies come in all shapes and sizes. Different crimes are assigned different punishments because no single punishment fits them all. If someone commits a heinous crime like murder, we do not have to worry about his rights after prison because he probably will not be released. However, we can assume that many convicted of lesser felonies will never commit another crime. For example, a person who steals once might never steal again—why shouldn't that person be able to vote?

Felons have unique perspectives that deserve to be heard in elections. They have firsthand experience of the criminal justice system, thus their voices are extremely important. Furthermore, plenty of people who can vote have "dangerous" or "irresponsible" views—if we allow neo-Nazis and racists to vote, why should those who have committed crimes be left out? Finally, felons do not make up a large enough proportion of the population to have an effect on elections without at least *some* support from noncriminals, thus they are unlikely to be responsible for the passing of anything especially radical.

CONS

There is no such thing as a "lesser" felony. We classify crimes in different ways to indicate their level of severity—the least harmful crimes are classified as misdemeanors. They command lighter sentences—in some cases, community service or even a fine will suffice. With these missteps, society is more able to forgive. A felony, on the other hand, is by definition serious and deserves a more serious punishment, including disenfranchisement.

Letting felons take part in such a serious and consequential process as an election is dangerous. If someone has shown herself to be as immoral, antisocial, and irresponsible as a felon, she is in no way competent to help decide the course of an entire nation. Voting is an immense responsibility—there is a reason we do not allow minors, who we deem immature and irresponsible, to cast ballots.

OTHER MOTIONS:
Felons should not be allowed to vote
Disenfranchisement is always wrong

RELATED MOTIONS:
   Prisoners should be allowed to vote

WEB LINKS:
- Nakagaw, Scot. "Felony Disenfranchisement: The Roots of Exclusion." <http://www.safetyandjustice.org/node/195>. Article providing historical background on the issue.
- ProCon.org. "State Felony Voting Laws." <http://felonvoting.procon.org/view.resource.php?resourceID=000286>. Summary chart on laws.
- The Sentencing Project. "Felony Disenfranchisement Laws in the United States." <http://www.sentencingproject.org/doc/publications/fd_bs_fdlawsinusMarch2010.pdf>. Overview and latest information on changes in sentencing laws.

Gas Guzzlers, Ban

Motion **Ban cars getting under 30 MPG**

Introduction Between 2000 and 2010, monster cars dominated the roads. SUVs, vans, trucks, even Hummers based on military vehicles began appearing everywhere as status symbols. Despite the outcry from environmental groups about the single-digit miles per gallon of some vehicles, what finally slowed the sale of such vehicles was the rising cost of fuel. In a bid to reduce emissions, many countries, including the United States, have raised minimum fuel efficiency standards to be met within the decade. However, this will not address the thousands of gas guzzlers already on the road or that will continue to be sold until new regulations take effect.

Debating the Motion Many countries already have bans in place or are gradually imposing them; both teams should research them.

Proposition: The proposition must define *car* (does it include personal trucks, vans, or SUVs, for example) and should outline a time frame for the ban. The team also should be clear on whether this proposed ban would affect the manufacture of new cars, cars already on the road, or both.

Opposition: The opposition does not need to argue in favor of gas guzzlers! Instead, it could argue that a ban would actually be harmful, for a variety of reasons including cost and availability. The team could also argue that such a ban is unnecessary: new fuel economy standards worldwide combined with increasingly efficient technology means that these cars will phase themselves out naturally and thus no contentious legislation is necessary.

PROS

Gas guzzlers should be banned because they are simply too costly to maintain. The fuel alone can cost hundreds of dollars a month.

CONS

People can choose how to spend their own money. If people can afford the cost of running these cars, then they should be allowed to have and use them.

PROS

Driving these cars is irresponsible because petroleum is a nonrenewable resource. These cars are called "gas guzzlers" for a reason—some of them get as little as eight miles to the gallon. We should not waste petroleum when we know that at some point in the future, it will simply be unavailable.

These cars are extremely bad for the environment. They spew unnecessarily high amounts of emissions into our atmosphere—we have many choices of vehicles that can carry the same number of people or the same amount of equipment and yet be more efficient. By allowing some people's selfish actions to continue, everyone suffers the ill-effects of the damage done to the environment. We need to enact a ban to protect everyone from these kinds of vehicles.

Removing gas guzzlers would increase road safety. Currently, many accidents involve a large car like a SUV and a smaller one. When large cars are banned and everyone is driving smaller cars, everyone is safer on the road.

By banning gas guzzlers, we can force car designers and manufacturers to produce more efficient cars. Car companies would be forced to offer new models with better fuel economy; this would spur them to work to create fuel-conserving technologies. Such improvements would make all cars better and allow us to conserve fuel while we work toward improving the environment.

CONS

As the availability of oil and gasoline decreases and the price of fuel rises in response, people will stop driving these cars of their own accord. Right now, we have enough reasonably priced fuel available, thus banning these cars is pointless.

While it is not ideal that these vehicles consume so much fuel, they are necessary in certain circumstances. When driving through rough terrain or hauling large equipment, such powerful vehicles are necessary. Small, energy efficient cars sometimes can't do the job. If you have a lot to haul, is using several small cars to carry the load more environmentally sound than using one SUV? In some cases, these vehicles are actually the most effective and thus environmentally responsible way to get the job done.

These cars are big—bigger is better because bigger cars keep us safer. In driving conditions that are less than ideal, a larger car can save lives. They are safer in crashes with other cars and some can even hold their own against large trucks—situations where smaller cars would crumple like a soda can.

While car companies are scrambling to develop new cars, they would almost certainly lose revenue. Such loss might cause some companies that cannot innovate fast enough to go under. This would result in a huge loss of jobs, not only for those who work for the failed companies but for all those employed in related industries

OTHER MOTIONS:

We must ban gas guzzlers

The government should set tougher fuel economy standards

RELATED MOTIONS:

Driving vehicles with low fuel economy is unethical

WEB LINKS:

- Autopia. "Ban All Cars Getting Less Than 35 MPG?" <http://www.wired.com/autopia/2008/02/ban-all-cars-wi>. Article discussing the pros and cons of the ban.

Genetically Modified Foods

Motion **Genetically modified foods do more good than harm**

Introduction Genetically modified foods are those that have had changes introduced into their DNA by genetic engineering techniques. These techniques are used to increase the nutritional value of foods, to make crops resistant to disease, and to produce more food with fewer chemicals. Genetically modified foods are controversial. Proponents maintain that they are hardier, grow well in more adverse conditions, and have many other benefits. Opponents worry about safety and environmental issues.

Debating the Motion Both teams need to research the processes used to modify foods and the kinds of foods usually modified. Because these processes are controversial, they will find a lot of arguments on both sides of the issue. But beware! A lot of misinformation is circulating on this topic, so teams should be cautious in their research and make sure that they are using only reputable sources.

Proposition: The proposition does not need to argue that genetically modified foods are all good or risk-free but that simply, on balance, they do more good than harm. The team also might want to specify what they mean by *good*.

Opposition: The opposition has the option of either proving that the harms outweigh the benefits of genetically modified foods or of showing them to be neutral, neither beneficial nor harmful. Because this technology is relatively new, provable harms are few, so the opposition will need to look at projected difficulties described by reputable agencies.

PROS

Genetically modified foods are the best tools we have for combating hunger. The nearly 7 billion people on Earth need to be fed every day. Genetic modification allows us to grow crops that are more resistant to weather, more nutritious, and less prone to rot. It could be especially useful for nations with rapidly growing populations and extreme weather conditions, such as in sub-Saharan Africa and Southeast Asia.

CONS

Genetic modification does not increase crop yield; besides, the problem of world hunger is attributable to unequal distribution of food, not a lack of it. First, a 20-year study conducted by the Union of Concerned Scientists found that genetic modification had no substantial impact on the amount of food produced in the U.S. Other organizations' researchers in countries such as India have come to similar conclusions. Second and more important, farmers of the world already produce enough food to feed everyone. The problem is that countries like the U.S. consume more than their share, while countries in the developing or undeveloped world get the short end of the stick. To combat world hunger, we need better ways of distributing food equitably—simply producing more food does not attack the root of the problem.

Genetically modified foods are better for the environment than regular crops. One of the biggest struggles we face is the problem of pesticides—they are often necessary to protect crops from insects, but they are highly toxic and can greatly damage the environment. Genetically modified foods reduce our reliance on chemical pesticides because we can modify crops to be naturally pest resistant.

Genetically modified plants can cross-breed with other plants, producing "super weeds" and can also be dangerous for the ecosystem. First, while resistance is wonderful when it occurs in the plants that we want to grow, it is dangerous in plants that we consider menacing and that could damage our crops. Resistant plants can cross-pollinate with weeds when their pollen blows, creating super weeds that themselves are resistant to any attempts to eradicate them. Second, genetically modified plants can harm the food web. For example, skylarks in Britain were greatly harmed by the introduction of genetically modified sugar beets. Because the beets could resist weeds, the amount of weeds was greatly reduced, and skylarks, who rely on the weeds' seeds, were forced to find food elsewhere. Also, animals that eat genetically modified crops can be harmed by the built-in pesticides.

Intellectual property rights are a distinct issue from genetically modified food. Corporations may be trying to exploit the use of genetic-modification technology, but that does not mean that the procedure itself is wrong or harmful. This is a separate ethical and legal debate.

Corporations and multinationals can use patents to exploit the developing world. No legal consensus exists about whether genetically modified crops can be patented, so some companies are forcing farmers to pay royalties in exchange for using their seeds. Genetic modification gives big business one more way to profit at the expense of small agriculture.

Genetic modification can increase the nutritional value of foods, which means we can eat less while still getting important vitamins and minerals. For vegetarians or people who lack access to meat, iron and protein could be found in fruits and vegetables. For kids who are picky about certain less attractive but necessary foods, their nutrients could be put into simple foods like apples and oranges. By combining the benefits of some foods with the better taste of others, we can make everyone healthier.

Fruits and vegetables could be genetically modified to contain vaccines against dangerous diseases. We struggle right now to adequately vaccinate people around the world against various controllable diseases. This struggle is, in part, because vaccinations and other medicine are expensive and require specific modes of transport and storage for them to be administered and work effectively. Scientists now think they can put vaccinations and medications into food through genetic modification. Imagine apples that could also vaccinate against polio or measles! Apples are easier to store, easier to transport, and safer to administer. We could help vaccinate millions and keep people from dying of preventable diseases.

Genetically modifying food can also make some people very sick. By combining the genes of multiple foods, we run the risk of transferring genes from plants that may cause reactions in humans to ones that generally do not—thus, making these "safe" foods risky for some. Some plants, like peanuts or strawberries, are notorious for the number of allergens they contain. Other foods, like apples, are less likely to cause allergic reactions. For example, when we combine the genes of peanuts with tomatoes, we run the risk of making relatively safe tomatoes into an allergy risk.

Putting vaccines in food poses potential risks as well. The chance of someone accidentally taking a traditional vaccine is small—most people do not normally interact with needles and refrigerated vials so they could never mistake a traditional vaccine for something normally eaten. But with vaccines taking the form of ordinary foods like apples, a definite risk arises of vaccination foods being mistaken for ordinary foods. People will wind up taking medicine that they do not need and that could actually harm them.

OTHER MOTIONS:

Genetically modified foods do more harm than good

Ban genetically modified foods

RELATED MOTIONS:

Genetically modified foods are the wave of the future

Genetically modified foods are unethical

WEB LINKS:

- Biotechnology Institute. "Genetically Modified Food Crops." <http://www. biotechinstitute.org/resources/pdf/yw10_1.pdf>. Detailed overview of the technology and the issues surrounding their use.

- ProQuest. "Genetically Modified Foods; Harmful or Helpful?" <http://www.csa.com/ discoveryguides/gmfood/overview.php>. Background and arguments on both sides of the issue.

- World Health Organization. "20 Questions on Genetically Modified (GM) Foods." <http://www.who.int/foodsafety/publications/biotech/20questions/en/>. Q & A providing background on the topic.

Gentrification

Motion
: **Gentrification does more harm than good**

Introduction
: Gentrification is not a new idea, and has been occurring for centuries. Gentrification is the socioeconomic change that comes to a neighborhood when wealthier people move in and indirectly push poorer people out because rents and housing prices increase as more people want to live in the neighborhood. Although the term often carries a negative connotation, proponents argue that gentrification improves blighted neighborhoods, providing benefits to current residents who do not move.

Debating the Motion
: Both teams need to research the process of gentrification and find notable contemporary examples. They also need to look at the long-term impact of gentrification on neighborhoods and cities as a whole.

Proposition: The proposition must clearly define what they mean by *gentrification* and present the specific harms associated with it. Remember, the topic is not just that gentrification is bad but that it is harmful.

Opposition: The opposition has the option to either paint gentrification as neutral or as a positive.

PROS

There is no benefit to improving a "bad" neighborhood if, ultimately, its residents are simply compelled to move to another bad neighborhood. As the local cost of living increases, the original population is unable to keep up. Struggling neighborhoods exist because some cannot afford better; a process that gets rid of blighted areas by simply pushing people out does not fix the problem, it only masks it.

CONS

Gentrification does not entail forced removal. Whether people leave for more affordable housing or because they are paid to do so, they make their own choice to move. Furthermore, the extent to which original residents move out is exaggerated. A study conducted by Lance Freeman, an urban planning professor at Columbia University, found that low-income, less educated residents are actually least likely to move out of gentrified neighborhoods. For those who do choose to move, their home values will have drastically increased, earning them a large profit when selling a home.

A neighborhood loses part of its culture through gentrification. In part, gentrification has a negative connotation because it takes neighborhoods that, though perhaps run-down, have personality; they offer something unique that gives residents an emotional attachment. Gentrified, suburban, middle-class neighborhoods lose this uniqueness, replacing it with cookie-cutter homes.

Gentrification creates racial and social tensions. As the middle- and upper-class people move in, current residents feel they are being pushed out. Take the example of the controversy over the IKEA store built in Red Hook, Brooklyn. Long-term residents wanted it—the store would create jobs and generate revenue for local business. New, gentrified residents were opposed because the store ruined the waterfront view of Manhattan. Middle- and upper-middle class people have different priorities from poor and working-class residents, creating tension and bitterness.

Gentrification helps only the wealthier incoming residents. As they are the ones with money, they will be the ones whom police and civil services help and protect. The original inhabitants often find themselves harassed into leaving and are forced to move into even more dangerous neighborhoods. An increase in safety for new residents does not help the old ones if they are not there to enjoy it. In terms of the neighborhood economy, gentrification raises prices because the store rents rise. The original residents of the community can no longer afford to live there—and have to move.

Blighted and broken neighborhoods do not have "charm." No one wants to live someplace with smashed street lamps, gang shootings in the street, and robberies at all hours. People move from run-down neighborhoods when they can afford to do so because these neighborhoods, while romanticized by outsiders, are not desirable places to live. Gentrification changes that.

Gentrification is integration. As explained above, many former residents remain in gentrified neighborhoods—and enjoy the benefits that come with the change. Cities benefit from having racially and economically mixed neighborhoods. Gentrification does this by creating a mix of low-income and middle-class individuals and families living in the same neighborhood—all desiring a safe and pleasant place to live. Gentrification gets rid of the system of elite neighborhoods with nearby "ghettos."

Gentrification is beneficial because middle-income residents are better able to fight for services. They also have more money, thus buying more from the local retailers and paying higher taxes. This middle-class presence helps establish better schools, community safety organizations, public services, renovated parks, and public places, etc. Gentrification improves a neighborhood—everyone benefits!

PROS	CONS
Gentrification negatively affects local businesses. Businesses reflect the local population—low-income residents shop differently from middle- and upper-class ones. Businesses that have been in the neighborhood for decades are forced to shut because they do not appeal to new residents; people lose their livelihood because of the displacement of the previous population.	*Gentrification is good for local businesses.* It brings in people with more money to spend. Furthermore, if some businesses are forced to shut, that means demand for those businesses products or services has declined and they are unnecessary—we believe that it is better for useless businesses to be replaced by ones that people actually want.

OTHER MOTIONS:

Gentrification is unethical

Gentrification does more good than harm

RELATED MOTIONS:

Community organizations have a duty to fight gentrification

Businesses should seek to promote gentrification

WEB LINKS:

- Footnotes. "The Double-edged Sword of Gentrification in Atlanta." <http://www.asanet.org/footnotes/apr03/indexthree.html>. Article discussing the problems associated with gentrification.

- PBS. "What Is Gentrification?' <http://www.pbs.org/pov/flagwars/special_gentrification.php>. Article describing the process of gentrification as well as pros and cons.

Health Care, Universal

Motion **The U.S. should have universal health care**

Introduction In 2010, Pres. Barack Obama signed into law an important health care reform bill. Among other mandates, the bill requires most Americans to purchase health insurance and expands Medicaid coverage. Although not as expansive as many European health care models, this act has caused a great deal of controversy in the United States, with some critics arguing that it is too close to a "universal" model, while others maintain that is not "universal" enough. Those opposed to truly universal health care argue that such a large program wastes government resources and violates individuals' liberty. Those who want a more expansive model argue that health care is a fundamental right and that the current system does not go far enough in ensuring that every American is covered (for example, there is no public option).

Debating the Motion Remember that this topic addresses the issue of universal health care, which is not the same as the health reform measure the U.S. adopted in 2010. The United States does not have universal health care. Many other countries already offer universal health care, so both teams should research these—not only to offer examples of how it works in other places but also to see what criticisms and problems exist. Both teams should pay attention to the complaints people have about their health care coverage. Both teams should also look into the history of health care reform in the U.S.

Proposition: The proposition must explain what they mean by universal health care, what kinds of medical services it would cover, and how medical providers will be compensated. They should also indicate how such care would be paid for. This topic will require an especially comprehensive case to counter the opposition, so the team should not be afraid to spend slightly more time than usual setting up the case before introducing arguments.

Opposition: The opposition has the option to argue that paying for health care is simply not the government's responsibility regardless of the benefits; alternatively, the opposition could argue that better ways can be found or established for people to gain access to affordable health insurance. A lot of the criticism about universal health care in the U.S. is speculative because we do not actually have such a system in place, so looking at internal criticism from big national health service organizations in countries like Canada, France, and the U.K. will help the opposition present proven arguments.

PROS

Health care is a basic human right. The rights to life and liberty are both dependant on a relatively high degree of health—people who are ill cannot have full lives. Furthermore, the United Nations has recognized medical care as a right. A country like the U.S., which was founded with the goal of protecting individuals' rights, ought to ensure that every individual has access to health care, but even in the new system, not everyone is covered; in addition, few cost controls have been proposed for insurance premiums.

Most other developed countries provide universal health care and it works well for them. Citizens have a higher quality of life and do not need to worry about seeking treatment for serious health conditions. The French universal health care system, for example, was ranked top in the world by the World Health Organization, while the old U.S. system—and corresponding measures like life span and happiness—regularly received low marks. Although the 2010 reforms have not been properly evaluated, they still lack the expansiveness of successful foreign systems.

A single-payer system would have no for-profit companies, thus health care providers would do what was best for the patients, not the bankroll. In a market system, insurers are often reluctant to cover those individuals who most need care—such as people with pre-existing conditions—because insurers know that such individuals will cost more money. Insurance companies are eager to cover individuals who are less likely to need expensive services and procedures because they will make a greater profit from them. Even in

CONS

The most important right that needs to be protected is the right of citizens to decide the government's role in their lives. It violates individuals' autonomy to force them to pay for something they do not want, yet universal health care would require all Americans to pay taxes to support it. We grant that certain public services, such as a police force, are necessary for civic society, however, as much as possible, individuals should have the right to decide how and on what to spend their money.

Yes, other countries offer universal health care, but we don't know that those systems provide quality care. Wealthy citizens of these countries often invest in private health insurance to receive the level of expert care we expect in the United States. Further, those who do use the government insurance either by choice or necessity often complain about wait times, services, abuses to the system, and substandard care.

If insurance companies were less competitive, the result would be less incentive to do research leading to new cures and medical innovations. If the government covered all costs, the need to compete and thus develop better and more cost-effective methods of treatment would disappear. Competition is necessary in any industry and is essential in health care, where we all must rely on advances to keep us healthy and treat devastating diseases.

a system like "Obamacare," which requires insurance companies to take all applicants, the existence of competition still means that health care providers have an incentive to cut corners or deny service—placing profit before patients' health.

Universal health care would save money. First, it would encourage people to seek medical care early, thus removing the need for more expensive treatments and operations later. For example, finding out about heart problems early could give a patient the chance to change his lifestyle and prevent the need for open heart surgery or even a heart transplant. Second, a single-payer system would have less bureaucracy—for example, Medicare's administrative costs are less than 2 percent of its total budget.

Universal health care would increase taxes. European systems may cover more people, but European taxes also tend to be far higher than those in the U.S. We already spend lots of money on programs like Social Security, and people are already struggling to make ends meet—they don't need higher taxes.

In a universal system, doctors would be more motivated to enter fields such as preventive care. The highest-paying, and consequently most attractive, medical specialties are often those that involve the fanciest operations, like plastic surgery. However, the most important kind of care is preventive—basic health care that ensures that people do not need more expensive operations later on. If the government set salaries with an emphasis on primary care, it could encourage doctors to practice in these fields.

In a universal health care system, doctors' salaries would be set by the government, probably at a lower rate, thus providing less of an incentive for students to enter the medical field. Doctors in some fields would certainly make less money than they do in a market system and, given the high cost of medical school, this would probably be a serious deterrent to those considering becoming health care professionals. Fewer doctors would be the result.

OTHER MOTIONS:

Universal health care is a basic human right

State-funded health care does more harm than good

RELATED MOTIONS:

It is the government's responsibility to provide health care

WEB LINKS:

• BalancedPolitics.org. "Should the Government Provide Free Universal Health Care for All Americans?" <http://www.balancedpolitics.org/universal_health_care.htm>. Overview of the debate.

• Underwood, Anne, and Sarah Arnquist. "Health Care Abroad: France." <http://prescriptions.blogs.nytimes.com/2009/09/11/health-care-abroad-france/>. Explanation of the French health care system, an oft-cited example of universal health care.

• U.S. Department of Health and Human Services. <http://www.healthcare.gov>. Explains the new U.S. health care system.

Health Courses for Students

Motion

Colleges and universities should require health courses for students with unhealthy BMIs

Introduction

Many people are aware of the potential risks that arise from an unhealthy body weight. In an effort to promote the health of its students, Lincoln University in Pennsylvania required all students to undergo a physical examination for graduation and to take a health course if their body mass index (BMI) was over 30, indicating that they were in the obese category. (The BMI is an indicator of body fatness based on a ratio of an average person's weight to height.) Controversy arose because the course was not required of every student, only those deemed to be obese. As efforts are made to combat the bulge that is overtaking the country, education venues are often on the front lines, but should they be? Proponents argue that universities need to educate their students for a successful life and basic health is as major a part of this mission as job-specific coursework. Opponents argue that universities are overstepping their bounds.

Debating the Motion

Both teams should become familiar with the controversy surrounding Lincoln University's requirement. While its policy was aimed at obese individuals, both teams would do well to also consider cases involving underweight individuals. Additionally, the topic of BMIs is controversial in itself, so teams should research the history and current guidelines given by the AMA or other accredited medical bodies.

Proposition: The proposition team should specify what is entailed in the mandatory health courses and also what constitutes an "unhealthy" BMI. A specific plan is a must; investigating the Lincoln University controversy can help you shape that plan. Additionally, because the opposition may attack the concept of the BMI, be prepared to defend its use in your plan.

Opposition: In opposing this motion, you have both general lines of argument to pursue as well as those specific to the elements of the proposition's case. In general, the opposition has the option of disputing the value of the BMI in determining health or arguing that imposing a course on a specific group is discriminatory. The opposition can also argue that such courses are necessary but for everyone, not just a select group. The opposition also can argue against specific elements of the proposition's case.

PROS

Universities have the right to ask their students to adhere to certain regulations. No one is forced to go to college. Students have chosen this specific school—part of that choice involves consent to the school's rules. If you elect to go, you can expect to follow the school's regulations.

The job of the university is to educate, which includes teaching general life skills. Many schools now require students to have counseling and to use their career services. For students who clearly do not know how to manage their own eating and exercise, schools should require health courses the same way they require freshmen to live in the dorms as a necessary life learning experience.

Universities already require other courses in certain situations. Students who are suspected of or have been proven to be abusing drugs, alcohol, or even struggling with managing their anger can be required—as a condition of permitting them to stay enrolled—to take courses that address their issues. Requiring overweight or underweight students to take a health course is the same—remember, poor health is a risk to a student.

Requiring a course will help students avoid stigmatization in later life. Sadly, our society stigmatizes people who are overweight or obese. The university would actually be helping its students by requiring them to deal with these issues so that once they leave the relatively safe environment of the school, they will be able to manage their weight and thus not experience discrimination.

CONS

Universities have the right to make rules but they do not have the right to discriminate. Requiring only those students with BMIs outside the normal range to take a special course is discriminatory. Wouldn't everyone benefit from learning good health habits?

The job of the university is to educate all its students. Colleges do not require only certain students to have counseling or use their career services. Nor do they require only certain freshmen to live in the dorms. If schools think it important to teach general life skills, they should make it a required course, like some schools do World Civilization and other core subjects.

The major difference here is that those issues mentioned by the proposition—drugs, alcohol, anger—pose a distinct danger to members of the university community and to the public at large. Thus, the university has not only the right but also the duty to protect others. Obese or underweight individuals do not pose such sweeping risk to others and, therefore, should not be required to take a course from which the rest of the students are exempt.

These courses are dangerous because they unfairly stigmatize people who are not of average weight. Sticking a bunch of "fat" people or "skinny" people in a course together calls attention to them. Surely these students will be isolated and bullied. Such experiences could cause them long-lasting emotional damage, which would negatively affect their ability to be successful in life.

PROS	CONS
Courses for all would be a waste of resources in a time when universities are struggling to make ends meet and tuition costs are soaring. Those who already manage themselves do not need these services; we can target those who do using far fewer resources.	*A responsible school would require health courses for everyone.* The United States is one of the most obese countries in the world! Everyone needs to know how to maintain a healthy lifestyle. If everyone were required to take a course, no one would be stigmatized. We can also target those who may not yet be unhealthy but would become so as they age and their metabolism changes.

OTHER MOTIONS:

Health courses should be required in universities

K–12 students with unhealthy body weights should be required to take special health classes

RELATED MOTIONS:

Universities should not require PE classes

WEB LINKS:

- CNN. "College's Too-fat-to-graduate Rule Under Fire," <http://www.cnn.com/2009/HEALTH/11/30/lincoln.fitness.overweight/index.html>. Article discussing both sides of the issue.

- WebMD. "How Accurate Is Body Mass Index, or BMI?" <http://www.webmd.com/diet/features/how-accurate-body-mass-index-bmi>. Background information connected to the issue.

International Baccalaureate

Motion **U.S. high schools should use the International Baccalaureate System**

Introduction One of the myriad fixes proposed for the hurting U.S. public education system is the International Baccalaureate (IB) program. While some proponents point to the international advantage IB could provide, others write it off as a fad. In some places, this idea is still very new, while in other parts of the United States, the IB program is already common. The question now is whether schools should be made to implement IB across the country.

Debating the Motion Students should familiarize themselves thoroughly with the history of the IB and what the high school level exam entails today. Additionally, both sides should be prepared to lay out a plan, both for the implementation and an alternative for the opposition.

Proposition: The proposition should lay out a plan for implementing the IB program. As the country already has schools using it, researching those schools' programs will help to give a framework. The proposition's plan should also give a time frame for implementation and address issues such as training teachers in new materials and modes of instruction.

Opposition: The opposition can argue either that it is unnecessary or harmful to require IB or it can create its own counter case for standardizing high school education and exam programs. They could also argue for the status quo: that different curricula and testing systems are an advantage and make our education system diverse and thus richer.

PROS

Implementing the IB program allows us the benefits of a national exam without requiring the resources to create one from scratch. Many believe that to save our struggling school system, the United States needs a national exit exam as a requirement for graduation. Such an exam would ensure that students actually met minimum requirements and prevent them from "slipping through the

CONS

U.S. schools already employ huge amounts of standardized testing, yet our students continue to do poorly by international measures. Implementing the IB, which includes a long series of difficult, high-stakes exams, would only add another unnecessary layer of standardized testing—without addressing the roots of the problem, for example, badly paid and trained teachers or enormous class cracks." U.S. schools could use the national IB exams as such a test. IB has a proven record of being a rigorous and successful program, so we know before implementation that it would be a good evaluative tool.

The IB program could help improve academic standards in this country. American children often lag behind their counterparts in other countries, and many have heard the claim that the U.S. education system is an inch deep and a mile wide. A rigorous and in-depth program like the IB could improve classroom learning by fostering the inquiry and critical thinking that IB classes demand. It would also have rigorous standards for students and teachers alike.

Using the IB will allow our students to become world citizens. The IB is used by many countries throughout the world; indeed, its very title tells its global nature. Studying the same curricula as other students across the world gives our children common ground with their foreign counterparts, promotes a more international perspective in our increasingly globalized world, and could provide access to study at foreign institutions for U.S. students who desire it. At the same time, IB programs can be tailored to local standards, so students would continue to learn about their own country and region.

An investment in education is the best investment we can make. Provided the IB is effective, as we have demonstrated in other arguments, the result—a more educated populace—can do nothing but good for our nation and its economy. Better-educated individuals would be qualified and able to get more high-paying jobs and make the United

sizes. And, exit exams have been shown to discriminate against minority students. Perhaps what the U.S. needs is less standardized testing and more emphasis on actually engaging students in discussion and learning.

The IB is indeed a strong program, but it is too restrictive. If a student wants to do the IB, she must commit to the entire program, whereas AP classes are signed up for on an individual basis. True, the IB is a rigorous and successful program but offers relatively little choice, thus it does not allow students to tailor curricula and pursue subjects in which they are particularly interested. Students should enjoy learning—an overly restrictive curriculum can prevent this.

The IB will require our students to spend less time learning about their own country. Some classes will still focus on the United States, particularly at higher levels, but, in general, the IB is an international program. Encouraging a global perspective is good, but students also need to maintain their national identity. It stands to reason that Americans should learn more U.S. history than students in other countries. Under the IB, however, students across the world study nearly the same subjects.

The implementation of this program is extremely expensive. It is not possible to implement just one or two IB courses, so schools would have to adopt the entire program. In addition to the costs of the exam itself, making IB mandatory would require an expensive overhaul of the current curricula and systems in place in many schools. Additionally, $10,000

PROS	CONS
is not a huge amount in the grand scheme of running a school—consider that state test prep programs cost that much each year for the workbooks alone!	additional and costly training for teachers. Furthermore, it costs about $10,000 for a school to apply for IB authorization and another $5,000–$8,000 a year to maintain accreditation.
Many schools already use the international baccalaureate, but many of these are either private schools for the wealthy or charter schools for the poor. If this program is offering so much success to certain groups in this country, we should make it available to *all* children to level the playing field. Every child deserves a good education—what is unfair is to allow some students to participate in an IB program while denying it to others.	*Simply because many schools use IB already does not mean all schools should implement it.* Many schools use many other systems with great success, and we cannot jump on every fad that comes and goes in education. If parents want their children to participate in the IB, they should lobby local school boards or start their own schools, but why should we insist that every child take part in IB when they already have completely adequate instruction?

OTHER MOTIONS:

The IB is a better tool for getting into college

U.S. high school students should be required to take the IB exams

RELATED MOTIONS:

The IB does more good for students than APs

All U.S. high schools should use a standard curriculum and have exit exams

WEB LINKS:

- Chesterfield County Public Schools. "Benefits of an International Baccalaureate Education." <http://chesterfield.k12.va.us/Schools/Midlothian_HS/ib/info/benefits.htm>. Outlines benefits of IB.

- Fioriello, Patricia. "Pros and Cons of International Baccalaureate Program." <http://drpfconsults.com/pros-and-cons-of-international-baccalaureate-program/>. Description of the program with four arguments for and against it.

- International Baccalaureate Organization. <http://www.ibo.org/>. Outlines pros and cons of the IB.

Junk Food Tax

Motion   **States should implement a tax on junk food**

Introduction   Most Americans oppose any increase in taxes, but one popular way being proposed to raise money for states struggling to balance their budgets is a so-called junk food tax. Similar to taxes on tobacco and alcohol, the junk food tax creates more revenue for government while discouraging bad habits—in this case, eating junk food. While health advocates and state budget officials celebrate this, large corporations and small businesses alike are crying that such tax will be too great a burden and some opponents are claiming it would disproportionately hurt the poor.

Debating the Motion   Several places have already implemented taxes on specific kinds of junk foods such as sugary drinks, so both teams should become familiar with these taxes. The term *junk food* is vague; both teams should define this term. Teams should also look at the effects of the tax.

Proposition: Definitions are especially important for the proposition. The proposition should begin their case outlining what foods are considered junk food: Does the term mean restaurants like McDonald's and cookies at the store; does it include beverages like sodas and juice drinks? Suggesting the specific tax would also be helpful; the team could look at existing soda taxes or even extrapolate from tobacco taxes for suggestions on how much to tax.

Opposition: The opposition should research the impact of taxing items to control behavior, for example, taxing cigarettes. They should also investigate who would be affected by the tax to demonstrate the potentially classist aspects of this tax—which many argue will disproportionately affect the poor. The opposition should look into the effects on those working in food service and related industries, like transportation and delivery. Also, the opposition can argue against the validity of the proposition's definition of the term *junk food* and the tax rate they propose.

PROS

Taxing junk food will raise needed revenue. In our society, we cannot escape junk food! From candy to cookies, from fast food chains

CONS

The tax will hurt the economy and jeopardize jobs. This proposed tax is just a tax like any other—it takes money out of average citizen's to quick munchies and the ice cream man on the corner, junk food is everywhere. Given its overwhelming presence, taxing it is undeniably a good way to raise money. Even if the tax were small, the amount of junk food we consume is so great that states and municipalities could generate so much additional income from such tax that they could fund schools, hospitals, public transportation . . . the possibilities are nearly endless!

The increased cost will make people think twice about unhealthy eating. We have already tried many ways to deter people from overindulging in unhealthy foods. From posting calorie counts to printed warnings to health courses in school, many previous attempts to help individuals make healthier choices (and possibly avoid obesity) have failed. So, we have one more option that is relatively fail-safe: hit people in the wallet.

Taxes do work as a deterrent. For example, since we began heavily taxing tobacco products, smoking has decreased. If imposing high taxes on tobacco products—arguably much more addictive than junk food—worked, such taxes will surely decrease junk food consumption.

Any program or tax that guides the poor to make healthier choices will have immediate benefits. The poor are less able to pay for

pocket by putting a premium on goods that many people buy regularly, even daily. Additionally, a tax will put a drag on existing producers and possibly deter new producers from investing in our country.

The tax won't help stop unhealthy eating. Those people who want alcohol and cigarettes still buy them. People will still buy and eat junk food. It will just cost them more to do so and, sadly, those least able to afford to spend extra will be hit the hardest.

You can't prove that taxes are a deterrent. Smoking has gone down, but that doesn't mean that higher tobacco taxes led to the decline. Many other factors might have contributed or caused the decrease, like public campaigns and increased knowledge of the dangers. In fact, given all the antismoking measures in place, it is impossible to tell which one really made a difference—the taxes might have nothing to do with it! We might experience the same with junk food—if we do see a decline in the purchase of junk food, such a drop would probably be the result of growing awareness of health issues and not to taxation.

This proposed tax amounts to nothing more than a tax on those citizens least able to pay it. The poor consume greater amounts of junk

PROS	CONS
health care, so better food choices will help them maintain their health and thus lessen or even avoid health care costs later in life.	food. In neighborhoods where good-quality food may be unavailable, stores and restaurants usually offer only processed and junk foods. This new tax will unfairly burden those who already can barely afford what they need.

OTHER MOTIONS:

Sugary drinks should be taxed

Taxing junk food is unethical

RELATED MOTIONS:

Junk food companies should pay higher taxes

WEB LINKS:

- Grist. "Study Suggests Junk Food Taxes May Beat Healthy Food Subsidies." <http://www.grist.org/article/study-suggests-junk-food-taxes-may-beat-healthy-food-subsidies/>. Article discussing the benefits of taxing junk food.

- New Yorkers Against Unfair Taxes. <http://www.nobeveragetax.com>. Site presents information in opposition to a beverage tax.

- Reuters. "Battle Lines Drawn Over Soda, Junk Food Taxes." <http://www.reuters.com/article/idUSTRE5806E520090901>. Article presenting arguments on both sides of the issue.

Juvenile Offenders in Adult Courts

Motion   **Juvenile offenders should never be tried as adults**

Introduction   In recent years, trying minors in adult courts has become easier and easier. Some states have no current limit on how young an "adult" offender can be, with children as young as ten being tried in adult courts. Advocates of trying minors in adult courts argue that serious, especially violent, crimes require very serious punishment, and the only appropriate venue is adult court. Opponents argue that because of the inherent differences between children and adults, we cannot prosecute them at the same level.

Debating the Motion   Both teams should familiarize themselves with the major differences between the juvenile and adult criminal courts as well as laws that permit juveniles to be tried as adults. Creating a simple chart outlining which ages, which crimes, and what punishments are allowed by state will allow both teams to draw general conclusions. Research also needs to be done into the physical and psychological differences between adults and youths of various ages.

Proposition: The proposition must explicitly state what is meant by *juvenile offender* by clarifying at what age a person would stop being a juvenile. It might also lay out a plan for exactly what changes would be made to the juvenile system to allow for adequate punishment of serious offenders.

Opposition: The opposition has the option of arguing against the specifics of the proposition's case, such as their definition of *juvenile* or arguing against "never" by demonstrating that, under certain circumstances, trying juveniles as adults is appropriate.

PROS

Juveniles must be cut some slack for their actions because they do not fully understand right and wrong. Research has shown that juvenile offenders do not have the ability to understand the consequences of their actions as fully as adults. For example, very young children may not realize that when they shoot someone, death is permanent. Therefore, even if they commit a serious crime, they do not deserve the same punishment as an adult.

CONS

That is no excuse for murder, rape, or other serious crimes. We might refrain from judging teens for obnoxious behavior, but juveniles do know the difference between right and wrong. They are capable of understanding that killing someone is wrong.

PROS	CONS
We need to rehabilitate young offenders, not punish them. Young brains are still growing and changing, so juvenile offenders are capable of changing. Because minors are still in formation, the right care and treatment are more likely to rehabilitate them than they would an adult. As such, they should be tried in the juvenile courts, which focus on rehabilitation as opposed to pure punishment.	*Some teens cannot be rehabilitated.* Minors who have committed numerous violent crimes and are simply disturbed cannot be helped by the juvenile court system. For individuals who will continually pose a danger to society, a more serious punishment is necessary. These extreme cases should be dealt with in adult court because that is the only venue equipped to handle such hardened criminals.
Sending a child to an adult facility is a recipe for the making of a hardened criminal. In an adult jail, the juvenile will be influenced by adult criminals. Juveniles who spend time in adult prisons learn from adults how to be better criminals. Thus, they are even more dangerous when they get out of prison.	*Juveniles who are tried as adults will be deterred from committing future crimes if they spend time in adult jails.* After going to an adult jail, there is no way they will want to go back.
If juvenile courts are currently inadequate for dealing with all child criminals, then juvenile courts should be reformed. Juvenile courts are useless if they cannot address the most serious juvenile offenders.	*Some crimes need more serious punishment than can be imposed by juvenile courts.* For example, most punishments in juvenile courts cannot go beyond a criminal's 18th birthday. However, some juvenile offenders need harsh punishments and some crimes need more serious punishments than a handful of years in a youth facility. In these extreme cases, justice demands that juveniles be tried in adult courts.
Juvenile courts impose lesser punishments for a reason—putting a child in prison for an adult sentence renders them incapable of ever functioning in the outside world. If, for example, a 12-year-old were sentenced to 30 years in prison, she would spend her developmental years behind bars. Even if this person were perfectly rehabilitated, she will enter society at 42 years of age without any real-life experience.	*Parole programs exist for this purpose.* Criminals are gradually reintroduced into society through a halfway house. Furthermore, the damage that may be done to the offender is outweighed by society's right to security; the minor has demonstrated extreme criminal behavior and cannot be allowed to live freely.

PROS	CONS
Trying juveniles as adults will deter other juveniles from committing serious crimes. If other kids see that they will be punished harshly, they will be less likely to commit serious crimes.	*Trying juveniles as adults will not deter other juveniles from committing serious crimes.* Many serious crimes, such as assault or murder, are crimes of passion, with the offenders heedless of the consequences of their actions at the moment of the crime—so deterrence will not work.

OTHER MOTIONS:

Murderers should be tried as adults regardless of age

Trying minors as adults does more harm than good

RELATED MOTIONS:

Serious crimes deserve serious time

WEB LINKS:

- American Bar Association. "Juvenile Justice: Facts and Figures." <http://www.abanet.org/media/jjqa.html>. Fact sheet on the system and juvenile crime.

- BNET. "Should Juvenile Offenders Be Tried as Adults?—Rehabilitation at Issue." <http://findarticles.com/p/articles/mi_m1272/is_2668_129/ai_69698409/>. Article arguing that trying young offenders (12 and under) as adults may not be good policy.

- Carter, K. C. "Should Juvenile Offenders Be Tried As Adults?" <http://www.talonmarks.com/2.6585/should-juvenile-offenders-be-tried-as-adults-pro-minors-or-not-no-excuse-for-murder-1.742297>. Article in favor of trying juveniles as adults for serious crimes.

Letter Grades

Motion **Schools should eliminate letter grades**

Introduction Working hard for an A and dreading a D or F are deeply engrained in American students. In fact, it is hard to imagine schools without letter grades. But some schools have abandoned them in favor of other systems. Some use standards-based systems where teachers use a list of skills a student should have and check off each a student has mastered. Others use a levels method, where children are assessed on their ability to handle a particularly difficult book or complex math problem. Still others have students create portfolios of their work to present to high school or college admission boards, the same way a designer or architect would show a potential client a portfolio. Many of these systems are quite successful.

Debating the Motion Both teams need to investigate the alternatives to letter grades systems, researching how these systems work and how they have been implemented, as well as the benefits and drawbacks of each.

Proposition: With this topic in particular, the proposition must begin by narrowing the scope of the word *school*; if they choose not to narrow the scope, they must indicate the age ranges they will be discussing. Because many criticisms of letter grade systems are available, the proposition can simply make a general case against them. However, a stronger case would include proposing an alternative. Such alternative should include the new system as well as information about how it will be implemented, specifically addressing issues of time frame and budget.

Opposition: The opposition has different options, depending in large part on what the proposition presents. The opposition can defend the letter grade system as good or claim that it is neutral—that is, no better or worse than the alternatives—and therefore not worth investing time and money in abandoning the status quo.

PROS	CONS
Letter grades create dangerous divisions and shame. A student with a reputation of being an F student is going to be treated differently,	*Any kind of measurement system can cause students to feel not good about themselves.* If a student doesn't perform to the standards of her

by teachers and other students, than is an A student. Letter grades are unfair because a letter grade cannot show the circumstances of the student receiving it. Perhaps a lower grade was caused by exceptional circumstances in a student's life. The feelings of shame, of failure, and of being a poor student can remain with children for a long time—even a lifetime. Getting rid of letter grades would allow us to look at students in a more fair and balanced way.

Ridding ourselves of letter grades removes pressure from students to always get the A. While it is great for students to be motivated, if the only motivation is achievement of a certain letter rather than gaining a thorough understanding of new material, then students are concentrating on the wrong goal. Pressure to get a good grade can often damage the ability to learn because the stress can negatively affect a child's work and health. Getting straight As is such a deeply entrenched idea that switching from letter grades would instantly remove a large burden and thus free students to spend more energy on learning content.

Letter grades are inaccurate. There is a huge difference between 70 percent and 79 percent, yet both are considered to be a C. Letter grades would lump students with these two scores in roughly the same category, even though one student has performed considerably better and the other needs more assistance from the school. These broad categories don't help any students,

school, teachers and administrators should be concerned and take a closer look at that student. But even if schools used an alternative method, a child who always performs at the lowest level or who has met fewer standards than his peers could still be singled out and made to feel like a failure. Merely switching from letter grades does not solve this problem.

Removing letter grades would actually result in increasing pressure on students. Letter grades give us a broad picture of what a child is doing within a 10 percent range. So, if a student performs poorly on a couple of assignments, she can still get a good letter grade at the end of the semester because all grades are averaged over the term. By using a system that measures work more closely—for example, by using raw percentages in place of general letter—students will actually feel more pressure to perform exceedingly well on each measured item of content. Students might not be satisfied with 90 percent (which under a letter system is an A) and easily might feel forced to try to turn that 90 into a 91, then a 92. This actually increases performance pressure and distracts from focusing on real learning and actual content.

While some differences may be seen between the child at the lower end of a grade range and the child at the higher end, these kids are still within a similar range. In a perfect world, school staff would sit together and determine the best plan for educating each individual child. However, this is not the case in the real world. Schools usually have hundreds or even thousands of children attending; thus, schools because teachers and administrators cannot be truly aware of each child's needs and therefore cannot help each child in the best way possible.

Letter grades are, in essence, just a way of comparing students. A school can look at an A student and decide he is more worthy than his neighbor—who only received a C. However, to improve our education system, we need to take the focus off comparisons of large groups and concentrate more on the needs of individual students. Using other approaches—such as standards or learning benchmarks—allows us to really look at an individual child's abilities. It also helps to ensure that she gets the support she needs to become a better student. This focus will improve the quality of education in the long run because it will meet children where they are rather than trying to stuff every child into a one-size-fits-all mold.

need broad ranges to group children. Letter grades allow schools to group students in the best way to help them learn and achieve.

It is an unfortunate fact of life that students are in competition with one another. Students have to be comparable in some consistent way so schools, universities, and employers can pick the most capable candidate. Letter grades are a simple way to achieve this evenhanded comparison. Grades are already widely used, so that a level of consistency can be and is achieved.

OTHER MOTIONS:

Ban letter grades in schools

Schools should use a standards-based approach to grade students

RELATED MOTIONS:

Schools should switch to authentic assessment programs

Schools should not compare students based on performance

WEB LINKS:

- Culbertson, Linda Doutt, and Mary Renck Jalongo. "But What's Wrong with Letter Grades?" <http://lrs.ed.uiuc.edu/students/jwbates/Lettergrades.htm>. This paper offers alternatives to traditional assessment and grading systems.

- Family Education. "Are Letter Grades on Their Way Out?" <http://school.familyeducation.com/assessment/educational-philosophy/56197.html>. Article on the trend toward abandoning letter grades.

Martin Luther King, Jr. Day

Motion **Martin Luther King, Jr. Day should be a mandatory school day**

Introduction Few can deny the impact that Martin Luther King, Jr. had on the United States. Most people agree that a national holiday should be devoted to this champion of peace and equality. People differ, however, on how best to honor King's life and celebrate his accomplishments and how best to keep his spirit of activism alive. For many students and adults, Martin Luther King, Jr. Day, which is celebrated on the Monday closest to his birthday (January 15), is a three-day weekend to use to celebrate or relax. For others, the holiday represents a renewed call to action against the inequalities that remain. Some activists claim that a better way to honor King would be to require a day of school devoted to learning about King and the changes he and others helped to bring about in U.S. society. This would be especially helpful because many children have heard his name but are not quite sure who he was or why we celebrate him.

Debating the Motion Both teams might find it interesting to research how people actually spend MLK Day. They can research special events and programs, as well as poll school friends and teachers. Both teams might also want to consider the effect of the passage of time on the holiday. Has it changed the way we celebrate the holiday?

Proposition: The proposition should present a specific actionable plan detailing which schoolchildren would be required to go to school, how long they would be there, what they would learn, and who would teach it.

Opposition: The opposition's case might hinge on the fact that Martin Luther King, Jr. Day is a holiday. Traditionally, how people celebrate a particular holiday varies. The opposition might also present an actionable counter plan for what should be done on that day.

PROS	CONS
The best way to celebrate King is to have schools teach about him and others like him. A day off school is not the best way to commemorate the activism and accomplishments of a great man. Nowadays, a day off is likely	*Families need time to remember and honor King's life and achievements in their own way.* While some students may choose to play video games all day, who is to say that this isn't their way of celebrating Martin Luther

to be wasted on video games, television, and texting. Doing nothing all day does not honor him.

Without proper school programs, the significance of King is lost. Many students know his name, but they have only vague ideas about who he was and what he did. A group of fifth-graders recently declared that King was famous for freeing the slaves! We must ensure that students everywhere know what he was fighting for—not least because that fight continues today. Since schools clearly aren't finding time to teach about Dr. King in class, time can be made on this special day.

In school, students can be taught what is necessary to carry on his legacy and continue to fight for a just society. The struggle to end racism and promote equality is not over. Many students want some advice on how to start becoming active around these issues. A special day in school devoted to teaching students how to honor the man and his legacy and how to continue his fight for equality is the best way to commemorate King.

Families may not have the tools to help their children understand King's legacy. Parents' own knowledge might be limited or, even if they are well-informed, they might not know how to explain Dr. King's importance to a young child. A school will have the best resources for teaching children of all ages about the struggle for equal rights—instituting a day where all students can engage in learning together will be a most valuable experience for all involved.

King, Jr.? It would be worse still to rob those families who want to celebrate by traveling to places associated with King and the civil rights movement.

A school is not the only place where Dr. King's significance can be taught. He is publically celebrated around his birthday in many ways—with rallies, television specials, and museum exhibits. For families who worry that their children do not know about King, this is a great opportunity for them to take time to attend one of these events and talk about him.

Family members may have personal memories to pass on to children and grandchildren that are more valuable than a classroom lesson. Grandparents might remember having been to one of King's rallies or marches or remember being active in their own youth for some cause. With a day off, families can take their children with them to be active in the causes that are important to them. Making it a national day of service as opposed to another school day is the best way to carry on his commitment.

Lots of resources are available to help families educate their children about the civil rights movement. Rather than making a "day of learning" mandatory, schools could offer voluntary programs for kids and their parents to learn together. Churches, museums, and other cultural institutions can also provide tools to help families learn about King.

PROS

Martin Luther King, Jr. fought to ensure that all people were treated equally; where better can this be seen than in schools? In big cities or even small towns, the one place that brings people of all races, backgrounds, and religions together is the school. By definition, the group around you at home or a church is much more uniform. When you spend a day in school, you are literally surrounded by diversity, which is exactly what Dr. King fought for. It is the best way to celebrate him.

A day of learning about King will highlight the need for more inclusive curricula. Spending a day discussing King will emphasize the importance of learning about the civil rights movement and integrating King's theme of equality and justice into many subjects. Even once we have a better curriculum, a day of learning would still be useful: schools already routinely devote time to other holidays—each year in December students learn about the festival of Hanukkah, for example. Such days reinforce the importance of the topic.

CONS

True, a school is more diverse than a family but sadly, especially in the most diverse schools, students self-segregate. At a school with people of all different backgrounds, students are even more prone to seek out and befriend people like them. A better way to celebrate and enhance diversity would be service programs outside of schools, where students work with people who are different from themselves to do an important job, like raising money for a worthy cause, fixing a building, or planting a garden for a charitable organization. Simply leaving students to their everyday cliques is no way to celebrate what Dr. King was fighting for.

Days like Martin Luther King, Jr. Day or events like black or women's history month are belittling because they support the idea that all of the accomplishments of traditionally marginalized groups can be put into little slots of time—that they are not important enough to be included in the curriculum throughout the year. King was so important to our history that the civil rights movement and its accomplishments should be at the forefront for the entire school year. Insisting that everything about him can be learned in one day is almost offensive. He fought hard and effectively for equality, but we do not give him (or other minorities or women for that matter) an equal place in our curricula. As long as special "set aside" days exist, they stand as a barrier to better, more inclusive curricula, which are what are truly necessary.

OTHER MOTIONS:

Martin Luther King, Jr. Day should be a required day of service

Civil rights curricula should be required in schools

RELATED MOTIONS:

School curricula should include more minority figures

WEB LINKS:

- Greater Philadelphia Martin Luther King Junior Day of Service. "2010 Annual Report." <http://www.mlkdayofservice.org/>. Article reviewing an alternative to a school day devoted to King.

- Strauss, Valerie. "Despite Lessons on King, Some Unaware of His Dream." <http://www.washingtonpost.com/wp-dyn/content/article/2007/01/14/AR2007011401026.html>. Article reviewing how schools and students recognize the holiday.

Meat, Eating

Motion   **Eating meat is unethical**

Introduction   Most all-American dishes are meat-based, from hot dogs to hamburgers to fried chicken to barbecued brisket. Yet, many Americans are increasingly concerned about how animals are treated in the meat industry. Many argue that eating the meat of animals that have been mistreated is wrong; others point out that the meat industry has severe negative effects on the environment. Nevertheless, most Americans continue to eat meat, arguing that it is not unethical to eat meat because meat is beneficial to health.

Debating the Motion   Research could be geared to animal rights issues, but should also focus on the meat industry itself since the industry produces waste that affects the environment. This topic focuses on the ethics of eating meat, so the arguments should center not on whether eating meat is good or bad for health or the environment but on whether any moral truths can be drawn from each argument for or against eating meat. This does not mean health and environment arguments should not be made, but rather that they must be linked to the subject of ethics to be relevant to the topic.

Proposition: The proposition has two options when defending a topic on ethics. The first would be to establish a blanket definition of morality and relate all arguments to this definition. This might actually be the trickier of the two options. In creating a definition of morality, be careful not to use a literal definition taken from a dictionary. Rather, pick a major ethical theory such as the greatest good for the greatest number or the ends justify the means, etc. The second option would be to create arguments first and then link each one to a major ethical theory.

Opposition: The opposition does not need to establish meat eating as ideal habit, only that it is not immoral. They can present meat eating either as ethically neutral or beneficial. Options for running a counter case are similar to the hints for the proposition: either pick one ethical theory and defend all arguments on this ground or find ways to link arguments to a variety of ethical theories.

PROS

Killing animals is wrong. We would never kill a human where it could be avoided because

CONS

Killing animals to feed people is not morally wrong. The proposition gives animals the we value life; animals, too, have lives. Killing animals for their flesh is not necessary—human beings in modern society can easily survive and prosper without eating animal products, therefore, choosing to kill animals is not morally defensible.

Killing animals for food is inefficient. Animals consume large amounts of grain for the meat they produce; it takes 16 pounds of grain to produce one pound of meat. Seventy percent of U.S. grain is grown to feed farm animals; fish on fish farms are fed five pounds of wild-caught fish for every one pound of farmed fish produced. Twenty percent of the world population could be fed on the grain and soybeans fed to U.S. cattle alone; worldwide, cattle consume the calorie equivalent of 8.7 billion people. Rather than use so much of our resources to produce meat, we could conserve these resources and attain the same nutrition through vegetarian options.

The production of meat causes enormous environmental damage. Approximately half the U.S. land mass is used in some way to raise animals; making space for grazing animals has led to massive deforestation globally. More than one-third of fossil fuels in the U.S. are burned in the meat industry, and according to the Environmental Protection Administration, 80 percent of ammonia emissions in the U.S. come from animal waste. Eating meat is not simply a personal choice; these environmental harms affect everyone.

Most meat comes from factory farms, which are unethical in the way they raise animals. They pose enormous health risks through their use of antibiotics and their crowded conditions provide a breeding ground for new

same moral weight as humans—this is not the case. Animals are not as conscious and therefore do not deserve the same consideration. We disapprove of wanton killing, but meat is part of a balanced diet; many people struggle with disorders like anemia (low iron levels), which are best treated through consumption of red meat.

Using grain and beans to feed animals is not inefficient because these do not act as substitutes. We cannot simply take the grain used to feed cows and give it to people instead; humans require a variety of nutrients. Although nutrients found in meat can also be found in tofu and soy, vegetarians and vegans tend to be deficient in iron, protein, calcium, and vitamin B_{12}. The world currently does not have an issue with efficient production of food; we currently produce enough food to feed the global population. Starvation is the result of problems and inefficiencies in distribution. However, replacing meat with grains would not affect distribution.

All farming causes environmental damage. If we were to require everyone to follow a vegetarian diet, we would need space to grow more plants and grains. The process of razing forests and clearing land to create fields destroys native ecosystems. Farming causes damage, but we must accept such alterations in the natural landscape if we are to feed people.

If there is a problem with the system, we should fix the system, not opt out of it. When Theodore Roosevelt read Upton Sinclair's *The Jungle*, a novel about the horrors of the Chicago meat-packing industry in the early twentieth strains of bacteria. Furthermore, even if killing animals for food is not inherently wrong, we must still treat animals in a way that respects their capacity for pain and suffering. Animals on factory farms have their beaks sliced, teeth clipped, or genitals removed without any pain relief. They are given powerful doses of drugs so that they grow faster, but their hearts and limbs cannot keep up—as a result, they are often crippled or suffer heart attacks when only a few weeks old. Because humans have a higher level of consciousness, we have a greater responsibility to the Earth—endorsing the meat industry and all its horrors is unethical.

Research increasingly shows that diets heavy in meat put humans at increased risks for health problems—cancer and heart disease, for example. While an adult may choose to eat meat and incur these risks, it is wrong for parents to feed children meat before they are old enough to make their own decisions. Parents have a moral obligation to keep their children healthy, and thus should raise them on vegetarian diets.

century, he pressured Congress to create the FDA to fix that industry. Similarly, meat-eaters today should pressure the government to force the meat industry to comply with stricter regulations. This would most likely lead to an increase in the price of meat, which would lead to a decrease in meat consumption and the problems associated with it. Total abstention from meat is unnecessary; we simply need better regulation.

These studies mix up causation and correlation. Vegetarians and vegans are often healthier than meat eaters, but this is partly because people who actively choose to be vegetarians generally are more health-conscious in the first place. Furthermore, because they have fewer options, they *have* to be more conscious of what they eat to make sure they get proper nutrition. Vegetarianism is not necessary to be healthy—one merely needs a balanced diet, which can include meat.

OTHER MOTIONS:
Eating meat does more good than harm

RELATED MOTIONS:
The meat industry is bad for the United States
Animals deserve the same rights as humans

WEB LINKS:
• Niman, Nicolette Hahn. "The Carnivore's Dilemma." <http://www.nytimes.com/2009/10/31/opinion/31niman.html?_r=1>. *New York Times* op-ed piece on the meat industry and climate change.
• Time Magazine. "Should You Be a Vegetarian?" <http://www.time.com/time/covers/1101020715/story5.html>. Article offering arguments on both sides of the issue.

Metric System, Adopting

Motion   **The U.S. should adopt the metric system**

Introduction   The U.S. is one of only three countries that officially does not use the metric system. Americans are used to measuring in Fahrenheit degrees, miles per hour, and gallons of milk, and would be hard-pressed to suddenly understand the weather forecast if it were give in metric units—how hot (or cold) *is* 40° Celsius? However, not using the metric system definitely has drawbacks in terms of our ability to work with others. This debate is not new. In 1975, Congress passed an act that committed the country to converting to the metric system—more than three decades later, it has yet to happen.

Debating the Motion   Teams should research what combination of U.S. customary units and metric units other developed countries use—many countries that technically use the metric systems still retain measurements such as feet, pounds, and miles. In addition, teams should look into the cost of converting to metric and the problems involved. Finally, they should research existing legislative proposals for conversion.

Proposition: A plan is a must for this topic. It should present a time frame for conversion, including which elements of the system we might adopt first and any overlap period in which the U.S. would use both systems. It should also discuss how the plan would be implemented and enforced. The proposition could also argue for a limited adoption of metric units to reach consistency with countries like the United Kingdom, which uses a combination of both systems.

Opposition: The opposition does not need to argue against the metric system but rather against its forced adoption. The opposition can encourage the teaching of the metric system, note its ease of use, and champion its continued use in the fields of sciences. The main case for the opposition will be to argue that adoption is impractical and that many difficulties would be encountered in forcing the general public to adopt the system.

PROS

Switching to the metric system is totally doable. We have already made successful inroads in what is arguably the best place to

CONS

Switching to the metric system would be almost impossible. Alas, since the government pledged to switch to the metric system, soda begin: food. Soda, cereals, and other food-stuffs are measured in liters and grams; if we can successfully switch to the metric system with basics like food, we can do it with everything else.

Switching to metric is necessary for easier and more accurate communication with other nations. Because nearly all other countries use the metric system, tourists in the U.S. struggle to make sense of distances, speeds, and temperatures. This is equally so in cases where U.S. citizens travel to other countries and cannot understand the metric measurements. Let's make life easier for everyone and commit to the switch!

This change will save us money. We won't have to waste resources translating the measurements on imports and exports that invariably use the metric system. And, we won't be at risk for multimillion dollar disasters like that with the Mars Climate Orbiter, where miscommunication about measurement systems resulted in the loss of millions of human-hours in work and millions of dollars in technology investments.

The metric system is easier to use because it is made up of units of ten and thus can be easily multiplied and divided. . American have notoriously poor math skills, so utilizing a simpler system will be better for everyone.

Large segments of the population already use the metric system, so converting will be easy. Scientists and others involved in technology already use the metric system; students are taught to use it in school. It is not a

bottles represent the sole gain made in more than 20 years. If 20 years are needed just to get people used to soda measured in liters, then switching over all other units of measurement will take untold centuries and is not worth the effort.

The U.S does not adopt policy based on the needs of tourists. U.S. citizens are used to our customary units and we should keep these to ensure convenience for our own citizens. Americans spend very little time in other countries, and those who do can familiarize themselves with the metric system. We should do what is easiest for most people: keep our imperial units.

The cost will be enormous. The cost of translating a few labels will pale in comparison with the investment needed to teach and get a country of 300 million used to an entirely new and almost completely unfamiliar system. Further, the Mars Orbiter incident was a freak accident: most scientists, even in the U.S., use the metric system, so, generally, we do not have to worry about miscommunications among scientists.

The imperial system is easier to use than the metric. It is hard to divide a meter into 3 equal parts because 3 does not go evenly into 10, but a foot can be easily divided in many ways because 12 is divisible by more numbers.

Scientists and students make up only a small part of the population. The concern isn't for those who are learning and using the metric system already. We worry about the average Joe who has spent his life using feet and

PROS	CONS
big leap from those segments to the whole population.	pounds and suddenly must switch to meters and grams. Where will the money and support come from to help the average person adjust? The drain on resources is not worth it when our current system works just fine.

OTHER MOTIONS:

The U.S. should set a deadline for switching to the metric system

Ban the U.S. customary system of measurement

RELATED MOTIONS:

The U.S. should ban the metric system

WEB LINKS:

- National Institute of Standards and Technology, Technology Services. "The United States and the Metric System: A Capsule History." <http://ts.nist.gov/WeightsAndMeasures/Metric/upload/1136a.pdf>. History of the effort to adopt the metric system, with Q & A in support of adoption.

- U.S. Metric Association. <http://lamar.colostate.edu/~hillger/>. Site provides links to a wide variety of sources in support of the metric system.

Minimum Wage

Motion **Increase the minimum wage**

Introduction As the nation rapidly industrialized at the turn of the nineteenth century and as immigrants eager for any kind unskilled worked poured into the country, the U.S. became a nation of sweatshops. The rise of the unions and public outcry over low wages, long hours, and unsafe working conditions brought about labor laws, including a minimum wage. The minimum wage has increased over time, yet many critics argue its increase has not kept pace with the economic changes in the nation. Opponents argue that increasing the minimum wage is bad for the worker and the economy.

Debating the Motion Business and labor organizations have weighed in on this issue, and both teams need to research their arguments. The teams should research the change in the minimum wage over time and how this compares both with the increase in cost of living and inflation. They should also research the impact that changes in the minimum wage have had on employers and job availability.

Proposition: The proposition should define what the increase would entail and the time frame wherein these increases would take place. Legislation like the Fair Minimum Wage Act of 2007 paved the way for a series of increases; the proposition could use this measure to help create a plan. Also, minimum wages can differ from state to state, so the proposition should be clear about whether they are talking about federal or state changes.

Opposition: The opposition can argue either not to increase the minimum wage or to decrease it. Keeping the wage constant would entail showing that the minimum wage is a good and is sufficient at its current level. Arguing to decrease the minimum wage might entail referencing a struggling economy and how a decrease is necessary to save businesses. The opposition could also mount a counter case by declaring that there should be no minimum wage.

PROS	CONS
All workers need to earn a wage that covers at least the necessities of life—food, rent, and utilities. A person working a standard workweek	*Most minimum wage earners are not supporting a family.* According to 2008 Labor Department findings, only 1.1 percent of

at minimum wage in the United States would earn less than $16,000 per year—if he is supporting a family, they will be considered under the poverty line. The minimum wage has not kept pace with the cost of living and needs to be increased to allow families and individuals to survive.

Increasing the minimum wage would give low-income wage earners a salary that is sufficient so that they do not need welfare benefits. Most welfare programs require participants to work; rather than have people work at low wages and then give them a handout, we should help them to earn enough money to support themselves. This saves the taxpayers' money as welfare benefits would decrease.

An increase is needed to help disadvantaged groups. Today, most minimum wage workers who rely on their hourly work as a primary source of family income are women and minorities. On average, minorities receive lower-quality educations and are less able to afford post–high school training, while women's career paths are often interrupted by child rearing, and they still earn less on average than their male counterparts for doing the same jobs. By denying these groups enough money to properly care for their families, we are extending the cycle of poverty; their children will be similarly

individuals working 40 hours per week or more earn minimum wage; approximately 66 percent of minimum wage earners receive a raise within a year. Teens are five times more likely to earn the minimum wage than adults. Most people working for the lowest wages are teenagers and college students because they are unskilled, work part-time, or work seasonally. They often are less reliable than older workers and don't depend on the income as their sole means of support.

If there is an obligation to support the poor, that obligation belongs to society, not businesses. If a shopper sees a shirt that is only worth $5.00, but costs $20.00, she can refuse to buy it. Similarly, if an unskilled worker's labor is only worth $3.00 an hour, businesses should not be forced to pay $7.50. If the public thinks that someone has to help these low-skilled workers, the public has to accept higher taxes. Furthermore, taxpayers would most likely not save money through an increase in the minimum wage because they will simply pay more for goods—higher labor costs result in higher prices.

Minorities are hurt most by increases in the minimum wage. Minimum wage increases lead to higher unemployment, and minorities become unemployed at a higher rate. In September 2009, an increase in minimum wage was combined with a poor economy—teenage unemployment hit 25.9 percent. For black teenage males, however, the unemployment rate was 50.4 percent. A minimum wage may seem like it increases salaries, but for many minorities, it drives wages down to $0.00.

disadvantaged and are more likely to earn low wages. Besides, much of what the opposition suggests shows a correlation, but does not prove a causal relationship between increased wages and increased unemployment.

A higher income allows low-wage families to spend more money, stimulating the local economy. The phrase "you have to spend money to make money" holds economic truth; by increasing the minimum wage, we increase the spending power of many families. Because low-income families tend to live in economically depressed areas, this spending will be particularly beneficial by stimulating these areas.

In terms of economics, it is better to establish a society where the employed can support themselves than to have the poor work at measly wages and then receive a government handout. Furthermore, the balance between supply and demand is not as rigid as the opposition claims. Especially in a bad economy, employers have the upper hand in negotiations. With more workers than jobs, even if a worker is worth a higher wage, employers do not have to pay more because they know someone else will take the job for less. This is the reason minimum wage laws were initially enacted; waves of immigration in the late 1800s created huge competition for jobs, allowing employers to exploit employees.

Increased income for low-wage earners increases the price of goods. If labor costs more, production costs more; business owners must increase prices to remain in business. As a result, people are able to buy fewer goods with their money, so an increased income does not actually help low-wage earners or local businesses.

The minimum wage is bad economics. Credible economic analysis demonstrates that an increase in the minimum wage increases unemployment. In the United States, wages are determined by a balance of supply and demand—if a worker's skills are worth more than the minimum wage, that worker can demand higher pay. If an employer thinks the worker is worth that pay, he will pay it. If not, the worker will find a different employer. But if a worker's skills are not worth the minimum wage, employers will simply find a more skilled worker and the poorest of society will be out of a job.

OTHER MOTIONS:
The minimum wage does more harm than good
The minimum wage should be set to match inflation

RELATED MOTIONS:
Implement a living wage

WEB LINKS:

- Economic Policy Institute. "Fact Sheet for 2009 Minimum Wage Increase." <http://www.epi.org/publications/entry/mwig_fact_sheet/>. Article listing the benefits of the wage increase.

- U.S. House of Representatives, Joint Economic Committee Report. "The Case Against a Higher Minimum Wage." <http://www.house.gov/jec/cost-gov/regs/minimum/against/against.htm>. Report by the then-Republican-controlled committee on the issue.

Movie Rating System

Motion **The movie rating system should be abolished**

Introduction Radically progressive films in the 1920s and early 1930s shocked conservative groups who called for a censor board that put in place the Hays Code, which dictated what could and could not be shown in films. Many critics objected to the code on the grounds that it limited freedom of expression; in 1968, the Motion Picture Association of America (MPAA) replaced that code with a system that assigned ratings (and prohibited access) to films. The system has continued to evolve, so that we now have G (general audience) appropriate for all viewers; PG for slightly more mature films; PG-13 for those 13 and older; R for mature content; and NC-17, which bars anyone under the age of 17 from seeing the movie, even with parental supervision or permission.

An MPAA panel views films and determines the ratings based on language, violence, nudity, and sexuality; depictions of crime; drugs and drug paraphernalia; and a number of other items. Panelists are parents with no special film knowledge or ties to the film industry. Filmmakers can appeal their rating to a board composed of producers and other film specialists. The rating system is controversial. Critics say it should be abolished because ratings are not assigned objectively; films with sexual themes are given more restrictive ratings than those with excessive violence. The MPAA says ratings reflect mainstream values.

Debating the Motion Both teams should research the history of the movie rating system and why it was established. Teams should also research movie rating systems used in other countries and research controversies surrounding the ratings of particular films.

Proposition: The proposition should begin by offering an alternative case—the proposition must show that a new system is so at odds or so different from the current system that the MPAA legitimately needs to be abolished so a new fresh system can be put in place. The proposition also has the option to argue simply to abolish the system and not replace it. In proposing this, it would be necessary to gear arguments toward showing that any system is unnecessary or that any system constitutes a form of censorship rather than simply pointing out the flaws in the current system.

Opposition: The opposition has three choices in how to debate this case. First, it might defend the current system. Second, it could argue that the system can be fixed and that it should not be abandoned without a viable alternative in place. Third, depending on the strength of the proposition's case, it could show that the proposition's plan is either no better than the current system, so there is no need to change, or that their plan is actually worse.

PROS

Our current rating system needs to be abolished because it is not accurate. In particular, ratings that displease major studios can be manipulated through clever campaigning on the part of the studios without any changes actually being made to a film's content. Ratings can be bought by big companies, thus, patrons of mainstream movies have no way of accurately knowing what to expect of a film in terms of its content and level of violence.

The current system is skewed, reflecting the worst in American society. It is harshly stacked against even innocuous sexual material, for example, yet allows grotesque amounts of violence. Members of the MPAA have even admitted this! It is ludicrous to think that somehow seeing a naked breast, which is healthy and natural, is worse than seeing torture and killing depicted, yet the rating system works to hide one while permitting the other. We know that letting children see excessive violence desensitizes them—surely a harm. The current system lets children watch extremely violent films with relatively nonrestrictive ratings—in other countries, such films would be rated for adults only.

The system does not give filmmakers clear guidelines so they can make films with the ratings they want. As a result, assigning ratings becomes very subjective. If no objective, comprehensive set of rules is readily available, the public cannot trust a rating.

CONS

This is simply not true—we have no concrete proof that ratings can be "bought." While it is true that ratings that displease a studio can be changed, this is not accomplished by buying people off. Rather, studios have the option to reedit and reapply or to appeal. If either of these actions results in a changed rating, this does not indicate corruption but rather displays the sensible flexibility of the MPAA.

The system is not skewed; it reflects American social values—which is as it should be. Our culture is more conservative about nudity and sexuality than violence and the ratings reflect this. Each country needs to evaluate each film within its own social context—our rating system makes sense for the United States.

Each film is unique, so to have one set of inflexible guidelines would not do at all. What is needed are common sense and the objectivity to assess each film fairly on its merits. Besides, publishing hard and fast guidelines could have negative consequences.

PROS	CONS
	Unscrupulous filmmakers could develop scripts that contain much objectionable content but still technically get a less restrictive rating, resulting in children seeing completely inappropriate material.
Our current system discriminates against smaller and independent film companies. Because MPAA members are often those with ties to major studios, obviously these studios get more latitude. Independent studios, on the other hand, are seen as competition to the studios in which many members have a vested interest and are thus treated more harshly. Independent studios often lack the funds to either purchase desirable ratings or to reedit the film and then appeal a restrictive rating.	*The MPAA strongly disputes conflict of interest within its membership.* All films are judged on their content, not on which studio made the film. If an independent filmmaker is concerned that a film she will be making may get an inappropriate rating, she can put the cost of a possible appeal into her budget. Costs of possible appeals should not be a reason to insist that the MPAA be disbanded, but rather a lesson in fiscal responsibility for all studios and filmmakers.
The ratings make little sense. They draw an arbitrary line between a 12-year-old and a 13-year-old—does some major developmental leap happen on a 13th birthday? Are children then suddenly mature enough to handle higher levels of violence, foul language, or nudity? If material is not appropriate for children, then turning 13 will not make it so. These nonsensical ratings really do not provide much guidance at all and so should be done away with.	*Age distinctions are arbitrary but are nonetheless necessary.* A line needs to be drawn somewhere to give us a rough idea of what a film might include so that we don't have young teens lumped in with college students. The real reason for this guide is so that parents can have an idea of whether or not the film is appropriate for their child. These are only guidelines—they leave the choice to parents while providing as much information as they can so that the parents' choices can be informed ones.

OTHER MOTIONS:
The MPAA rating system does more harm than good
Movie rating systems are outdated

RELATED MOTIONS:
The movie rating system is a form of censorship

WEB LINKS:

- Bowles, Scott. "Debating the MPAA's Mission." <http://www.usatoday.com/life/movies/news/2007-04-09-movie-ratings-main_N.htm>. Article summarizing MPAA efforts to address the criticism of its rating system.

- Bowman, Donna, Noel Murray, and Jim Ridley. "Broken Code: Why the MPAA Ratings Code Should Be Overhauled." <http://www.nashvillescene.com/nashville/broken-code/Content?oid=1184941>. History of the code and arguments for its abolition.

- Motion Picture Association of America. <http://www.mpaa.org/>. Association that rates films explains the rating system.

National High School Graduation Exam

Motion **The United States needs a national high school graduation exam**

Introduction In recent years, in an effort to improve levels of learning, states and localities have required students to take standardized tests to evaluate their progress. The No Child Left Behind Act, for example, requires students be tested every year from grades 3–8 and once in high school. Some experts suggest that the United States needs a national high school graduation exam. A national graduation exam could help standardize and improve the quality of U.S. education and ensure that students are prepared for college. Others question whether such an exam is necessary and if it would actually measure college readiness; in addition, such proposed tests would necessarily require standardized content be taught nationwide, even though regional differences in content are arguably beneficial.

Debating the Motion Since this topic is about a type of standardized testing, researching the pros and cons of standardized testing is essential. Many other countries already have national exams; debaters should examine how these exams are structured and what effect they have on school curricula. Both teams should also research how standardized exit exams affect graduation rates.

Proposition: As part of their first speech, the proposition should present a plan explaining what kind of exam they would require and what content it would test. Using exam guidelines from other countries or models like the International Baccalaureate will be helpful in creating a workable plan. The team should include a timeline stating how much time schools would have to meet certain benchmarks in order to preempt the opposition's implementation concerns.

Opposition: The opposition has a number of options. The first is to argue in favor of the status quo: a national exam is unnecessary and states should continue policies that target the needs of the local population. Second, the opposition could argue that the exam is unnecessary because national alternatives like the SAT, the ACT, and Advanced Placement exams already exist. Third, such an exam could actually be harmful. Finally, the team could propose a mixture of all the negative positions. Most of the arguments below could be framed to fit any of these positions, but a good organizational tactic would be to pick one overarching position and relate back to it.

PROS

A national test would ensure that high school graduates are prepared for college. A college student with a poor high school education will struggle, become discouraged, and be likely to drop out. A national exit exam would test knowledge in core subjects as well as academic skills (essay writing, critical thinking) that are necessary for college; if students do not pass, they are not ready to be graduated from high school. This would decrease the college dropout rate.

These exams do not take the place of a national graduation exam. The SAT and ACT are private exams; schools are not required to teach to their standards. The students who excel on these exams typically prepare outside school, using costly tutors or preparation programs. Thus, these tests unfairly favor the wealthy. Students must also pay a fee to take these exams, which makes it hard for schools to insist that their students take the test. One national exam would allow low-budget districts to focus on teaching students material that will be on that test and allow schools to require students to take the exam.

A national exam would encourage standard learning expectations countrywide. We already know that standards for learning are different in larger and wealthier schools than in smaller or poorer ones. However, we also know that schools across this country use widely different methods for teaching key subjects like math and reading. The more successful school systems appear to utilize consistent teaching methods. We see this proven in successful local schools and in countries with students achieving at a high academic level. A national graduation exam would promote this consistency, which would, accordingly, improve learning across the board.

CONS

Not all high school students will attend college. College is not the right choice for every student—some would be better served by acquiring a skilled trade rather than pursuing a degree. Low-performing students, who are already at the highest risk of dropping out, are likely to be discouraged if they are held to a college-level standard merely to graduate from high school. These students would simply be more likely to drop out before receiving even a high school diploma.

A high school exam is not necessary; the SAT and ACT evaluate a student's college preparedness. Advanced Placement exams, International Baccalaureate exams, and SAT subject tests evaluate a student's mastery of academic material. Because these exams are administered by outside agencies, school boards (which already often operate on an insufficient budget) are not burdened with the expense of testing. The fact that most schools do not teach up to these standards is a problem with the schools, not the test. Rather than create more tests, we should focus on having students excel on the ones that exist.

A national test might create loose standards in terms of content, and one simple test could not help to standardize teaching in all schools in the country. State testing has already shown this to be true—every student in the state takes the same test, yet even among schools in the same district, teaching remains inconsistent. If the state tests cannot bring about even local change, a national test surely cannot.

PROS

Test-taking skills are essential once a student leaves school. Students will take driving tests, tests for employment, etc. In any test, an individual will do better if he can use strong test-taking strategies and can perform under pressure. Teachers do not sacrifice "real learning" by teaching test-taking skills. No amount of strategy will substitute for actual knowledge—plus students benefit from learning to communicate what they know. Although testing puts pressure on high school students, teenagers—like all people—respond to incentives. Teens are more likely to study and master the material they are taught if they must pass a test to graduate. Standardized tests can test critical thinking skills and thereby do not compromise real learning. New York State Regents exams contain multiple-choice sections as well as an essay, both of which evaluate a student's analytical skills.

Other countries with superior education systems use standardized graduation tests. The Organisation for Economic Co-operation and Development ranks the United States 33rd globally for reading, 22nd for science, and 27th for math. France, the Netherlands, and the U.K. are all consistently ahead of the U.S. and all use standardized exit exams. These exams ensure an educated public, providing a better workforce and informed citizenry. The U.S. education system is notoriously inefficient, thus using one national standard will help compare schools nationwide to identify problems and ensure a baseline quality of education for all.

CONS

High-stakes standardized testing puts excess pressure on children and changes the curriculum for the worse. Schools face serious consequences for poor test results and put extreme pressure on students to perform well. Already many schools encourage weak students to drop out so that standardized test scores remain high—standardized tests create a perverse incentive to dismiss the students who need the most attention. Furthermore, students learn critical/creative thinking and research skills much better through class presentations, creative projects, and research papers than through tests. Teachers are forced to put less emphasis on these assignments because they must cover material that will appear on standardized tests.

Other countries have different goals in their education systems. In countries like Korea, the U.K., and France, students focus on subjects related to their future careers. Americans, conversely, value a well-rounded education that allows high school students to appreciate all fields before choosing a major interest. Furthermore, only some of these countries use exit exams—Finland, considered to have one of the best education systems in the world, uses little standardized testing. Last, these rankings are based on standardized tests. Obviously countries that focus more on testing will have students who test better, but these tests do not capture the full value of a critical-thinking approach to education.

OTHER MOTIONS:

The U.S. should develop and put into practice a high school exit exam

Students should be required to pass a national exam to graduate

RELATED MOTIONS:

Students are tested too much

The SATs do more harm than good

WEB LINKS:

- California Department of Education. <http://www.cde.ca.gov/index.asp>. Offers full information on the high school exit exam as well as scores and statistics about student performance.

- Education Commission of the States. "Exit Exams: Pros and Cons." "<http://www.ecs.org/html/IssueSection.asp?issueid=108&subissueid=159&s=Pros+%26+Cons>. Arguments on both sides of the issue.

- Singapore Ministry of Education. <http://www3.moe.edu.sg/corporate/eduoverview/PreU_ALevelCurri.htm>. Website detailing the A-level system, the national high school age curriculum and testing program utilized by students in the U.K. and other Commonwealth states. This framework could be useful for the proposition team in creating their case, while criticisms of the A-level system could provide specific examples for opposition arguments.

- Tucker, Jill. "High School Exit Exam Gets Boost as More Pass." <http://www.sfgate.com/cgi-bin/article.cgi?f=/c/a/2009/07/09/BALI18L4GF.DTL>. The state of California already uses an exit exam—whose efficacy currently is being debated.

No Child Left Behind

Motion   **No Child Left Behind does more harm than good**

Introduction   At the prompting of the Bush administration, Congress passed the No Child Left Behind (NCLB) Act in 2001 to improve the quality of U.S. education. The statute requires each state to set its own educational goals and measure the success of its students using standardized tests in major subjects like math, reading, and science for children in grades 3–8. To hold schools and states accountable for the progress of their students, the act ties federal education funding to how well students perform on these tests. Many say the measure will improve an education system that does not prepare U.S. students to compete in the twenty-first century. Others argue that the emphasis on testing leads to "teaching to the test" and puts real learning on the back burner.

Debating the Motion   Both teams must be familiar with the provisions of the No Child Left Behind Act. They should also research the experience their state—as well as large states such as New York, California, and Texas—has had with the law. Teams also should compile statistical evidence to support their position. Remember, though, that statistics usually can be manipulated to support either position, so use them strategically and carefully. Remember, too, that this topic is not discussing whether NCLB is bad or good, but rather whether the program has been harmful or beneficial.

Proposition: The heavier burden definitely falls on the proposition, which needs to support the motion that NCLB has been harmful overall. Remember that it is not necessary to say that everything about NCLB is bad; what is necessary is to demonstrate that, on balance, the NCLB has been more harmful than beneficial. Thus, demonstrating that the legislation has been 51 percent harmful compared with 49 percent beneficial would meet that goal.

Opposition: The opposition can support either a neutral or beneficial position—or a combination of both. The opposition also has the option to recommend changes to NCLB that would address any harms the proposition suggests. This tactic would require offering a counter case—which would require a very solid grounding in the policy particulars of NCLB.

PROS

Schools have had to cut corners to implement programs proposed by NCLB. Thus, NCLB ultimately is harmful. New programs are being put in place haphazardly while existing, successful programs are being cut to fund NCLB. Because NCLB requires constant standardized testing, many schools are now investing in test preparation programs like Kaplan and Coach. These programs cost thousands of dollars and must be purchased anew each year. These funds have to come from somewhere and too often the money set aside for instrument purchases, art supplies, or even the salary for more teachers is used. So, now, the schools are caught in the worst of all possible situations—the new programs are ineffective and they have lost valuable older programs.

NCLB's focus on standardized and often multiple-choice testing has forced schools to emphasize test-taking skills rather than content or important thinking and learning strategies. This harms the quality of our students' education because our education system is already notorious for presenting a lot of content and teaching it poorly rather than presenting smaller amounts of content and teaching it well. Requiring the teaching of test skills robs students of even more opportunities to actually learn content and analytical skills.

NCLB has forced schools to cheat in order to meet their state standards and receive full federal funding. Because NCLB imposes harsh consequences on schools that fail to improve fast enough, great pressure is applied to teachers and administrators to make sure that their students pass the standardized

CONS

Forcing schools to budget carefully is an important outcome of NCLB. When schools are required to implement new programs without additional funds to support them, schools are forced to focus on what is important and to carefully evaluate the effectiveness and necessity of old programs that may have just remained out of habit rather than because they were beneficial.

Test-taking skills are necessary to do well in life, so it is good that the NCLB has promoted them. Students will use test-taking skills not just in school and college, but to get into advanced programs like law, medical, business, or graduate school. People need to take tests for citizenship or a driver's license, so these skills will be useful for a lifetime. Further, all the test-taking skills in the world are useless without knowledge of content. Children are clearly being taught the material because they need that information to pass tests!

Cheating happens in school—the NCLB is not the sole cause of cheating. Stories of teachers giving students answers for any one of a number of reasons, including the school's reputation, to keep funding, or to meet NCLB guidelines, can be found all over. The good news is that these incidents are rare.

tests. Teachers give students answers because schools believe this is the only way they can avoid losing funding or being shut down. Not only are teachers setting children a poor example, but the students are being cheated out of actually learning content.

To meet NCLB guidelines, several states such as Maine and New York have lowered their standards. If students are struggling, states often take the path of least resistance by making the tests easier rather than working with students to improve and expand their knowledge and skills. Thus, even though test scores may be going up, students are actually learning less. In practice, states that lower their standards are actually being held less accountable than those with stricter standards. In the long term, students from states with low standards will not be able to compete with those from states—and countries—with higher standards.

NCLB's assumption that standardized tests are the best way to assess students is flawed. Poorly made tests unintentionally assess what they should not be testing and contain hidden biases. For example, math tests with hard vocabulary can cause failure among students who are actually quite capable. A reading that uses the word *moss* would favor a suburban child who has probably seen moss over a very bright urban child who never has. This type of testing leaves so many out.

The chief harm of NCLB is that it prevents us from seeking better alternatives. Many schools are afraid to try something new that will not generate perfect test scores immediately. Brilliant curricula that might show great

The most important point is that these situations are not unique to, and therefore cannot be considered a result of, NCLB.

Many states accused of lowering standards, including Maine and New York, deny that they have done so. In response to NCLB, some states have reassessed their standards, but that does not necessarily indicate a harm. U.S. education is often accused of being a mile wide and an inch deep—we force kids to learn lots of material but none of it well. Revising standards to emphasize core content could raise the quality of education by increasing real understanding instead of encouraging students to be jacks of all trades and masters of none.

Many of the tests created to match NCLB learning goals are "content valid," meaning they test exactly what they mean to test. Past controversy over poorly written tests has led to better quality. The fact is, however, that with or without NCLB, many state and city school systems, as well as universities, use standardized tests as a primary tool to broadly measure academic success. If states and universities already use such tests, we can't say that standardized tests are a harm caused by NCLB.

Do not declare NCLB ineffective! Time is needed to see growth. To improve our education system, schools need to get behind the program. Besides, just because NCLB hasn't fixed our education problems overnight

PROS	CONS
progress in the long term may be dropped in favor of far more mediocre programs that show immediate gains.	doesn't mean it has done more harm than good—it might simply be ineffectual, which is a neutral outcome, not a harmful one.

OTHER MOTIONS:

NCLB does more good than harm

Standardized testing does more harm than good

RELATED MOTIONS:

Repeal NCLB

Ban standardized tests

Tying funding to test scores is beneficial in the long run

WEB LINKS:

- Care to Vote '08. "The Controversy: Has NCLB Been Successful or Has It Failed?" <http://www.carleton.edu/departments/educ/Vote/pages/Pros_and-Cons.html>. Offers arguments on both sides of the issue as well as links to sites discussing the successes and failures of NCLB.

- Dillon, Sam. "Federal Researchers Find Lower Standards in Schools." <http://www.nytimes.com/2009/10/30/education/30educ.html>. Article discussing how states have lowered their standards as a result of NCLB.

- U.S. Department of Education. "Mapping Educational Progress 2008." <http://www2.ed.gov/nclb/accountability/results/progress/index.html>. Data on the academic progress of U.S. schools.

Non-standard English in Schools

Motion   **Non-standard English should be allowed in academic courses**

Introduction   If you can win a Grammy award or a Pulitzer Prize with works of art expressed in non-standard English (dialects, for instance), why can't you submit an essay to your English teacher written in non-standard English? Proponents of English dialects argue that these increasingly valid forms of expression constitute inclusion and validation for traditionally marginalized student populations. Others argue that allowing non-standard English into schools only does "on the fringe" populations a disservice by keeping them basically on the outside and ensuring that their future progress will be limited because they have not mastered mainstream spoken and written English.

Debating the Motion   Both teams should investigate the research on the value of non-standard English in education. They might also speak with a literacy specialist in the school who probably can discuss the issue.

Proposition: The terms in this motion are very vague, so the proposition will need to present a plan in which they discuss what they mean by the standard and non-standard English. Does non-standard English mean dialects, slang, something else—text messaging terms, for instance? The plan should state what the proposition means by "academic courses" and the grade levels the motion would apply to.

Opposition: The opposition could argue against the motion in general or against the proposition's plan, but the best course would be to combine the two. Because there are many arguments against the use of non-standard English, the opposition should present these, but to ensure maximum clash, it should also attack elements of the proposition plan. For example, it might challenge the proposition's definition of the term *non-standard English* or dispute the situations in which the proposition is advocating its use.

PROS

Permitting the use of non-standard English will help keep students in school. For students who come to school speaking flawless mainstream English, this topic is not very

CONS

Accepting non-standard English in the classroom will not help the dropout rate. Students do not drop out because they do not speak standard English but because they relevant, but we must recognize that dropout rates are highest among those who don't speak standard English. Allowing students to express their thoughts in class in the form of English they are most comfortable with can reduce dropout rates because these students will be more engaged and because they may feel (and even become) more accepted by their teachers and classmates.

Expressions that were once looked down on as improper English are now considered perfectly fine. English changes all the time. With all the words derived from technology coming into use, admitting common words from dialects into English classes is the next logical step for an ever-changing language.

Non-standard English words and phrases are used in daily life in pop culture. Popular songs and literature, even books that are read in school courses, use English dialects and slang. If these forms of expression are good enough to be used by genuine artists or by authors studied in school, they should be all right to use by students.

So many students, particularly in middle and high school, suffer from poor self-esteem. The negative consequences include the failure to apply to good colleges or to apply to any college at all. Allowing natural forms of expression encourages students and helps them increase their sense of self, which has huge influences on future success.

don't find school relevant or because they come from families that do not value education. What these students need is not lower standards that allow dialect or slang in the classroom—they need better education and community outreach to learn at the highest level they can.

This is exactly the kind of idea that has led to the degradation of the language! Already so many beautiful aspects of English have been lost, like using the subjunctive. The job of English teachers and educators is to protect what is left of this language. We do not want the English language to deteriorate further!

Schools need to prepare students for the real world—the narrow sphere of arts and entertainment is not the world that most will be working in as adults. The number of successful musicians and writers is very small; most students will not find a career in these fields. Schools need to prepare students to be attractive to employers—most of whom require the use of standard English. Without the ability to communicate in standard English, most students will not be able to make a decent living.

Students can be encouraged and develop high self-esteem without lowering standards. Teachers can recognize English dialects and explain that these forms of communication are fine with your friends and family but not in the world of formal spoken or written expression or at a job. Many schools teach "code switching"—which permits students to keep their dialects while also learning standard English. This entails teaching students that they speak different codes every day: one for family, one for friends, and one for school and business. Students are taught when to turn off the non-standard English code and switch to the code of professional mainstream English.

Non-standard English actually is the standard in many schools. School populations are changing; in certain environments, dialects are much more common among the students and even staff than is standard English. Schools should work to accommodate students' needs and wants rather than force students into a mold. Schools could still teach standard English, but recognition of the more common local language should also be included in course work.

Like it or not, standards are necessary to give a bigger picture of what students can do. Such standards also allow for comparisons between students so they can compete fairly for college spots, jobs, etc. A strong foundation in standard English is a requirement for any of the above. In addition, if every region taught its own dialect, moving between regions for schooling would be almost impossible because a pupil would need to learn a "new" language in each place. Teaching dialects would be a sad disservice to students.

Permitting the use of non-standard English would encourage students to accept diversity. Why not let students express themselves in class as they do among family and friends—it would help to expose students to people different from themselves. Using only standard English masks the differences in culture and lifestyle that might exist between students in a school; hiding such differences robs students of a chance to learn about other ways of life. Learning these lessons early will help bring about more tolerant and culturally aware adults—and will go a long way toward decreasing the self-segregating tendencies of school cliques.

Allowing the use of non-standard English in the classroom and for assignments actually serves as a way to further push groups apart. Not only does it highlight differences that bullies could take advantage of, students who don't learn standard English in school can't compete with those who do. In a way, permitting non-standard English is just a tool to keep the marginalized people "in their place" and promote the success of those children who come from families who already live in the mainstream.

OTHER MOTIONS:
Forcing children to use standard English does more harm than good

RELATED MOTIONS:
Slang should be allowed in school

Slang has degraded the English language
Slang is a natural progression in any language

WEB LINKS:

- Barford, Vanessa. "Mind Your Slanguage." <http://news.bbc.co.uk/2/hi/uk_news/magazine/8388545.stm>. Discusses the debate over slang in schools; interviews mostly teachers who believe it is inappropriate.

- Henry, Julie. "School Bans Youth Slang and Sees Exam Results Soar." <http://www.telegraph.co.uk/education/2435923/School-bans-youth-slang-and-sees-exam-results-soar.html>. Report on one British school's positive experience in banning slang.

- Linguistic Society of America. "LSA Resolution on the Oakland 'Ebonics' Issue." <http://www.stanford.edu/~rickford/ebonics/LSAResolution.html>. Defends the Oakland school board's 1996 decision to recognize African American vernacular English in schools.

Nuclear Power, U.S. Switch to

Motion **The United States should switch to nuclear power**

Introduction One of the major ways for the United States to both reduce dependence on foreign oil and emissions is to switch to nuclear power for generating electricity. The United States is the largest producer of nuclear-generated power in the world, but nuclear power constitutes only one-fifth of the power used here. Getting approval to build new plants is extremely difficult, both because of community opposition and strict government restrictions. These restrictions were put in place after accidents at operating plants at Three Mile Island in Pennsylvania and Chernobyl in the Soviet Union raised concerns about the far-reaching consequences of nuclear accidents. New technologies, however, have made nuclear power safer. Breakthroughs have finally been made in producing energy through nuclear fusion—the same way our Sun creates energy. Scientists predict that fusion will be even safer than the current fission reactors and offer even greater potential for creating energy. Given the potential, some think the United States should lead the way in going nuclear despite the risks.

Debating the Motion This is a research-heavy topic. In addition to looking into the history of nuclear power and current scientific developments, both teams should look into the risks and benefits. They should also research the cost-benefit of nuclear power versus other fuels.

Proposition: The proposition has two options. It could argue that a certain percentage of energy should come from nuclear plants or that the United States should go all nuclear. In either case, it should present a plan that lays out the time frame and describes how it would handle obsolete coal- and petroleum-fired plants and why it would do so.

Opposition: The opposition does not need to argue against nuclear power, although it can. It might argue that nuclear power is neutral, neither better nor worse than other forms of power, thus spending money to create new plants is unnecessary. On the other hand, the opposition could argue that nuclear power is bad and that our current system is better or that we need to create a new system—one that relies on solar, wind, and water power, for example. As always, a combination of all of the above is another way to go.

PROS

Switching to nuclear power will drastically decrease our dependence on foreign oil. Most of our energy still comes from burning fossil fuels—of which we have comparatively little. We must rely on foreign imports for oil. This is a national security risk because a major international incident could jeopardize our oil supply.

Nuclear plants produce far less waste than fossil fuel plants. According to the Union of Concerned Scientists, a typical 500-megawatt coal plant generates more than 125,000 tons of ash and 193,000 tons of sludge each year. More than three-fourths of this waste is disposed of in unlined, unmonitored landfills, and byproduct elements like arsenic can leach into drinking water. Disposal of these dangerous byproducts also is a huge concern. If concerns are voiced about the disposal of nuclear waste, the increased use of nuclear energy will encourage researchers to find safer and more effective ways to deal with it. Ultimately, nuclear energy will be even safer and greener than it already is, bearing in mind that it is already much greener than coal- and oil-generated energy.

The use of nuclear energy will allow us to improve our air quality and our environment—which will provide health benefits to all. Nuclear power plants release relatively low amounts of carbon dioxide and greenhouse gases into the atmosphere—far lower than plants powered by oil and, especially, coal. The improvement in our air quality would reduce problems ranging from asthma rates to acid rain.

CONS

The United States already has the tools to reduce its dependence on foreign oil without resorting to dangerous nuclear power. It has ample coal resources; untapped sources of oil also exist in our country. We have the resources, now we just need to be willing to use them.

Although nuclear plants may produce less waste, the waste they produce is far more dangerous than the waste produced by coal or oil. In fact, the waste from nuclear power plants is radioactive and can remain so for hundreds of thousands of years! No matter how we dispose of this kind of waste, the byproducts of producing nuclear energy pose enormous health and environmental hazards that are just too dangerous to be worth it.

Even if nuclear power plants can reduce emissions, nuclear power is still far more detrimental to the environment in the long run. The increase in radioactive waste coupled with the risk of another disaster like Chernobyl would cause greater damage to the environment than the emissions released by oil and coal plants. Increased radioactive pollution would cause cancer rates to skyrocket, not just in humans but in animals as well. Compare this to possibly reducing asthma rates and you can see that nuclear power is not worth the risk.

Nuclear power plants produce cheaper energy than coal and oil plants, generating power that is 4 to 10 times cheaper per kilowatt hour. For consumers struggling to make ends meet, lower bills for basic necessities like power can make all the difference. It would also save always cash-strapped local governments money.

Nuclear power can tide us over until other sources are developed. Fossil fuel resources are dwindling, but nuclear power uses uranium. And, we have enough uranium to last us hundreds of years. Nuclear plants will provide us enough time to develop alternative energy sources.

Even if nuclear power is cheaper, the initial cost of building a single plant is well into the billions of dollars. Only a small fraction of our energy comes from nuclear power right now, thus the cost would be hundreds of billions or even trillions of dollars to build enough plants to power the country. Decades would pass before anyone would see savings, while in the meantime power costs would soar.

We should be focusing on developing less dangerous sources of long-term energy—renewable energy sources such as solar and wind power, for example. Granted, we have not sufficiently developed these technologies, but rather than spending money on building new nuclear plants, the government could fund incentives to perfect safer renewable energy. Until those alternatives are workable, we can continue to use coal and oil.

OTHER MOTIONS:

Nuclear energy does more good than harm

Ban all nuclear power plants

RELATED MOTIONS:

Nuclear energy should be included in low-emission energy initiatives

WEB LINKS:

- McCarthy, John. "Frequently Asked Questions about Nuclear Energy." <http://www-formal.stanford.edu/jmc/progress/nuclear-faq.html>. Background information on the topic.
- Online Digital Education Connection. Nuclear Energy. "Nuclear Energy: Advancing or Destructive?" <http://www.odec.ca/projects/2003/chiuw3w/public_html/tech.html>. Article describing nuclear reactors and offering the pros and cons of nuclear energy.
- World Nuclear Association. "The Economics of Nuclear Power." <http://www.world-nuclear.org/info/inf02.html>. Article arguing that nuclear power is cost-effective.

Official Language, English as

Motion **Make English the official national language**

Introduction While about half the nations of the world currently have official national languages used in conducting legal, legislative, and bureaucratic proceedings, the United States does not. Some promote English as the official language as a unifying measure, while others consider it a sign of disrespect to the non-English-speaking immigrants who helped build our nation. National language bills rarely get serious attention because they are often used merely as distractions or time-wasting ploys during contentious legislative sessions. However, since immigration reform has become an increasingly important issue, more attention has been paid to the debate about an official U.S. language.

Debating the Motion Both teams need to be clear about the difference between *national languages*, *official languages*, *nationally recognized languages*, and similar terms. They should also research the history of this issue and legislative proposals to make English the official language.

Proposition: The proposition should begin with a definition of what is meant by an *official language* and offer a plan for implementing the motion that might include a time frame, resources for nonnative speakers, etc. Looking at specific proposals for making English the official language can help provide a framework for creating a case.

Opposition: The opposition might want to look into historical reasons why the U.S. has not previously adopted a national language. The opposition has a number of options in defending their side. The first is simply to argue that the U.S. does not need an official language. The second would be to create a counter case in which the opposition might suggest that a number of languages be made official; several countries, including Canada, have multiple official languages, so researching these will help give a framework for a counter plan.

PROS

An official language would eliminate bureaucratic obligations to serve residents in their language. Because we do not conduct our governmental processes in any one specific language, money is wasted on translating

CONS

Declaring English to be the national language does not magically eliminate the needs of non-English speakers. For example, if we print tax forms only in English, non-English speakers will most likely simply file their and printing alternate versions of every form from election notices to driver's license applications. Declaring English as the sole national language would give agencies the right to conduct all business in English.

A national language is a unifying factor. Our flag and national anthem unify people in their patriotism and bridge political and socioeconomic differences. Many other nations have a national language as a symbol of cultural pride—the United States should demonstrate its pride in its culture by recognizing the language that pervades every aspect of our lives.

Establishing an official language would pressure immigrants to learn English, helping them to adapt. While most immigrants learn English to get well-paid jobs, some live in isolated communities of immigrants and do not learn English. Such immigrants do not assimilate, which reduces the benefits of our heterogeneous population.

If we do not take measures to preserve English as our language, we risk losing our heritage. This country's history is bound not only to the English language, but specifically to American English, which reflects our own nation and culture. From our differences in pronunciation to our differences in spelling, American English is our own and must be preserved.

taxes incorrectly. In the long run, having civil servants waste their time attempting to correct mistakes caused by a language barrier will cost more than it would to simply translate forms.

The United States is a nation of many languages. What really unites us is our celebration of the rich culture that is created by our diversity. To exclude those who wish not to or cannot express themselves in English only alienates them. Furthermore, many other countries that have official languages recognize multiple languages as a symbol of respect to all within their borders.

Immigrants will try to learn English whether or not it is the official language because it is necessary to success. English is a difficult language; creating additional pressure to learn it puts undue stress on immigrants who, generally, must work harder to get by as it is. Isolated communities are few and far between and, in any case, are unlikely to change their culture simply because the government has declared an official national language.

English need not be the sole national language to be preserved as part of our history. Furthermore, an even more important part of our heritage is our culture of immigrants and diversity. The United States was built upon the backs of immigrants—most of whom did not speak English—who came here in search of a better life. To suddenly declare one national language implies that those who speak other languages are less American; it shows disrespect to immigrants and thereby disrespect to American citizens.

OTHER MOTIONS:

The U.S. does not need an official national language

The U.S. needs an official language

RELATED MOTIONS:

Spanish should be an official language in the United States

WEB LINKS:

- "Do You Speak American?" <http://www.pbs.org/speak/seatosea/officialamerican/>. Overview of the issue with links to other sources.

- Time Magazine. "Law: No Official Language." <http://www.time.com/time/magazine/article/0,9171,969432,00.html>. Article presenting arguments on both sides.

- U.S. English. "Official English." <http://www.us-english.org/view/2>. Site offering arguments in support of the motion.

Oil Dependency, Ending Foreign

Motion **The United States should set a date for ending dependence on foreign oil**

Introduction Fossil fuels are a nonrenewable resource that will be exhausted sooner or later; the fact that they come to the United States from often unstable and unfriendly parts of the world makes them all the more unreliable and unattractive. This country has long known that it needs to end its dependence first on foreign oil and then on petroleum-related products altogether. Some suggest that setting a concrete deadline for abandoning fossil fuels will force us to turn our full attention to developing alternative energy sources.

Debating the Motion Because this topic is a hotly debated one, teams should research what kinds of deadlines have been suggested and who has suggested them. They should also research projected dates for running out of fossil fuels.

Proposition: The proposition should offer a specific deadline based on projected scarcity of fossil fuels and improvements in alternative technologies. This will allow them to speak to many of the opposition concerns about the feasibility of alternatives.

Opposition: The opposition does not need to argue against an end to dependence on foreign oil; the team could argue that setting a specific deadline would be harmful. On the other hand, the opposition could argue that a deadline is not necessary. A combination of these two approaches is also possible.

PROS

Setting an absolute deadline sends a strong message to the American public that the problem of global warming is real. The lack of a detailed plan to end our dependence on oil suggests that oil consumption is not an immediate issue. Not every American appreciates the urgency of the situation. We must not run out of oil before we can replace it with other sources of energy; the way to spur action is to set a realistic and public goal so that

CONS

While goal setting is great, concrete plans cannot be made in every situation. We cannot know exactly how soon we will be able to employ alternate technologies on a vast scale, and we cannot predict what our economic and political relations will be like in several years. If governments decide not to share technologies with us or if unforeseen circumstances hamper research progress, we may need to rely on an old, well-known everyone has a strong reason to work toward achieving it.

Setting a date will push the United States to do what it knows is needed. We know that we rely heavily on fossil fuel and that this resource cannot last forever. Nevertheless, we have been slow to develop alternative technologies and work to create an energy-delivery infrastructure that operates on other forms of energy. The deadline will push us toward what we need to accomplish.

We should set a date because we now can. We now have a number of realistic energy alternatives—and we will continue developing more. In addition to the advances in nuclear technology that have put us on the threshold of fusion, we also have access to increasingly affordable and effective wind and solar technologies—not to mention ethanol. Much of our current alternative energy technology did not exist 20 years ago. Now that these choices are available, setting a date is reasonable.

Setting a date for ending dependence on foreign oil encourages oil-producing nations to restructure their economies. If countries know when the U.S. is planning to cease buying their oil, they can find alternate sources of income.

source such as oil. When our energy independence depends on the doings of a globalized and interconnected world, it is foolish to stick to an inflexible schedule.

With no way of accurately predicting the future, setting a deadline would be foolish. Although fossil fuels are finite, we might develop technologies that run on small amounts of oil that would allow us to stretch our supply almost indefinitely.

While these alternatives may be improving, they are not yet ready to take the place of fossil fuels. We have no way of knowing when any of those other sources of energy will be improved enough to replace fossil fuels as a main source of energy. Just because a lot of progress has been made recently does not mean that we won't encounter a major stumbling block in the near future. These alternatives have not advanced enough to accurately predict when we will be able to stop relying on foreign oil.

Telling those countries that currently provide us with oil that we will not be needing that commodity in the near future may sour our relations with them. Many countries—particularly in Asia—have a growing demand for oil, thus, oil-exporters will have no real need to restructure their economies. On the other hand, using foreign oil can be important diplomatically. If the U.S. is a big importer of a country's oil, the country has to deal with us. Without foreign oil, the U.S. could put itself in more danger from unstable and unfriendly regimes. This could

PROS	CONS
	disrupt our oil supply sooner than we had planned and could ruin our relationships in what is already a volatile region of the world. Our security could be compromised in addition to leaving us without fuel!
A goal will help encourage the innovations necessary to move us away from fossil fuels. With a deadline approaching, time and resources will be reallocated to developing alternative energy technologies, some of which may have been overlooked in the past because we were complacent about our sources and ready availability of energy. Just as goals about emission cuts have induced automakers to develop increasingly fuel-efficient cars, so will a date for ending our dependence on foreign oil spur us to make solar, wind, water, and nuclear fuels economically and technologically viable and safe.	*The government and private industry can provide grants and incentives for those perfecting greener technologies.* Once alternative energy is viable, we could perhaps set a date, but development of greener technologies and setting a date by which we are independent of foreign oil need to be done in this order, not vice versa. This deadline cannot be set before we are assured of a working and efficient alternative.

OTHER MOTIONS:

The United States should set a date for ending its use of fossil fuels

The U.S. should stop relying on foreign fuel

RELATED MOTIONS:

Dependence on foreign oil does more good than harm

WEB LINKS:

- Lefton, Rebecca, and Daniel Weiss. "Oil Dependency Is a Dangerous Habit." <http://www.americanprogress.org/issues/2010/01/oil_imports_security.html>. Article discussing the problems associated with oil dependency—and arguing for clean fuel alternatives.

- U.S. Energy Information Agency. "How Dependent Are We on Foreign Oil?" <http://tonto.eia.doe.gov/energy_in_brief/foreign_oil_dependence.cfm>. Background information on the topic.

Penny, Abolish the

Motion **End the use of the penny**

Introduction The penny is special among U.S. coins. Its copper color makes it stand out from all the other silver-colored coins. Yet with inflation, fewer and fewer items can be purchased with a penny. Ironically, not even a penny is worth a penny these days, with the U.S. mint spending almost 2 cents to make a single penny. Some argue that the penny should be permanently retired.

Debating the Motion This topic is interesting because it appeals more to emotion and sentiment than to factual or statistical-based arguments. Fittingly, emotion and sentiment are the two main reasons while we still have a penny. Many have taken sides on this debate, so a quick search of the web will provide information that will be useful in finding anecdotes and quips. The hard facts of this case involve research into time and cost-effectiveness. But this topic, more than almost any other in this volume, is an exercise in rhetoric: How well do you present your case to a judge?

Proposition: The predominant arguments for the proposition will revolve around the expense and inefficiency in manufacturing and using the penny.

Opposition: The opposition can pursue two lines of argument: the expense involved in abolishing the penny and its historical and emotional value.

PROS

The production of pennies is a drain on resources and taxpayers' money. The simple fact is that nowadays it costs more than a penny to make a penny—almost twice as much. Thus, the government is losing colossal amounts of money in producing this coin; indeed, in 2007 alone, the government lost $31 million in the production of 6.6 billion pennies. Especially given the current economic crisis, we cannot afford to be so wasteful. Time for the penny to go!

CONS

Producing fewer pennies means producing more nickels, which are just as expensive to make. If pennies are no longer in circulation, the government will need to increase the production of the next smallest denomination coin to keep the same amount of money in circulation. Given that the cost of production of a nickel is about 9 cents, there is reason to believe that the government will save very little—or nothing—by eliminating the penny.

Losing the penny will make cost calculations and divisions easier, saving both time and effort. Adding up lots of tiny numbers can be difficult. In fact, Citizens for Retiring the Penny estimates that the average American spends nearly two-and-a-half hours per year handling, or waiting for people to handle, pennies. And, as any economist knows, time equals money. For example, if cashiers could count out change more quickly, stores might need fewer workers to keep checkout lines moving, thus fewer salaries would have to be paid and merchandise prices could be reduced.

Preserving the penny for "cultural" reasons is sentimental and nonsensical. There is no logical reason to continue a wasteful practice just because "things have always been done that way." Furthermore, what was a good practice hundreds of years ago is not necessarily a good practice now—having a penny made sense when a penny was worth something but times, and inflation levels, have changed.

Any increase in prices will be very tiny, given how worthless the penny is today. The sad truth is that the penny just has no point anymore. In days of old, a penny could actually purchase something. From penny candy to penny buns, to penny ribbons and penny arcades, in the bygone era pennies were useful. Penny items were like the dollar menus of today. Now, you cannot buy anything for a penny! It is over the top to claim that

How foolish to say that the tiny amount of time saved from not having to count out pennies will make transactions any easier! The proposition forgets that we are advocating the removal of the penny and not all coinage. Even if we are left to deal in nickels and dimes, change from a $5 bill for a $1.35 purchase will still require the cashier to count out a nickel, a dime, and two quarters; these coins will still require consumers to dig out their change purses. Saving two hours over the course of a year will have a very small impact indeed on money and/or convenience.

Saying good-bye to this beautiful coin that celebrates one of our greatest leaders is a great blow to our national heritage. The penny has existed since the founding of our nation and has borne the face of Abraham Lincoln for more than one hundred years. The penny has a long history and has become an important part of American identity. Indeed, according to the U.S. government, the 2010 design of the penny is "emblematic of President Abraham Lincoln's preservation of the United States as a single and united country." It has too much cultural significance to be eliminated.

Eliminating the penny will lead to increased prices. Those little extra numbers between 5s and 0s are going to have to go somewhere—without the penny, the price of most goods will probably go up to the next highest 5 cents, resulting in subtle changes in prices that can really add up. Two extra cents per item doesn't seem like much, until you figure that on a family grocery shopping trip alone, you might buy 100 little items,

PROS	CONS
a few extra cents added to some purchases will result in any serious change to a family's finances.	upping your cost by almost $2. Add those extra $2 to every shopping trip made in a lifetime and clearly the consumer is going to have to pay big time for losing the penny. Poor consumers in particular will be affected, since they often make more frequent, smaller transactions.

OTHER MOTIONS:

The U.S. should act to save the penny

The U.S. should abolish the nickel

RELATED MOTIONS:

The U.S. should abandon coinage for paper money

WEB LINKS:

- Americans for Common Cents. <http://www.pennies.org/>. Provides much information about the penny, including a survey showing that Americans support keeping the penny.

- Barrett, Maggie. "Professor's Research Supports Eliminating Penny." <http://www.wfu.edu/wfunews/2006/2006.07.18.w.html>. Article reporting on research that eliminating the penny will not raise prices.

- Consumeraffairs.com. "The Penny's End Is Near." <http://www.consumeraffairs.com/news04/2006/07/penny_sense.html>. Article supporting the elimination of the penny.

Physical Education, Mandatory

Motion   **All schools should make physical education courses mandatory**

Introduction   The obesity rate is rising in the United States at an alarming pace, particularly among children. According to the Centers for Disease Control, an estimated 17 percent of children and adolescents aged 2–19 years are obese. One of the many solutions offered to address the problem is requiring physical education (PE) courses in schools. For all those kids for whom physical education/sports is either their favorite or most hated class—for most kids it is one or the other—the subject of mandatory PE is a very timely topic.

Debating the Motion   This topic is very vague: *physical education* and *school* are all-encompassing terms. Both teams should be aware of what could potentially be meant by physical education and which type of schools should be required to have mandatory programs. How physical education is defined differs widely. In many places, it refers primarily to gym class. In other places, it includes health and personal wellness courses. Both teams should be prepared to talk about physical education in all its forms.

Proposition: The first proposition should begin by narrowing the scope of the terms *schools* and *physical education*. The proposition should then offer a clear plan about what will be entailed in PE classes, who will be required to take them, and which schools will offer them.

Opposition: Because the terms of this topic are so broad, the proposition has a lot of leeway in creating its case. Accordingly, the opposition needs to be especially well-researched and flexible; team members must be ready to talk about students from toddlers to graduates and PE courses ranging from running laps to cooking healthy meals. If the proposition does not narrow the scope of *PE* and *schools*, the opposition should define all terms as broadly as possible, thus increasing avenues for argumentation.

PROS

Physical education, which includes personal wellness classes, should be mandatory in all schools K–12 because a school has the specific responsibility of educating its students to achieve a better life. One of the major predictors for quality of life is physical well-being.

CONS

The job of a school is to provide an academic education. That task requires specialists—professionals who know how to teach specific subjects. Education in academic subjects cannot be provided outside school by other sources, like parents. Parents, on the other

In the long run, teaching all kinds of academic topics does not help students if they don't learn how to make the choices and decisions that keep their bodies healthy. Further, because many parents lack the necessary education about healthy eating and living, a child's only opportunity to acquire such knowledge would be in school.

Because students now have little free time, the school must provide them the chance to exercise or play. The length of the school day is increasing. In the past, students could play or exercise after school; now they return home only to do hours of homework.

Although physical education programs require a hefty investment in equipment and professionals with the correct training, that investment will pay off in the long run. The cost of PE programs is minor compared with the cost of treating all the children who will, without education in making good life choices, become unhealthy and obese adults. Obesity is a serious problem. It increases the likelihood of cardiovascular disease and diabetes and so raises health care costs. It also increases business costs because obese individuals are more likely to miss work and take more disability leave than those of normal weight. Investing in physical education now will actually save the country millions of dollars in the long run!

hand, are quite capable of providing the kind of information that children learn in most PE and wellness classes: they can serve healthy meals instead of fast food and make sure that their children exercise. If unsure, parents have access to many resources to help them educate themselves and their children about physical fitness and health: the Internet, government outreach programs, or even their pediatrician.

If students do not have time after school to exercise or play a sport, they must better manage their time. Granted, the amount of homework assigned has increased, but so has the amount of time that students spend watching TV, playing video games, or surfing the web. Homework isn't the cause of our nation's steadily expanding waistlines; the cause is that students have replaced strenuous after-school activities with stationary ones. If a student can make time to chat on the phone or play video games with his friend, he can make time to exercise.

Physical education programs are very expensive, and, in the face of school budget cuts, we would do better to spend our money on more important subjects—math and reading, for example. Because physical education courses require teachers with specific training and certification, lots of equipment, and the use of vast quantities of space, they are an enormous drain on our limited resources. Why, six or more new classrooms could be built in the space it takes for one gymnasium! Today, students cannot get adequate attention from their teachers because of large class sizes. Let's take the money assigned to PE programs and use it to build more classrooms, hire more teachers, and reduce class size.

The only way to improve the current quality of physical education is to mandate and regulate it. Because the United States has no nationally mandated standards for PE and some states have no standards, many schools simply find an extra body to watch students play (or not play!). With mandated national standards, such as those developed by the National Association for Sport and Physical Education, the quality of PE would improve at the same time that the number of courses offered would be increased.

Physical education and personal wellness must be taught by professionals. Parents are not well enough informed to do so—misinformation about diet or lack of training in sport safety can lead to health problems and injury. Physical education teachers know what children are physically capable of doing at specific grades and ages. They can respond appropriately to injuries and, better yet, know how best to prevent them.

Even if we concede that physical education is necessary, making physical education in its current state mandatory is a poor choice given its low quality. Having children exercise and eat healthfully are admirable goals, but our current programs won't let us achieve them. Physical education curricula are poorly thought out and what staff they have are not trained. We do not have enough good curricula or enough good teachers to fulfill this mandate; replacing rigorous academic courses with mediocre physical education and wellness classes cannot be good.

Achieving general wellness is not rocket science. While supervising the diet of a professional athlete or the training for an extreme sport may require special expertise, families should be able to provide both the healthy meals and the opportunity for activities that almost always result in reasonably good health and lifelong healthy habits.

OTHER MOTIONS:

PE should be mandatory in public schools

All K–12 students should be required to take gym

RELATED MOTIONS:

PE should be required for college students

Personal wellness classes should be required for unhealthy students

WEB LINKS:

- AllBusiness. "New Reports Find Physical Education in California's Schools Is Failing Our Kids." <http://www.allbusiness.com/services/business-services/4023405-1.html>. An overview of PE programs in California, with fact-finding about current efficacy and recommendations to change problem areas.

- Armour, Nancy. "Mandatory P.E. Class Not Enough to Fight Fat." <http://articles. sfgate.com/2009-06-21/news/17210256_1_gym-class-physical-education-pe>. An overview of nationwide mandatory PE programs that questions their efficacy, concentrating on lack of oversight and no standardized curricula.
- The President's Challenge. <http://www.presidentschallenge.org/educators/program_ details/physical_fitness/qualifying_standards.aspx>. The Presidential Fitness Challenge serves as a fitness curriculum for many schools since most states lack a standardized curriculum. The goals found here can help provide a framework for creating a practical plan.

Plastic Bags, Banning

Motion   **Ban single-use plastic bags**

Introduction   Single-use plastic bags are either a boon or a nuisance depending on how you look at them. On the one hand, they can be a convenient way to carry groceries, a hygienic way to wrap meats on the way home from the store, and useful around the house for holding trash. On the other, plastic does not break down in landfills. Plastic bags contribute to trash in public spaces in cities and parks and litter our roads—who hasn't seen a flurry of plastic bags swirling in the wind and fluttering from their resting place in bushes? Some cities, including San Francisco, have banned stores from offering them. Stores complain that such restriction is an unfair burden, forcing them to provide costlier alternatives, while shoppers bemoan forgetting their tote bags on the way to the store. Despite complaints, ever more cities are considering imposing this ban.

Debating the Motion   Both teams should research specific examples of bans to discover how they were implemented and what programs have proved most successful.

Proposition. The team needs to offer a plan for the ban that would include a time frame and any exceptions to the ban they think appropriate. Remember, when proposing any sort of ban, the proposition may choose to recommend an immediate total ban or ban only certain items in certain situations, as long as their definition of *ban* is broad enough to allow for a healthy debate.

Opposition: The opposition team does not need to argue that plastic bags are good, just that they do not need to be banned. Depending on the proposition's case, the opposition team might also argue against specific elements. For example, it might argue against any exceptions the proposition has allowed; alternatively, if the proposition proposed a total ban, it might argue that the proposition should have allowed exceptions.

PROS	CONS
Plastic bags pose a real hazard to wildlife and in landfills, while alternatives to plastic bags are all environmentally sound. Tote bags can be washed and reused and can also be made	*Plastic bags can be used in an environmentally responsible way as well.* Many stores that use a lot of plastic bags, such as supermarkets, now have recycling bins, just as they have for

of fair trade materials harvested from sustainable farms, while paper bags made of recycled paper will biodegrade and can be recycled. Plastic is made from petroleum and never breaks down.

cans and bottles. The bags are then recycled into numerous products, including tote bags. Further, not all alternatives are as environmentally friendly as they seem. Some totes, for example, are made of cotton, which is a crop that is notoriously unsustainable, exhausts the land on which it is grown, and causes environmental degradation in its processing. Paper bags are made from wood pulp—trees have been destroyed to make them.

Loose plastic bags floating around towns and cities are a menace. They are a danger to animal life and never biodegrade. Even if people say they will reuse or recycle plastic bags, just look outside to see the danger these things pose.

If the concern is proper disposal, then we need littering laws and clean-up crews, not a ban on plastic bags. They are helpful in and of themselves; if the cause of the problem is human behavior, then we should regulate that rather than the bags.

By banning plastic bags in stores, we can increase responsible consumption. Many people wander into a store on the way home or on a whim. They often end up wasting money on things they don't need. Forcing shoppers to bring their own bags will cut down on wasteful shopping because they won't be able to carry unnecessary items.

Requiring the use of tote bags for purchases will actually increase irresponsible consumption. For those who are forgetful or who come up against an unexpected need, having to buy a new tote bag is a waste of money.

Banning plastic bags will make shopping more convenient. Tote bags or paper bags are sturdier, so shoppers won't have to worry about them bursting. We are banning something that isn't even the most helpful alternative for carrying purchases. With plastic bags gone, stores will have to offer the sturdier options. The ban actually helps shoppers, so having the ban is a good idea.

Other kinds of bags are not necessarily more convenient than plastic; indeed, there are times when a sturdy tote or paper bag won't do. Paper will fall apart in the rain and tote bags add weight and bulk to a purchase. Furthermore, plastic bags have benefits the alternatives do not. They are more sanitary than paper or canvas, especially for carrying raw meat or containers likely to leak. Bacteria could easily seep into the paper or cotton, breed, and spread—with plastic, a shopper can responsibly discard the contaminated bag.

PROS

A ban on plastic bags will help small businesses. Small businesses will make more profit in the long run if customers provide their own bags than if stores have to stock plastic bags. If the store no longer must provide plastic bags, costs will go down. The option of selling reusable totes also provides numerous benefits. It is another way for a store to add to its profits; tote bags carrying the store's logo also provide an opportunity for free advertising that can boost business.

CONS

A ban on plastic bags would hurt small businesses. Small businesses may not be able to afford to stock reusable totes. Totes are more expensive than plastic bags, and stores that have very little profit may not have the extra cash to buy them. If forced to stock pricey totes, they may not be able to stock some of the usual products they sell. Furthermore, stores that cannot afford to stock totes would be at a disadvantage. These businesses would have to rely on customers to bring their own bags. The inconvenience might very well cause customers to go elsewhere, resulting in a decline in profits.

OTHER MOTIONS:
  Plastic bags do more good than harm
  Ban paper shopping bags

RELATED MOTIONS:
  Tax the use of plastic bags

WEB LINKS:
- Gorn, David. "San Francisco Plastic Bag Ban Interests Other Cities." <http://www.npr.org/templates/story/story.php?storyId=89135360>. Article summarizing the response to San Francisco's ban on plastic bags.
- West, Larry. "Paper, Plastic, or Something Better? Reusable Bags Are Best for Both Consumers and the Environment." <http://environment.about.com/od/recycling/a/reusablebags.htm>. Article opposing the use of both plastic and paper and in favor of reusable totes.

Pledge of Allegiance in Schools

Motion   **Students should be required to recite the Pledge of Allegiance**

Introduction   While in the past it might have been common to hear the pledge recited in every classroom at the start of the day, the issue of whether or not to require students to participate in the recitation of the pledge has become increasingly divisive. Some schools still recite the pledge, others give teachers the choice to have their students do so or not—while still others have stopped the practice altogether. Now, however, the school-by-school decisions are being taken over by districts, and even states are imposing rules and passing legislation demanding the return of the pledge to classrooms. Both sides of the debate claim to be the more patriotic: on the one side, people are relying on the pledge as the ultimate symbol of faith in the United States, while those on the other side claim that nothing is more patriotic than the right to refuse to pledge.

Debating the Motion   Many legislative attempts have been made to impose the recitation of the pledge, so both sides should research what has been successful and what has failed. Both teams should also research whether reciting the pledge impinges on First Amendment rights.

Proposition: The proposition needs to present a plan that addresses who will be required to participate—how often, where, and when—so as to block general arguments such as those pertaining to freedom of religion.

Opposition: The opposition will have more or less ground to stand on depending on how carefully the proposition presents its case. If the motion is argued as is, without any additional policies or stipulations, arguing on grounds of constitutional freedoms would be best. This approach should be used even if the proposition has offered an opt-out plan, so being very familiar with constitutional protections is a must. Legal arguments aside, the opposition might also take the stance that reciting the pledge is an unnecessary exercise.

PROS	CONS
Reciting the Pledge of Allegiance at the beginning of the day sets a good tone. A consistent daily routine will mark the shift from home to school for kids. This mental shift is	*While much research supports having routines at the beginning of school as ways to turn students to learning and get them focused, why waste time by doing this with the pledge?*

necessary to get children focused on learning and working; in addition, the physical act will be beneficial to children who struggle with behavior disorders because it creates a concrete marker that helps them change from their more unstructured home behaviors to their more regimented schools tasks.

Many of the states and districts that require the pledge have created exemptions for students who have religious objections. These students have a right to sit quietly and respectfully while others participate in reciting the pledge. Because only a few would choose to opt out, students in general can still get the benefits of reciting the pledge daily while not compromising the rights of a few students.

So many students today take for granted the freedoms that the Constitution guarantees and protects. In an age where the media is more likely to portray discontent, patriotism is lacking. Reciting the pledge helps to increase love of country by highlighting and paving the way for the appreciation of the freedoms that Americans are guaranteed when so many others in the world are not.

The words of the pledge are powerful and express a message valuable not only to the country but also to a school. The calls for unity, liberty, and justice are as necessary in a school community as in the greater community.

Instead, students should start with a short review of items from the previous day's lessons or with a question or a problem to solve that will tie into new material. Such exercises will provide a better and more appropriate entry into the school day than rote recitation.

Requiring students to recite the Pledge of Allegiance violates their First Amendment rights of freedom of speech and freedom of religion. Naturally included in the right to speak one's mind is the right to keep silent when one chooses. Forcing children to recite a patriotic formula violates this right. The inclusion of the word *God* poses difficulties for atheists and a variety of religions whose believers do not speak God's name or who do not believe in pledging anything other than sincere and private words of prayer. Forcing them to violate the rules of their religion would impinge on these children's freedom of religion.

To nurture appreciation of the freedoms of the United States, schools would do better to help their students learn and understand our Constitution. Citizens who truly understand the structure of our country's government and its founding documents are more valuable to us than robots who recite. The best way to increase patriotism is through quality civic education, comprehensive U.S. history courses, and the study of the different systems of government in other countries.

While many students would like liberty and justice, they don't really exist for children. Children do not have the same constitutional rights as adults, and their rights are interpreted differently. Bringing attention to this

Reviewing and affirming these concepts daily in the pledge will allow schools to bring to the fore how the school lives up to these values.

fact might increase the natural conflict that can occur between children and adults in school, especially with older children in middle or high school who are learning about the Constitution and wondering why the amendments do not yet apply to them. Further, while it would be wonderful for students to feel a sense of duty to their country and school, it is not valuable if they do so simply because of words they chant each morning. Better for the school to engage in activities that create a real sense of community in the school—which will, in turn, inspire a real sense of pride and duty.

OTHER MOTIONS:

Requiring students to recite the pledge is unconstitutional

All students must recite the pledge

Reciting the pledge does more harm than good

RELATED MOTIONS:

Remove the words *under God* from the Pledge of Allegiance

WEB LINKS:

- Hudson, David L. "Pledge Allegiance." <http://www.firstamendmentcenter.org/speech/studentexpression/topic.aspx?topic=pledge>. Overview of the topic.

- ProCon.org. "Should the Words 'under God' be in the US Pledge of Allegiance?" <http://undergod.procon.org/view.resource.php?resourceID=000063>. Offers arguments on both sides of the issue.

Presidents, Non-native

Motion   **Non-native U.S. citizens should be allowed to run for president**

Introduction   From Alexander Hamilton to Arnold Schwarzenegger, U.S. history is rife with possible presidential candidates who are barred from running because they were born outside the United States. The Constitution permits only native-born citizens to run for president. Some argue that the Constitution should be amended to remove this provision.

Debating the Motion   Several measures on this topic have come before Congress in the past, so both teams should research the grounds for making these petitions and why they were unsuccessful. Both teams should also look at the individuals for whom advocates are wishing to change this constitutional provision.

Proposition: The proposition team should lay out a more specific plan than the motion states, including what kinds of stipulations that will be necessary to become president if place of birth is no longer a criterion.

Opposition: The opposition is upholding the status quo, so it should research why the provision was included in the Constitution. Remember, changing the Constitution is difficult and rarely done, so precedent about the reluctance to amend the Constitution can provide additional ground for the opposition case.

PROS

Permitting a foreign-born citizen to run for president would show the world that we believe in our core principles: all people are created equal. We do not have classes of citizenship. Americans believe that people should succeed not because of where they were born but because of merit and hard work. Permitting foreign-born citizens to run for president would show the world we have no limits on what an American can aspire to and attain.

CONS

Restricting foreign-born citizens from running for and serving as president is not at odds with our core values. The Constitution has restrictions on even native-born citizens, requiring individuals be of a certain age to sit in Congress or be president.

In a democracy, the people should be able to choose whoever they think is the best leader. Placing restrictions on who can run for office confines the populace's ability to structure their government as they see fit.

Some of our best politicians are foreign-born citizens; this restriction may rule out the best potential presidential candidates. Naturalized citizens often bring great ideas with them and are often more dynamic and committed to the American dream than complacent native-born citizens. It seems silly that someone like Arnold Schwarzenegger can govern California, the most populous state in the union, with the fifth-largest economy in the world, yet we could not trust him to be president.

Longtime citizens can be just as loyal to the U.S. as someone who was born here. Born-citizenship is not a guarantee of loyalty. Timothy McVeigh, who launched a terrorist attack killing 168 people, was born in the U.S. Many foreign-born children come to this country as infants and consider this country their only home; their loyalty is to the United States because they never really knew their country of birth.

A foreign-born individual could be a better president. Immigrants who come from oppressive countries appreciate U.S. liberties more than many native-born citizens. A foreign-born president would be less likely to take America's blessings for granted because she knows they are not guaranteed. Furthermore, knowing about another culture could be extremely helpful in certain circumstances, in the diplomatic realm especially.

If Americans were interested in allowing foreigners to run for president, there would be support for a constitutional amendment. No such movement exists because this democracy does not wish to allow foreign-born citizens to run for president.

In a country of more than 300 million people, we can find excellent native-born presidential candidates; we don't need to change the Constitution for the benefit of one or two individuals who may become prominent periodically. In every generation, only a very few of the individuals who could even remotely be possible presidential contenders are foreign-born: Arnold Schwarzenegger is the only individual mentioned in recent years. We should not change the Constitution for one individual.

To elect a foreigner, even a naturalized one, is a security risk. Undoubtedly a foreign-born citizen will love this country or she would not have become a citizen, but she may still carry some loyalty to her native country. This would be even more dangerous in situations where the politician is not aware of such split loyalty. The president must have unquestioned loyalty to only one country, the United States.

Only someone born in the country can truly understand it. People raised in other countries may well appreciate American freedoms, but only someone raised here has the knowledge of American society and civil traditions to lead it effectively.

OTHER MOTIONS:

Foreigners should be allowed to run for president

RELATED MOTIONS:

Foreigners should not be allowed to run for public office

WEB LINKS:

- Kasindorf, Martin. "Should the Constitution Be Amended for Arnold?" <http://www.usatoday.com/news/politicselections/2004-12-02-schwarzenegger-amendment_x.htm>. Article discussing the issue in the context of suggestions that California governor Arnold Schwarzenegger would be a strong presidential candidate.

- U.S. House of Representatives, Committee on the Judiciary, Subcommittee on the Constitution. <http://commdocs.house.gov/committees/judiciary/hju67306.000/hju67306_0.HTM>. Transcript on 2000 hearings held on the issue.

Puerto Rican Statehood

Motion   **Puerto Rico should become the 51st state**

Introduction   Puerto Rico, a territory of the United States, has a complex relationship with the U.S. Its residents have full citizenship, but they do not have full voting rights—for example, they cannot vote for president and Puerto Rico does not have a voting member in Congress. Since Puerto Rico became a territory more than 100 years ago, the status question—should it became a state, become an independent country, or remain a territory—has been a constant theme in the island's politics.

Debating the Motion   Both teams need to research the legal relationship between the United States and Puerto Rico as well as the political history of the island, which revolves around the question of status.

Proposition: The proposition might want to include a time frame for the incorporation of Puerto Rico as a state as well as a plan to minimize the political and economic impact that such a move might have on the existing states and Puerto Rico.

Opposition: The opposition has two distinct options in this case, either to argue against statehood or to argue for full independence for Puerto Rico.

PROS

It is unjust that Puerto Ricans have the same responsibilities as U.S. citizens, without having the same rights. For example, Puerto Ricans are subject to federal laws just as American citizens living in the 50 states, but they cannot vote in federal elections. Furthermore, Puerto Rico has only one nonvoting representative in Congress. Puerto Ricans deserve the full rights and protections that statehood would afford them.

CONS

In fact, the relationship between the U.S. and Puerto Rico is delicately balanced—plus, Puerto Ricans do not think being denied statehood is unjust. Indeed, they have consistently voted against becoming a state in referendums. Furthermore, Puerto Ricans can vote in all other elections and serve as voting delegates at the Republican and Democratic national conventions. The congressional representative can still vote in committees and speak. Finally, the U.S. government leaves most internal governing to the local Puerto Rico government.

If Puerto Rico were made a state, its citizens could be fully taxed, thus bringing in more money to the U.S. government. While Puerto Ricans do pay most taxes, all nonfederal employees are exempt from federal income tax. In fact, according to the U.S. Council for Puerto Rico Statehood, Puerto Rico costs the U.S. almost $10 billion each year because of payments to the island and lost tax revenues.

Whatever money we would gain from making Puerto Rico a state we would lose in the additional services that we would need to provide to it as a state. Full Social Security and Medicaid benefits, for example, would probably cost as much as any extra taxes could provide. The House Natural Resources Committee estimated extra federal spending could be in the billions and that taxes might not offset this since incomes in Puerto Rico are so low.

Puerto Ricans play an integral role in our military and so deserve full recognition as U.S. citizens. They have participated in the military in every major war in the last century. Indeed, they signed up for the Iraq War at a higher rate than the residents of many U.S. states. Puerto Ricans have earned their entry into the United States through their staunch defense of our interests and way of life.

Many of our nearest allies have also participated in nearly every major war we have fought, yet we do not extend to them offers to become states. If Puerto Rico shows such military prowess, rather than making it a state, why not grant it independence? Then it would be responsible for its own security and we can still count on it as a military ally.

The "language issue" is greatly exaggerated. English is one of Puerto Rico's official languages, as well as a required school subject. It is also widely used in banking and commerce. Furthermore, Puerto Ricans are already U.S. citizens, so using language as a reason not to make the territory a state is nonsensical.

It goes against the national culture to have a non-English-speaking state. Although the United States does not have an official national language, English is an important part of our identity. According to the 2000 Census, the majority of Puerto Ricans do not speak English well, thus Puerto Rico would effectively become the "Spanish-speaking state."

OTHER MOTIONS:
Puerto Rico should be granted independence

RELATED MOTIONS:
The United States should make its territories states
Puerto Rico does more harm to the U.S. than good

WEB LINKS:

- Puerto Rico Statehood Society. "The Problem with Puerto Rico's Current Political Status." <http://studentorgs.gwu.edu/prss/StatehoodIssues/>. Article in support of statehood.

- Swarts, Phillip. "Puerto Rico: The 51st State?" <http://news.medill.northwestern.edu/390/news.aspx?id=124793>. Overview article on support for statehood versus independence.

Rap Music

Motion **Rap music does more good than harm**

Introduction While rap music used to appeal to a relatively small niche market, today rap is everywhere. Rap is controversial for its lyrics, which sometimes glorify gang activity and contain intolerant messages against women, homosexuals, and other marginalized groups. While rap is decidedly more mainstream today, garnering attention from *Billboard* and even the Grammys, opponents still worry that rap can send the wrong kinds of messages to children.

Debating the Motion Both teams should find a solid definition of rap music. They should also research the history of rap, the stories of its most famous artists, and the lyrics of its most famous songs. Remember, also, that this topic is not about whether rap music is good or bad, but whether it poses harm to people and which people these might be.

Proposition: The proposition is seeking to show the benefits of rap music, so looking into educational uses and issues of identity among marginalized groups will provide solid support for their case. Also, because rap is closely associated with the public persona of the artist, looking into the good works of prominent rap artists would support the case.

Opposition: As with any topic about harms and benefits, the opposition has the option to maintain that rap is harmful, demonstrate that it is neutral rather than beneficial, or combine the two approaches. Remember, the team can concede some elements of the proposition's argument—such as a point the proposition might make about charitable giving—if the team can show that, on balance, the benefits of rap do not outweigh harms.

PROS

Rap music is beneficial because it is a healthy and socially acceptable form of expression. For those who cannot compose a symphony or paint a portrait, rap can offer an outlet and healthy channel for emotions in a format that is adaptable and readily understandable. Any venue that offers this outlet is, by definition, beneficial, because people maintain

CONS

The "good" use of rap is overshadowed by the more harmful aspects of this art form. If rap were used only to help people express their emotions and have the experience of working together constructively, then we would agree that it does more good than harm. But prominent rap artists use their music to proclaim vendettas, glamorize gangs and crime, emotional balance through constructive expression and through the experience of sharing their work with others.

Rap music can act as a good influence on kids growing up in rough neighborhoods. Many children lack role models of their socioeconomic and ethnic backgrounds and thus have little to inspire and guide them. Many rap artists from tough urban situations are successful not just as rap artists but also as entrepreneurs and can provide inspiration to kids who come from similar circumstances. Some rap artists also provide positive family influences on populations where single and young parenthood is common—several famous artists like Snoop Dogg and Ice Cube have been married to the same woman for decades and are raising healthy children to whom they are committed. Eminem is also known for being a stand-up father, caring for not only his own children but other children from his extended family. This gives fans an example of what families can be.

Rap music is important and necessary because it legitimizes experiences of minority and often marginalized groups. Mainstream culture often only concerns itself with the wealthy and ruling classes, representing and recognizing only their experiences. By failing to acknowledge the legitimacy of the experiences of nonmainstream Americans, we are relegating these individuals to the margins. The increasing popularity of rap allows the dominant culture to include the experiences of others, which is good for all of society because it makes the culture more inclusive.

and even celebrate the oppression of women, gays, and other groups. Because this kind of expression in rap is more predominant, we argue that it does more harm than good.

In the rap world, positive role models are relatively few and far between. For every rapper committed to his family, dozens more are promiscuous and engage in dangerous behaviors. Rappers are not realistic role models for children—who need concrete goals to enable them to choose a healthy path in life. Only a few can become stars; if children aspire only to be rappers, then they will ignore other, more realistic opportunities. We are setting children in rough neighborhoods up for failure if rappers are the only role models we can provide for them.

Rap music only serves to marginalize poor and minority populations even more. Because rap often relies on or even plays up stereotypes, it drives further wedges between people of different cultures or economic status. This poses a harm because stereotypes, in themselves, are harmful, spreading misconceptions and acting as barriers to true understanding between individuals and groups.

PROS

Rap artists contribute to their communities. Many rap artists come from poorer communities; once successful, they often give back to the places they came from. In poor communities with few resources, one person investing time, money, and public attention can make a huge positive difference in many lives.

Teachers have used rap to help struggling students. Rap is a form of poetry combined with rhythms and beats that can provide excellent tools for engaging children in learning to read and write. For students who struggle in school with these two basics, rap can be an enormous teaching tool.

CONS

Any benefit from their investment is counterbalanced by the often-unsavory message presented by rap artists in their music. What kind of message does it send to children when they are taught to idolize a rapper whose music promotes cop killing, the subjugation of women, and other harmful attitudes and actions? How does it make sense to name a school after a rapper who glorifies dropping out?

Rap is not the only form of art that teachers can use to engage students. Many other forms of music have more positive lyrics and a far better reputation; teachers can use these forms without fear of spreading the message that gangs and violence are the only way to survive.

OTHER MOTIONS:
Rap is good for children
Rap does more harm than good

RELATED MOTIONS:
Music artists have a duty to engage in socially responsible behaviors

WEB LINKS:
- Kirchheimer, Sid. "Does Rap Put Teens at Risk?" <http://www.webmd.com/baby/news/20030303/does-rap-put-teens-at-risk>. Study showing that watching gansta rap leads to violence.
- Rhodes, Henry A. "The Evolution of Rap Music in the United States." <http://www.yale.edu/ynhti/curriculum/units/1993/4/93.04.04.x.html>. History of rap.

Restaurants, Ban All-you-can-eat Establishments

Motion   **Ban all-you-can-eat restaurants**

Introduction   All-you-can-eat restaurants began at the turn of the twentieth century in predominantly working-class cities as a way for families to dine out at a reasonable price. At that time, the average American weighed 30–50 pounds less than today. With the United States facing an obesity epidemic, some question whether offering the all-you-can-eat option is really socially responsible.

Debating the Motion   Both teams will need to research creatively since this topic does not appear often in the news. In addition to examining buffets in general, research into cost-effectiveness, health concerns of buffets, benefits of buffets, and the psychology and science behind eating, obesity, and how people select food will help yield arguments and evidence.

Proposition: The proposition can argue for a total ban on these buffets or it might offer a plan that addresses concerns about unhealthy food and portion control while nonetheless keeping the restaurants open. This might include putting alternative low-cost, low-calorie food choices on the buffets or limiting the number of times a patron can refill his plate and also limiting portion sizes.

Opposition: Remember, the opposition does not need to support buffets as an ideal concept. The opposition might simply argue against the need for a ban and the difficulties that might arise in enforcing such a ban.

PROS	CONS
These restaurants promote waste. They allow people to fill a plate countless times and then not eat the food they have taken. Additionally, for food safety and quality reasons, the food on the buffet must be discarded periodically to keep the offerings both fresh and safe to eat. Buffets require preparing more food than necessary to ensure that there is	*Wasted food is not the fault of the restaurant.* Rather, the lack of ethical behavior stems from the attitudes of some irresponsible patrons who consistently overfill their plates. Given that the patrons are the ones at fault, wasted food cannot be used to prove that such restaurants are themselves harmful. Rather than ban such restaurants altogether,

enough; regular restaurants only prepare the meal once it is ordered. The socially responsible thing to do is to shut these restaurants so we can reconsider how we use our food resources and use them in a better way.

These buffets encourage unhealthy eating. Buffets usually include many processed, high carbohydrate, high calorie foods like pizza, pasta, and fried meat. Even salad bars are often flanked by containers of high calorie dressing. We all know the dangers of fast food restaurants—buffets are even worse because they take the poor quality of food and encourage the consumption of endless amounts for low prices. At least at McDonald's, once you eat the Big Mac, it's gone. At buffets, when you finish a plate, you're encouraged to go back for more!

The presence of so much food all at once encourages people to gorge. Research shows that we tend to overestimate what we can eat and to way overestimate what we *need* to eat. Many Americans already struggle with portion control—by placing so much food in front of people, restaurants are damaging even more our ability to gauge the right amount. At a restaurant where you order a dish, even if the portion size is larger than usual, when the food is gone, it's gone. At a buffet, on the other hand, the mere presence of an abundance of food and choices triggers a psychological need in many individuals to eat way more than is healthy. Banning these restaurants would help us fight the obesity epidemic in United States, a true public health threat.

making people more aware of what they waste would be a good move.

Buffets are not inherently bad for people and, indeed, often offer healthy alternatives. If people want to ignore steamed broccoli in favor of sweet and sour chicken, this is not the fault of the restaurant and not a reason for such restaurants to be banned. At best, it points to a need to recondition the American public's eating habits by focusing on healthier foods at home and in schools, so, when faced with a buffet, people can make wiser choices.

Granted, many people have issues with portion control, but we should not punish those who do not by closing certain types of restaurants. The way to address the issue of portion size is not to ban one single type of restaurant, especially since most restaurants are guilty of flouting nutritionist-recommended portion sizes with huge plates of food. Rather, education about portion size and strategies to encourage healthier choices (for example, providing smaller plates to trick the eye) are strategies for restaurants and for meals eaten at home—both would help get this country back on a healthier track.

People will still want to eat out, so banning buffet restaurants would not result in food-sector employees not being able to find work. The restaurant business is notoriously unstable, with huge turnover and failure rates. Thus, new restaurants are always opening to take the place of old ones. These newer restaurants will provide employment opportunities to waiters and chefs.

The mere presence of so many items on a buffet does not mean people will eat them. We already see this in the way that steamed vegetables languish while plate after plate of macaroni and cheese is devoured. In fact, studies show that the presence of a couple of comfort foods on a buffet will actually encourage people not to try a lot of other foods. Imagine a child who loves macaroni: at home, that macaroni would probably come accompanied by a vegetable. At a buffet, however, that same child has the option of piling up many plates of only macaroni.

Buffets are a food safety risk. Having foods sit out in the air for long periods increases the chance of food becoming contaminated; the proximity of many kinds of foods and many hands serving themselves increase the risk of cross-contamination. In addition, the nice warm spaces under heating lamps and over vats of steaming water provide the perfect incubator for bacteria and viruses. Those who eat at buffets are at higher risk of contracting food-borne illnesses. A ban is necessary to protect us from this unnecessary risk of serious illnesses like salmonella and E.coli.

Banning buffet restaurants will put thousands out of work. This country has numberless buffet restaurants—some have been community stalwarts for years. Employees, food suppliers, and equipment suppliers, as well as companies that transport the goods, will all suffer if this ban were to be put in place.

Buffets allow people to experiment and try new foods. All the options encourage diners to keep open minds. Ethnic buffets like Chinese, Japanese, and Indian expose people to new foods and cultures they might not try otherwise. Eaters reluctant to try different foods might not want to eat in a new restaurant where the one dish they pick does not suit them, but the choices at a buffet will support experimentation with food.

All restaurants pose a risk for food-borne illness. The key to remaining safe is not to ban one kind of restaurant, but to have tough food-handling and hygiene standards for all restaurants and for diners to exercise a little common sense. Sneeze guards, requiring a fresh plate every time, and having servers portion out food at buffets help restaurants to stay sanitary. Likewise, customers can keep themselves safe by using antibacterial soap or gel before eating, avoiding foods that look like they've been sitting out for a long time, and only eating at restaurants with satisfactory ratings from the Board of Health.

OTHER MOTIONS:

All-you-can-eat restaurants do more good than harm

All-you-can-eat restaurants do more harm than good

RELATED MOTIONS:

Ban fast-food restaurants

Restaurants have a responsibility to promote health

WEB LINKS:

- Canada.com. "Study: Food Portions—Your Eyes Really are Bigger Than Your Stomach." <http://bodyandhealth.canada.com/channel_section_details.asp?text_id=3594&channel_id=9&relation_id=30073>. Study demonstrating that the saying "eyes are bigger than the stomach" tends to accurately describe individuals' relationships with food.

- Caywood, Colin. "Buffets and Cross-Contamination." <http://www.foodsafetynews.com/2010/07/buffets-and-cross-contamination/>. Describes the health risks that all-you-can-eat buffets present.

- CNN. "Growing Trend: All-you-can-eat Sections at Big-league Parks." <http://sportsillustrated.cnn.com/2010/baseball/mlb/07/14/all-you-can-eat-ballparks/index.html>. Describes the growing popularity of all-you-can-eat restaurants in baseball stadiums, as well as concerns about their nutritional value.

- Kent, Tamsyn. "Rise of the All-you-can-eat Restaurant." <http://news.bbc.co.uk/2/hi/uk_news/magazine/8320043.stm>. News article on buffet restaurants—includes arguments on the issue.

Right to Know

Motion   **The right to know is more important than the right to privacy**

Introduction   Both the right to know and the right to privacy are built into our legal system. On the one hand, we have public records and the right to freedom of information, on the other hand, privacy laws aim to protect people from the potential harms of having too much information being public. As technology has evolved, it has made the rift between these two concepts worse and driven a wedge between the proponents of each one. In the past, even though information was public, real work was needed to find and gain access to it, thus ensuring that most records remained private by default. With the spread of the Internet and the use of digital archiving, information is now easily available and the face of this issue has changed, bringing people on both sides head to head.

Debating the Motion   In researching this topic, teams should look at what kind of information is generally in public records, which anyone can have access to, and look for legal justification for these open sources. Both teams should research issues surrounding legislation, such as the Freedom of Information Act, that gives the public access to government documents. Privacy laws vary from place to place, so teams should research these as well. The Internet plays a huge role in this topic, so both teams should research how it has affected both privacy laws and the right to know.

Proposition: This motion is vague, so the proposition team must define *right to know* and *right to privacy* before setting out arguments. Public records—for example, marriage licenses, court proceedings—deeds, are what most right-to-know advocates are talking about. However, both terms are sufficiently broad that they could be defined otherwise and apply to actions—such as paparazzi involvement in celebrity lives—rather than material set down in writing. The proposition might also want to look at the right to privacy controversy in general: some say such "right" is implied in our Constitution, while others argue that as it was not included, the signers did not mean it to be there and thus that we have no "right" to privacy.

Opposition: The opposition might argue that the right to privacy is more important that the right to know. Looking into particular matters that are usually private, such as closed court hearings, the withholding of victims' and the accuseds' names, and medical records, will help give an idea of why privacy laws are sometimes especially important. The opposition might also argue that neither privacy nor access is more important but that they are equal and must be weighed against each other in each situation.

PROS

The dangers of online theft are exaggerated. The 2005 Javelin Identity Fraud Survey Report found that the majority of identity theft still occurs offline. In fact, it is much easier to protect information online because online accounts can recognize potential fraud more quickly. In addition, individuals leave less of a paper trail, so fewer bills and statements are lying around with valuable information.

Making employment records open to the public is important so businesses can know what kind of people they are hiring. Resumes show a narrow picture and references are chosen by potential employees to portray them in the most flattering light. Open access to records of past work history would give employers a chance to make better hiring decisions. In addition, knowing that someone defaulted on her mortgage speaks about her responsibility and can give employers an idea of her trustworthiness.

Aggressively tracking politicians' actions allows us to better assess whether or not individuals are acting fairly. When the media print budgets, evaluations, internal communication documents, etc., we can better determine whether the powerful members of our society are doing their jobs efficiently and ethically and whether our elected representatives are acting in our interests.

CONS

Having so much information online makes identity theft much easier. It is not difficult in today's society to find out very personal details about strangers, such as phone number, address, work history, marriage records, Social Security number, and so on. With so much information readily available, it is far easier than in the past for criminals to steal others' identities.

The sheer volume of information means that employers may find information not relevant to a job but that could lead to potential discrimination. What business is it of most employers if someone defaulted on a mortgage? Also, paperwork online may not give a complete picture—special circumstances like identity theft, for instance, could give a negative impression of a person, and such information could cause good people to have their job prospects damaged. Employers have the right to know some information—but to know everything is neither responsible nor necessary.

Public scrutiny is good, but having too much information available on government activity can be a threat to national security. For example, the U.S. government has repeatedly criticized WikiLeaks, a website that posts anonymous leaks of documents not available to the general public. The government believes that this kind of indiscriminant release of information, for example the release of thousands of military records in 2010, could put citizens at risk.

PROS

Our greater knowledge increases our personal and neighborhood safety. We should know names of people involved, for example, in court cases—both to be aware if high-profile judges or others involved live nearby and to know if criminals live in our neighborhoods. Either of these causes a safety risk to nearby residents because retaliatory violence could cause damage in a neighborhood and criminals pose an obvious risk. Also, a right to view all records could allow the public to see a trend that the courts missed. Courts don't allow prior bad or criminal acts to be revealed during trials, but someone on a computer can draw conclusions by seeing that even though the guy next door has never gone to jail, he has been charged five times for the same crime.

CONS

Our justice system is based on the premise that an individual is innocent until proven guilty—not the other way around. No one should be convicted in the court of public opinion. Furthermore, people often react irrationally to information, harming the welfare or reputations of individuals. For example, knowing a man was on trial for rape, even if he was eventually found innocent, could completely damage his credibility and reputation, and even lead to violence and vigilante "justice."

OTHER MOTIONS:

The right to privacy trumps the right to know

The safety of the public is more important than an accused's rights

RELATED MOTIONS:

There is no constitutionally protected right to privacy

WEB LINKS:

- BNET. "When the Right to Know and the Right to Privacy Collide." <http://findarticles.com/p/articles/mi_qa3937/is_200609/ai_n17193518/>. Overview of the topic with arguments on both sides of the issue.

- Paulson, Ken. "Privacy vs. Public Right to Know." <http://www.firstamendmentcenter.org/commentary.aspx?id=22736>. Article on privacy concerns and the press.

School Day, Length of

The length of the school day should be increased

Introduction As some school districts struggle to improve performance, one suggestion is to make the school day longer. Many charter schools have a day that begins at 7:30 a.m. and ends at 5:30 p.m. Public schools usually have a six-hour day, with some city school systems, New York's, for example, having put in place required extra study time. Students are supposed to use this study time to work on subjects they are weak in and thus improve poor test scores and increase knowledge. We all understand that schools need to improve. Does more time spent in school and in study provide this improvement?

Debating the Motion As with any school topic, the teams should define what kinds of schools are included in the mandate. Both teams should research the current average length of school days and should also look at the way schools with longer days use their extra time. Charter school networks are a good source of research because these schools typically have longer days, but teams should look at how countries with longer days handle the time as well. Make sure to include studies of the impact of longer days on learning.

Proposition: The proposition should set out a detailed plan specifying what the new length will be and what they suggest the extra time be used for.

Opposition: The opposition has two major options. The easiest to pursue would be to uphold the status quo, that is, leave the length of the school day as it is. The slightly trickier alternative would be to advocate to decrease the amount of time students spend in school. Much of the argumentation and research to support this will come from research into the more successful education models from other countries that have shorter school days and school years.

PROS

The more time children spend in school, the more time they can spend learning. With additional hours, teachers can have their pupils practice more, review previous material, and engage in more rigorous and deeper study of

CONS

More time does not necessarily mean more learning. If the extra time is not used carefully, it will be wasted—simply filling the extra hours. Look at the results of many extended-day programs in the public schools—often a subject. New courses could also be added to the core curriculum. This greater choice of courses and more time to study will increase knowledge and proficiency and make it more likely that students will be able to compete in a global economy.

Increased time with students allows for greater influence on their habits. While some children come from highly educated households where punctuality, reading, speaking standard English, studying, organization, etc., are valued, some kids come from households where the family cannot or does not pass on these necessary life lessons. A longer day would also allow schools to work with children who have trouble with behavior. On average, students spend only six hours a day in school, and so schools have very little influence over them. Students spend more time at home—where they may have less helpful role models. Extending the school day allows children to see different ways of approaching tasks and responding to others. A longer school day could also increase the time the teachers have to teach acceptable behavior; good manners and good behavior will certainly help a child be successful in adulthood.

A smart approach to the school day can easily help solve the problems the opposition presents. Each day should have a recess or gym, have the pupils move to different rooms rather than sitting at the same desk all day, and also offer art, music, and "free time" to study or just read. All hours, including the extra ones, can be used with great efficiency.

teachers just babysit kids, allowing them to surf the web or watch movies. When New York City public schools were required to add an extra half hour to their day, chaos ensued, with individual schools scrambling to find an effective use for the time and bodies to cover the classes. The result was lots of free periods for kids and not a lot of additional learning.

Millions of students have no need of such guidance. Most students live in families with educated parents or parents who stress the value of good education and responsible behavior. True, some children need school to teach them behavior and life lessons, but completely changing a school's structure to address the needs of a small group makes no sense. After-school and before-school programs are available for those who need them.

A longer school day does not reflect the realities of child development. Studies show that kids can only pay attention for a certain amount of time each day. In addition, they can learn more easily at certain times of the day. Making the school day longer won't make attention spans longer or give already stuffed brains more room to take in more

Even if we agree that kids don't learn a lot more during an extended day, being in a school monitored by licensed professionals is still better than going home to an empty house or just hanging around on the streets. Years ago kids might have played outside, helped with chores, or even taken a part-time job after school. Most kids today don't have anyone at home to see that they don't get into trouble. At best, when kids get home from school, they play video games, eat junk food, or surf the web unsupervised. Without supervision, some may join gangs to find friendship.

More time in school can be used to provide tutoring, team sports, dance lessons, etc., to all students, not just those whose parents can afford to pay for these extras. Many schools have dropped music, art, sports, and other activities because they feel they need to focus on basic subjects like math or English. Extra time during the school day will give all children the chance to learn other skills—study a new language, join the debate team, or play a musical instrument.

knowledge. Any teacher or student can attest to the poorer work done and less attention paid during late afternoon classes. To extend the day even more would be a waste because students will not benefit and will be even more tired the next day.

Not all kids just sit around after school. Many *do* take part-time jobs; many others take care of their younger brothers and sisters. In addition, many children are involved in after-school programs that provide healthful snacks, help with classwork or homework, and give them a chance to exercise. Even if kids just watch television and play video games, these activities are not bad. Just like adults, children need down time to relax. They need time to play because they are kids. While playtime looks different now than 50 years ago, it is still play and is still necessary.

Extended days can actually keep children from engaging in valuable activities outside school. If the school day lasts until 5:00 or 6:00 p.m. or is extended to include weekends and summer terms, students won't be able to play on sports teams, take music or dance lessons, work on art projects, or even do extra work in subjects they find difficult. Many parents use after-school times and days off to be with their children or to take them to activities that interest their children and make them more well-rounded.

OTHER MOTIONS:
Public schools should increase the length of the school day
Extended-day programs do more good than harm

RELATED MOTIONS:

Saturday school should be mandatory

Decrease the length of the school day

Decrease the length of the school year

WEB LINKS:

- Ellis, Thomas I. "Extending the School Year and Day." <http://www.ericdigests.org/pre-922/year.htm>. Short, balanced overview of the topic.

- Fox News. "Obama Proposes Longer School Day, Shorter Summer Vacation." <http://www.foxnews.com/politics/2009/09/27/obama-proposes-longer-school-day-shorter-summer-vacation/>. Provides information about extended-day programs and compares the amount of time U.S. students spend in school with more successful academic programs in other countries.

- Miami-Dade County Public Schools. "Extended School Day. <http://drs.dadeschools.net/InformationCapsules/IC0705.pdf>. A fact-finding article, this contains many statistics as well as pro and con arguments about extended school days.

Schools, Year-round

Year-round schooling does more good than harm

Both students and teachers eagerly look forward to summer vacation. However, year after year, students and teachers end up spending a fair portion of time in the fall reviewing all that has been pushed out of mind by two or three months of glorious freedom. School systems in other countries, as well as many private and even some public schools, have switched to the year-round model—a misnomer for a calendar that often involves as many days off as the traditional U.S. school year but divides them into many small breaks. Supporters assert that year-round school would improve content retention and thus academic performance. Opponents assert that both students and teachers need recuperation time.

Both teams should research calendars for traditional and year-round school models to compare the number and length of instructional days and the length of vacations. Both should be careful to frame their arguments in terms of benefits and harms and not "good" or "bad."

Proposition: When presenting this case, the team should define exactly what is meant by *year-round schooling* since the term is somewhat misleading. The proposition should offer a sample calendar illustrating what they are suggesting. Narrowing this topic to a specific age range—elementary, high school—would also be prudent.

Opposition: Because this is a harms and benefits topic, the opposition has the usual two options: one of neutrality or one that directly opposes the proposition's case. The opposition can argue that year-round schooling is harmful or it can take the position that it does not matter.

PROS

The shorter breaks in the year-round schooling model enable students to retain more of what they have learned. If schools had shorter breaks, they would not waste the first month or two of the year reviewing old material. Over the course of a K–12 education, the time not spent reviewing would add up to an entire extra year of new learning!

CONS

Review is a necessary part of learning and occurs no matter how long or short a break. On Mondays, students review the previous week's concepts and work. Following winter and spring breaks, students review what they learned before they left. Shortening the length of breaks will not add extra learning time. By having small breaks throughout the

Shorter vacations would be particularly helpful in learning and retaining knowledge in subjects like math and science, which build very strictly on what was covered earlier. These are the very subjects in which the U.S. lags behind many nations. So, shorter vacations would be good for the country.

The year-round schooling model is more in line with an adult work schedule. Most adults outside of academia do not get long summer breaks. Finding care for children over the long summer vacation causes stress and financial strain on those families where both parents work normal 9–5 jobs. The year-round model removes that stress—because the small breaks are more easily accommodated in the parents' job schedule, they are more likely to be able to enjoy time off with their children. Spending time with children promotes family bonding, enables parents to transmit and reinforce their values, and removes the financial burden of paying a caregiver during a long summer break.

The year-round model helps students who come from low-income or poorly educated families. It helps to level the playing field among students by enabling teachers to give low-income children more sustained attention and instruction. When students of all economic levels have a long summer vacation, they lose academic ground. During the summer, some parents are able to enrich their children's experiences and advance their knowledge and skills—those families with low incomes and little education often cannot do so. The current school model was put in place

year rather than one long summer vacation, the proposition is increasing the number of major review sessions necessary!

Year-round school plans are not in line with adult work schedules; they have nearly as much vacation time as the regular school model, just scattered throughout the year. The fact remains that most adults do not have as much time off as children. Parents must pay for some form of child care anyway, whether it be for the traditional summer break, for a week, or long weekend each month. A long summer break is better financially for the families and for the intellectual and social development of children. Children can participate in camps and exchange programs that give them valuable experiences they could not have in a long weekend and the cost of a camp program is often cheaper than the hourly wage equivalent would be for the sitters that would have to be called for the mini-breaks in a year-round calendar.

Year-round schooling will help some students, while definitely harming others. Students who come from highly educated and wealthy families can gain more by being out of school than in because their families can provide richer and more varied experiences in combination with more individualized activities. Trips around this nation and abroad can provide real opportunities for cultural and language learning. Camps and learning programs can provide academic enrichment with materials and budgets most schools cannot afford. These when the U.S. was an agricultural nation and children were needed to work on the land during the growing season. The wealthy then used this time to take long family vacations. This model no longer functions well in a technological, 24/7, highly competitive global society—thus, our children are losing out and steadily falling behind.

The traditional school year was designed for reasons that are no longer valid: to free students to help on farms. In warm areas of the country, summers were too hot for children to sit in school before air-conditioning. Today, however, few, if any, students are needed on the farm and climate control is widely available. Therefore, we should adopt a new model that reflects the changes in technology and lifestyle—the year-round model that the proposition has already shown to be beneficial.

Year-round schooling also benefits teachers. One of the major causes of talented individuals abandoning careers in education is burnout. Teachers often struggle to make it from break to break—particularly if they serve special needs students or other challenging groups. Offering shorter but more vacations gives teachers time to recuperate and could help retain teachers. The year-round model gives teachers as much vacation time as the traditional model, so they would still have time to pursue personal goals and extend their education. Many colleges schedule courses on weekends and evenings so working adults can attend. In addition, since the amount of vacation time is the same in the year-round model, the benefit of a lot of time off would remain to attract people to the profession.

experiences help to broaden children's view of the world and deepen their knowledge. In addition, exposing young people to cultures different from their own at a young age will make them more valuable in our rapidly globalizing business and cultural worlds. Finally, such experiences will be of great value when students apply to colleges—which look for students with a variety of experiences and a broadness of outlook.

Although few now work on family farms, students still need and want to work. Summer jobs allow high school students to grow in independence while earning money to help pay for college. As for the climate issue, air-conditioning wastes energy and is very bad for the environment, so avoiding its use is preferable.

The current school model is vastly better for teachers for several reasons. The concentrated period of vacation time allows for the teachers to relax and recharge their batteries so to speak (which certainly contributes to teacher retention). It also allows teachers to further their education. Finally, the promise of a long vacation is one of the major considerations when young people and career changers look at the teaching profession. The profession needs to preserve those aspects of the job that will help them recruit more and better educators.

OTHER MOTIONS:

Year-round schooling does more harm than good

The United States should switch to a year-round school model

RELATED MOTIONS:

Quarter and trimester systems trump semesters

Extended school days do more harm than good

WEB LINKS:

- California Department of Education. "Year-Round Education Program Guide." <http://www.cde.ca.gov/ls/fa/yr/guide.asp>. Describes year-round schooling and offers pros and cons.

- Education Week. "Year-Round Schooling." <http://www.edweek.org/ew/issues/year-round-schooling/>. Offers pros and cons.

- NAYRE (National Association for Year-Round Education). <http://www.nayre.org/>. Website provides lots of information helpful to the proposition side.

- Newland, M. C. "Academic Impact of Year Round Schooling: An Annotated Bibliography." <http://www.summermatters.com/reviews.htm>. Details research and reviews the efficacy of year-round schools versus the traditional school year. The author opposes year-round schooling.

Second Amendment

Motion	**Repeal the Second Amendment**
Introduction	The Second Amendment to the Constitution states that "A well regulated militia being necessary to the security of a free state, the right of the people to keep and bear arms shall not be infringed." In part because of its vague wording, the amendment is very controversial. Gun rights' advocates argue that the amendment means that neither state nor federal governments cannot ban or severely limit citizens' ability to own firearms. Others argue that the amendment protects the collective right to bear arms in a militia. In response to gun violence, Congress and many states have passed laws that increase restrictions on firearms' ownership, while the courts have become sympathetic to gun owners' interpretation of the Second Amendment. A minority voice has come to call for the removal of this amendment from our Bill of Rights.
Debating the Motion	Both teams need to do extensive research into the history of gun control and court decisions on the issue. Organizations exist on both sides of the issue, so reviewing the arguments they present will help both teams frame their arguments. Additionally, the teams must know the exact wording of the amendment—the vague wording often plays a part in the debate on this topic.

Proposition: The proposition might want to offer a plan for repealing this amendment. If owning guns is no longer an individual right, under what circumstances would citizens be able to own guns and who would regulate gun ownership, states or the federal government? Looking at other countries like the U.K. where gun access is severely restricted will provide a framework for creating a workable policy.

Opposition: The opposition can either focus on upholding the Second Amendment as it is or they can run a counter case proposing a reinterpretation of its language. In both cases, the research suggested above would be helpful.

PROS	CONS
If guns are illegal, fewer people will own them. Fewer guns equals less gun violence and fewer accidental gun-related injuries and deaths. Most murders in this country are	*Honest citizens obey the law; criminals do not.* Banning guns will merely result in only criminals—the ones who commit violence—having them. We should not assume

committed with guns; banning guns will decrease the murder rate.

The Second Amendment is antiquated. The Second Amendment was written when a professional police force had not yet been organized, when people needed guns to hunt for food and protect isolated homesteads. The amendment was also more necessary because the United States, as a young country, did not have a fully developed military and so had to rely on militias. Professional police now protect citizens and are available almost instantly by dialing 911; Americans no longer rely on hunting as a source of food. Furthermore, if a police force is inadequate, we should focus on improving the police rather than have citizens fight criminals themselves. The Second Amendment is a holdover from a bygone time and now does more harm than good.

The Second Amendment prevents sensible gun control legislation. Repealing the Second Amendment would not automatically prevent individuals from owning or operating a gun. Rather, it would allow for better gun control so that those who truly need firearms could get them, but most citizens, particularly unstable ones, would have a hard time gaining access to a weapon with which they might do much harm.

people will not do something just because it is illegal. Take the example of marijuana in the U.S. (where it is illegal) and the Netherlands (where it is legal): a 2008 survey published in *PLoS Medicine* reported that 42 percent of Americans have tried marijuana, whereas only 20 percent of the Dutch have tried it. Finally, most murders are committed with guns simply because it is the most convenient weapon. If guns disappeared, murder would not stop. People would just use the next best weapon, for example, in the U.K. guns are not publicly available, so knife attacks are on the rise.

Crime exists in the modern United States. The average police response time is around 10 minutes—even slower in high crime areas. In an emergency, 10 minutes is too long—if one can even make the 911 call at all. The proposition implies that self-defense is unnecessary in urban areas, but sometimes police entirely lose the ability to control the population, for example, during riots citizens are left to fend for themselves. Finally, why ban civilians from hunting? It makes no sense—the federal government currently pays professional hunters to shoot deer and geese to prevent their populations from getting out of control. By letting civilians hunt (under reasonable regulations), the government saves money and does not waste the dead animal.

Repealing the Second Amendment is a slippery slope and is unnecessary. Without a constitutional provision, the government cannot be prevented from outlawing guns altogether. The Second Amendment does not forbid all regulation. Congress has passed extensive legislation banning "assault weapons," and many states have made handguns virtually impossible to attain legally.

PROS

The argument for self-protection via gun ownership leads to vigilantism, which is in direct opposition to the U.S. justice system. Legally, a homeowner cannot kill an intruder merely for invading the home—clear imminent danger is required. However, individuals are prone to panic; if they own firearms they are likely to kill—a dramatic overreaction to an intrusion.

Guns cause hundreds of accidental deaths each year and thousands of injuries. Many people buy guns to protect themselves, but are busy with other aspects of their lives and do not maintain necessary gun safety. They forget locks, leave guns loaded, leave guns in areas accessible to children, improperly use the firearm, etc. According to the Centers for Disease Control, almost 65,000 Americans suffered from firearms injuries and some 35,000 died in 2004, the last year for which statistics were available. We would do better to improve our police system and keep firearms away from those who cannot handle them.

In the modern world, a mere firearm is not going to stop an abusive government. Even gun rights proponents do not (generally) claim that individuals should be able to own machine guns, grenades, or other highly dangerous weapons. Governments generally have access to tanks, bombs, nuclear weapons, machine guns, and a great variety of other means of subduing a population. Firearms serve no purpose in checking government.

CONS

Self-defense is not vigilantism. This argument is not unique to firearms. If someone attacks me and I defend myself with a knife, am I a vigilante? Should we subsequently ban kitchen knives? Stopping an attacker in your own home is not vigilantism but simple enactment of the duty to protect one's family.

Guns are an equalizer. If a large, strong man attacks a small, slight female, she has little means of physical defense besides a firearm. Of course people who use guns for evil should be imprisoned, but attackers tend to prey on victims who are weaker—for many people, a gun is the only realistic means of protection. The Department of Justice estimates that guns are successfully used in self-defense approximately 1.5 million times per year in the United States—often, merely brandishing the gun is sufficient.

Individual gun ownership is a check on government. Although we do not expect citizens to revolt in the streets when government abuses occur, individual gun ownership is a psychological check. Respecting that individuals can responsibly exercise power indicates a government's acknowledgment that it is controlled by its people, not the other way around. Skeptics can look at the genocides of the twentieth century for proof. The genocides in Armenia, Nazi Germany, Soviet Russia, Red China, Nationalist China, Guatemala, Uganda, Rwanda, and Cambodia were *all* preceded by bans on targeted groups' firearms ownership.

OTHER MOTIONS:

Gun control is constitutional

RELATED MOTIONS:

The handgun ban is unconstitutional

The Supreme Court should reinterpret the Second Amendment

WEB LINKS:

- The Harvard Crimson. "Repeal the Second Amendment." <http://www.thecrimson.com/article/2002/5/15/repeal-second-amendment-when-two-thirds-of/>. Article arguing that the Constitution should reflect that gun ownership is a privilege, not a right.

- Salon. "Repeal the Second Amendment." <http://www.salon.com/news/opinion/feature/2007/04/18/second_amendment>. Article in favor of repeal.

- Second Amendment Foundation. <http://www.saf.org/>. Provides information in defense of the Second Amendment.

Single-sex Schools

Public schools should offer single-sex options

Introduction   Private schools offer the choice of sending your child to an all-boys or all-girls school. Some believe that the benefits of single-sex schools are so great that public schools should also consider offering some single-sex institutions. Although a system that offers targeted instruction appropriate to each gender's developmental strengths and ways of learning appears attractive, one of the concerns about having only one sex in the classroom is that real life involves both females and males, thus preparation for life (one of education's goals) requires both females and males in a school. Schools that taught boys and girls in the same classroom were once considered to be the most progressive—is the return to single-sex schools the next step in education?

Debating the Motion   Examples of single-sex schools abound and ample research is available on the effectiveness of these institutions. Both teams need to research specific programs and examples to back up their arguments.

Proposition: The proposition should define what ages, grades, or classes would be single-sex and what plan they might implement to ensure equal treatment of all students. Remember that it is not necessary to advocate for single-sex schools for all children. The proposition can define the ages and grades for when they think single-sex education is appropriate.

Opposition: The opposition needs to demonstrate why single-sex educational options are either unnecessary or actually harmful. The significance of arguments that show the harms of single-sex education is obvious. The opposition, however, must also remember that if it can show that single-sex alternatives are unnecessary, then single-sex education is certainly a negative because it will require time, money, and other resources to change the current system.

PROS	CONS
Single-sex schools are necessary in support of freedom of religion. The Constitution guarantees freedom of religion. States provide education and require children to attend school.	*Freedom of religion does not oblige the government to pay for special requirements.* The U.S. government doesn't provide wine for Christian communion or loudspeakers to

If school attendance is required, what happens to those whose religious beliefs demand that the sexes be separated? If our country truly supports religious freedom, public schools should accommodate them. Offering single-sex public schools allows religious families to practice their faith and their children to receive a free education.

Single-sex schools provide an easy way to take advantage of natural differences in learning styles between the sexes. Girls and boys progress at different rates. They grow at different times both in height and in the ability of their brains to learn and understand schoolwork. A single-sex school can take advantage of these differences by tailoring curricula to each gender. Public education should offer as much individualized instruction as it can because such attention will increase each child's ability to excel; single-sex schools can more easily provide such attention because they are dealing with children on the same basic developmental schedule.

Single-sex education can help learning because it takes away social competition that distracts from a school's mission of education. In middle and high schools in particular, interactions between growing boys and girls and the accompanying social pressures cause students genuine stress and anxiety. Desire to be liked and accepted by the opposite sex can cause students to stop paying attention in class and spend time out of school on appearance and social outings rather than studying and completing homework. Single-sex environments remove many of these distractions, thus allowing for greater focus on studies and more time to learn.

broadcast Islamic times of prayer. Parents have the right to practice any religion they choose, but if the requirements of their belief go beyond existing public services, they need to find alternatives. Those who require same-sex education can choose private schools or elect to home school their children.

While general developmental differences do exist, they are not universal. Single-sex environments might actually end up being less individualized because they expect students to conform to commonly accepted developmental models. Besides, one of the major benefits of putting both genders together is that as they develop different skills at different times, the advancement of one spurs the other to work harder to keep pace. The separation of the sexes might actually slow progress for both because it would take away the competition and challenging environment that encourages growth.

This argument ignores the fact that bullying and distractions often, even usually, occur between members of the same sex. Girls usually bully girls; boys usually bully boys. Single-sex institutions are more likely to have certain cliques taking advantage of others. If students don't fight over dates, they still worry about other issues. Simply removing a gender does not solve the problem of social distraction.

Single-sex schools do not isolate students from the real world; they provide the self-esteem needed to deal with it. Certainly the real world has both men and women. But exposure to the real world begins long before high school graduation; it starts with everyday encounters at places other than school—for example, extracurricular activities, your family, your friends' families, church, after-school jobs for older kids, and even common outings like grocery shopping. These experiences give children the necessary exposure to prepare them for a world that includes both women and men. Further, single-sex schools have enormous success in promoting self-esteem and accomplishment. A true key to success as an adult is a good sense of self, which is better provided by a single-sex school.

Offering the choice of single-sex education is a good use of money that will pay off in the long run because it increases educational quality and international standing. If students are taught at more developmentally appropriate levels, they will be more confident and will be more competitive in the world marketplace. The investment now will be returned when successful students provide innovations and leadership of a better quality than those provided by our failing school system.

Studies show that children in single-sex environments, particularly girls, perform better and have higher self-esteem. This greater self-confidence will better equip them to handle all the challenges of adulthood. What is a school's mission if not to prepare students for a good future?

Coeducational schools prepare students for the real world. The real world consists of both women and men. In most colleges and jobs, everyone has to deal with both genders. To learn in a single-sex educational environment keeps each gender from the opportunity to learn the social signals common to many members of each gender. This leaves students unprepared to succeed socially in the real world. If nothing else is learned during middle and high school, the ability to at least somewhat navigate the social scene prepares students for handling all the people they will encounter later in life. Single-sex schools do their students a disservice by denying them the experiences they need to survive.

The initial outlay of money to establish single-sex schools is too great; where would this money come from? Everything that is needed would be expensive—for example, training for teachers to be effective in single-sex environments, creating new curricula, refitting bathrooms in each school. Education budgets are already tight; this is financially impossible.

Studies also show that boys benefit from a coeducational environment. Changing everything to benefit one sex is not fair. To address concerns about sense of self, schools can use single-sex courses strategically within the coeducational environment, for example, separate health and self-esteem classes for girls and boys.

OTHER MOTIONS:

Single-sex schools do more good than harm

All public schools should be devoted to one sex or the other

RELATED MOTIONS:

Coeducational learning environments do not serve the needs of students

Single-sex colleges are obsolete

WEB LINKS:

- ETNI-English Teachers Network. <http://www.etni.org/singlesexedu.htm>. Links to articles on various aspects of the issue.

- GreatSchools. "Single-Sex Education: The Pros and Cons." <http://www.greatschools. org/find-a-school/defining-your-ideal/single-sex-education-the-pros-and-cons. gs?content=1139>. Article presenting arguments on both sides of the issue.

Smokers, Government Benefits and

Motion Smokers should not be eligible for government assistance

Introduction The United States has made huge strides in the battle against nicotine addiction. Laws about smoking in public are becoming increasingly strict, tobacco taxes are soaring, while many states and cities have public initiatives to help people quit smoking. Some are suggesting that to further discourage smoking, smokers should be denied government assistance if they become ill from smoking and cannot work. Smoking is a choice: Should the government be required to pay for the harms caused by poor choices on the part of its citizens?

Debating the Motion Research should be aimed at finding out the cost to the government in aid of a smoker compared with the cost of the average nonsmoker.

Proposition: The proposition should begin with clear definitions about who is a smoker. This would entail specifying how many cigarettes a person smokes on average and how long they have smoked, etc. Additionally, the proposition should explain which benefits would be lost and when, and if individuals who quit would be able to earn benefits back.

Opposition: The opposition might want to argue that smokers should not lose the rights to any government assistance, that they shouldn't lose specific benefits, or finally that they should be able to earn government services back if this is not already a part of the proposition case. A good focus for opposition research would be the civil rights of smokers.

PROS

Smokers use more government resources, so they should get less assistance. We all know that smoking is bad for you and that it puts people at risk for many health problems from heart disease to cancer. Smoking-related health issues are so great that they are a drain on government resources and public aid. This is especially so when smokers end up out of work due to their ill-health and need assistance for housing and food in

CONS

First, the purpose of government assistance is to help those who cannot help themselves; second, it's not clear that smokers are a drain on society to begin with. The purpose of government is to care for all its citizens and not to discriminate. Indeed, low-income families are a "drain on resources" since they pay less taxes, but no one would deny them government benefits such as food stamps because of it. It is people like smokers, who have a

Smokers, Government Benefits and | 229

addition to help covering their health care costs. They take a disproportionate amount of limited government resources, so they should receive fewer benefits.

Smoking is a choice, and it is fair for the government to decide not to reward it. It would be wrong for the government to deny assistance to those who needed it because of something outside of their control, like a congenital illness or an economic downturn. Smoking, on the other hand, is a choice. If people choose to smoke, they should also choose to pay for themselves.

If any money is directed to smokers, it shouldn't be to cover health care or other assistance, but instead should be spent on initiatives to get them to stop smoking. Then, if smokers choose to ignore these incentives, they shouldn't be eligible for any forms of assistance.

Denying smokers government assistance may encourage them to quit smoking or deter people from starting. Knowing that persisting in, or beginning, the habit will disqualify you from government assistance is a strong incentive for behavior alteration.

problem they can no longer control, that most need help. Besides, smokers pay high cigarette taxes, and many studies have found that they contribute more in this tax money than they cost in medical bills.

While smoking the first cigarette may be a choice, for many the subsequent cigarettes are not. Nicotine is highly addictive; individuals should not be punished for a foolish decision they made years earlier, possibly without understanding the risks.

Initiatives to encourage smokers to quit already exist. This plan is no different from the proposition's general position.

Individuals who try to quit and fail will be denied assistance for no good reason. For some lucky few, a lack of benefits may be all the motivation they need. But for those smokers who have been surrounded by cigarettes all their lives, come from generations of smokers, and have tried everything to quit, the benefits may not be a strong enough psychological incentive to overcome their physical dependency. In that case, denying them benefits is simply cruel.

OTHER MOTIONS:
The government should ban smoking
Smokers should pay higher taxes

RELATED MOTIONS:
   The government should not infringe upon smokers' rights

WEB LINKS:
- London Evening Standard. <http://www.thisislondon.co.uk/news/article-23410977-nhs-should-not-treat-those-with-unhealthy-lifestyles-say-tories.do>. Describes a similar debate in England.
- Meeker-O'Connell, Ann. <http://health.howstuffworks.com/wellness/drugs-alcohol/nicotine.htm>. Explains the addictive nature of nicotine.
- Velvet Glove, Iron Fist. <http://velvetgloveironfist.blogspot.com/2010/03/do-smokers-pay-their-way.html>. Reviews studies on the impact of smokers on society, concluding that smokers contribute more money in taxes than they cost in medical bills.

Space Program

Motion **Stop federal spending on the space program**

Introduction The National Aeronautics and Space Administration (NASA) has landed men on the Moon and explored outer space, significantly expanding our understanding of the universe. Its early programs galvanized the nation behind a massive commitment to space, but support for the program has declined amid growing concerns about costs as well as NASA's current effectiveness. Supporters of the program say it benefits the nation in many ways, from advancing science to creating jobs. Opponents say that NASA is ineffective and that in tight times the money could be better spent elsewhere.

Debating the Motion Both teams need to research how much money is spent on the space program and how this compares with government spending in other areas. They should also research the scientific advances that have come from NASA's research as well as how successful NASA has been in its more recent endeavors. Both teams should look at what alternatives exist should NASA and government funding disappear.

Proposition: The proposition has two options. The first is to argue that the benefits from the space program do not justify its cost. The second is to maintain that space exploration could be more effectively carried out by the private sector. The team also might argue a combination of the two.

Opposition: The opposition could argue that the government should continue spending as it has in the past or it might even argue for expanded funding for the space program. If the team argues the latter, they should be prepared to explain how they would use the additional funds. Suggesting an overhaul of NASA practices as part of a counter case might help against any arguments the proposition makes about the government agency's effectiveness.

PROS

There is no way to prove that the space program has increased interest in science. Correlation does not imply causation. It makes much more sense to develop stronger programs in math and science and recognize that our

CONS

Manned space missions encourage young people to pursue careers in science, a field in which the U.S. is lagging. The two major increases in the number of U.S. engineers, scientists, and mathematicians being trained in the science programs in schools need to be improved so that they are the equal of those of other countries. We should fix the root of the problem, not spend billions of dollars on showy missions that may not even work.

The money being spent on space programs—close to $18 billion per year—could be better allocated to increased funding for education, health care, and other important sectors. The needs of our children and the need to keep people healthy take precedence over the desire to look at stars. Space exploration might teach us more about the universe, but it does not create schools or get food on families' tables.

It's high time for the space industry to be privatized. The private sector is better able to make advances in this industry because of the lack of bureaucratic red tape that currently entangles NASA and impedes its progress. In addition, companies that are competitive with one another have greater incentive to develop technology more quickly and cheaply than does a nonprofit government-funded organization. For example, the Space Exploration Technologies Corporation is working on producing the cheapest and most efficient family of satellites to date.

With the economy in recession, the government must prioritize its programs and give money where it is most critically needed. While space

twentieth century came shortly after World War II and shortly after the U.S. landed men on the Moon. Such missions are inspiring, making technology and science more exciting to young people. It is worth investing money in space programs if doing so will strengthen U.S. performance in other important fields, especially when students from other countries are quickly overtaking ours.

First, the amount of money given to NASA is a tiny percentage of the federal budget; second, space exploration does benefit ordinary Americans. The amount of money given to NASA is minimal (0.52 percent of the federal budget) compared with the amount of money spent on social programs. In addition, studying ways to make space technology more efficient can lead to innovations in fields like energy and medicine. Many technological discoveries made by space scientists have furthered research in more "practical" disciplines.

Privatizing the industry comes with several risks. First, the government loses the ability to profit from any of the gains made in the fields of space-related technology. Also, many other nations have their own space programs—without a national program of our own there is nothing to stop U.S. corporations from selling their technologies and other advancements to another nation. Finally, a corporation motivated by profit may be more likely to cut corners to reduce costs—safety may be the loser.

We cannot simply get rid of programs every time the economy is in a tough place, only to invest enormous time and capital to restart research is interesting, it can hardly be considered an essential aspect of economic recovery efforts. If we were running a huge budget surplus, investing in NASA might make some sense. But in difficult economic times, we must realize that our priorities lie elsewhere.

The chances of a Near Earth Object or some other catastrophic event occurring are very remote. Even if the government was not tracking such things, other countries and private companies are; the fact is that with something that has the potential to affect the entire planet, a private company or other country would certainly share its knowledge with us. We would have all the information we need without having to foot the bill.

them when we are on surer financial footing. In leaner times, some programs or initiatives receive more money than others. We should at least ensure that our space program is up-to-date enough so that we can pursue more aggressive space exploration when the economy allows.

NASA still engages in research that might be necessary to save our lives. The chance of a Near Earth Object striking the planet is small, but as two small asteroids whizzed between Earth and the Moon in the summer of 2010, we know that it is a possibility. Scientists learn countless other facts and need to continue to be able to do research into near and far space if we are to keep up with other nations and even, perhaps, save the entire planet. The government must fund these lines of inquiry to save all our lives.

OTHER MOTIONS:

NASA is no longer functional

Space exploration is a waste of time

RELATED MOTIONS:

Space exploration is necessary for human survival

WEB LINKS:

- Brooks, Jeff. "Putting NASA's Budget in Perspective." <http://www.thespacereview. com/article/898/1>. Although the specific figures cited are dated, this article provides basic arguments in support of the space program.

- Livingston, David. "Is Space Exploration Worth the Cost?" <http://www.thespacereview. com/article/1040/1>. Article arguing that the program is worth the cost.

- NASA. "NASA Announces Fiscal Year 2010 Budget." <http://www.nasa.gov/ home/hqnews/2009/may/HQ_09-102_FY2010Budget.html> <http://articles.cnn. com/2010-02-01/tech/nasa.budget.moon_1_space-exploration-nasa-administrator-charlie-bolden-nasa-programs?_s=PM:TECH>. Budget figures.

Spanish Mandatory in Schools

Motion | **Teaching Spanish should be mandatory in schools**

Introduction | Foreign language instruction is increasingly common in many elementary and high schools; some proficiency in a second language is required to graduate by most colleges and universities. In a country that has no legal national language and that was built by immigrants speaking many languages, having all children learn at least one language besides standard English would seem to make sense. Some have suggested Spanish because its use is so widespread. But should it be required by all schools?

Debating the Motion | Many models of foreign language instruction are in current use in public and private schools, so both sides should search for examples that show both successes and failures in the acquisition of a second language. This general research can provide a basis for making Spanish-specific arguments on the proposition side and arguments for more generalized instruction on the opposition side.

Proposition: In addition defining the word *school*, the proposition should include a detailed plan about how the Spanish instruction will be implemented, for which children, for how long, etc. They might also want to address the ease with which Spanish could be learned.

Opposition: The opposition has two major strategies available. The first would be to dismiss the idea that second-language classes are necessary. For this approach, research the cost and benefits of current language programs. A second approach would be to propose a counter case: this would entail selecting another language as preferable to Spanish or arguing for the study of any second language. In this case, a skilled opposition could hijack many of the proposition arguments by conceding their arguments and then explaining how the benefits of language instruction proposed by the proposition actually support the opposition's counter case.

PROS

Learning Spanish would help us communicate with neighboring countries. Most of our nearest geographic neighbors speak Spanish. In Central and South America, and most

CONS

We don't need Spanish to communicate with our most important neighbor. While it is true that most countries in the Western Hemisphere are Spanish-speaking, we cannot of the Caribbean, Spanish is the dominant language. The pragmatic course would be to communicate with all our neighbors, thus Spanish should be taught to all students.

Learning Spanish would help us communicate with Hispanic Americans—one of the largest and fastest-growing population segments in this country. Given that so many in the United States speak only Spanish or are more fluent in it than in English, a knowledge of Spanish would enable all of us to communicate. You never know when you might encounter someone in school or business who only speaks Spanish; if you speak the language, you will have the greater advantage over someone who does not speak Spanish.

Spanish is a Latin-based language and, as such, offers many benefits to students. Knowledge of the Latin roots of words helps when taking standardized tests; such knowledge is also helpful in other ways—such as teasing out the meaning of unfamiliar words in everyday life. A good grasp of Spanish can also help Americans communicate in many European countries, given the similarities among all Romance languages.

Learning Spanish will help struggling students master English. Students who learn Spanish, which is grammatically simpler, will have that background to help them excel with the more difficult aspects of English grammar.

ignore Canada. The relationship between the United States and Canada is the closest and most extensive in the world. We share a 3,000-mile border and Canada is an important trading partner. If the purpose of acquiring a second language is communication with neighbors, then French would be more practical.

Mandating the teaching of Spanish would hurt Hispanic Americans. Creating widespread education reform simply to allow students in the United States to communicate with immigrants is an unwise move! It would set a dangerous precedent by removing the need for new immigrants to learn English. Immigrants need to be able to speak English to help them adjust to living here, to be able to get a job, and to be able to advance economically.

Why not learn Latin instead or learn Italian? Italian would also provide all the benefits of a Romance language and is the easiest language to learn to read.

The same benefits could come from studying any other language. Besides, at the end of the day, U.S. students still have to master English. Students who struggle already would struggle even more if their focus had to be split between two languages—how will these students survive learning two languages at once when they struggle to learn just one?

PROS

Given the benefits that we have already described of studying Spanish, it would be a worthwhile investment to have Spanish programs in every school. Getting such programs implemented would not be that hard. The United States has so many Spanish speakers, setting up a series of incentives to get some of them to become teachers should be relatively simple. Remember, federal and state governments already have programs to attract young people to careers in education.

CONS

Requiring Spanish in all schools nationwide would be close to impossible. Where would the money come from to hire new teachers? What about the difficulty in actually finding enough qualified Spanish teachers to cover every child in America? This would be an impossible task! If foreign languages must be required, keep a system like many schools have now—the schools decide which languages to offer and the students choose which languages to study. This way, all the teachers spread across the country who teach various languages will still have employment and can still teach a foreign language to kids who want to learn it.

OTHER MOTIONS:

Foreign language courses should not be mandatory

RELATED MOTIONS:

Students should be required to study a foreign language

Schools should eliminate Spanish-language courses

WEB LINKS:

- The Daily Courier. "Debate: Should Arizona Schools Require 2 Years of Spanish?" <http://www.dcourier.com/main.asp?SectionID=36&SubsectionID=1120&ArticleID=80879>. Newspaper essay in support of learning Spanish, with readers' comments.

- Early Advantage. "Brain Boost When Toddlers Learn Spanish?" <http://www.early-advantage.com/Articles/NYTreports.aspx>. Article presenting the benefits of learning Spanish at an early age.

- Ezine @rticles. "5 Benefits to Learning Spanish." <http://ezinearticles.com/?5-Benefits-To-Learning-Spanish&id=647365>. Article on the general benefits of learning Spanish.

Sports in Schools

Motion   Schools should decrease emphasis on sports programs

Introduction   School sports are as American as apple pie. In many high schools and universities, sports have a privileged place in the minds and hearts of students, staff, and alumni. At some schools, they might even have the most privileged position, even higher than that of academic programs. Some argue that an emphasis on sports is misplaced; others say it has benefits for the school and the student athletes.

Debating the Motion   Both teams should research high school and college sports programs, looking into the allotment of time and money afforded them. They might also want to compare the level of emphasis placed on sports in the U.S. with that in other countries. Both teams should also consider what is meant by the term *sports*: Do sports like golf really count? Finally, looking into what kinds of students are usually selected or recruited for teams might also provide interesting information.

Proposition: The proposition should think carefully about how they want to define the term *school* because arguments may differ depending on the definition. Some arguments, those about the loss of focus on academics, for example, will overlap, but some, such as the significance of income generated from sports or the morality of encouraging students to think they have careers in sports, may be more appropriate for college or high school. The proposition does not need to argue that sports in schools are bad or that they need to be eliminated, but rather that they need to be relegated to their proper place.

Opposition: Remember that the opposition does not need to argue that sports programs should take priority, but that the current emphasis is appropriate or at least not harmful.

PROS

Sports can cause serious harm to students, jeopardizing their ability to learn and function. The two major goals of a school should be academic excellence and the safety and well-being of their students. The latter might actually be the most important, because

CONS

Teaching children sports allows them to be healthy and safe. True, sports, like any kind of activity, can be dangerous. This is all the more reason to keep the focus on school sports. Sports are a part of society, and if kids don't play basketball in school, they're students who aren't safe and healthy cannot learn. The fact is that sports programs fly in the face of this goal: sports are dangerous! From the obvious dangers of being sacked by a linebacker to the dangers resulting from overtraining, improper oversight, and equipment failure, sports can seriously harm students. Schools should not be placing students in danger! Deemphasizing sports in schools will result in fewer students participating and thus fewer students injured. In addition, without pressure to have teenagers and very young men perform like professional athletes, the number of serious injuries can be reduced.

School sports divert funds that could be spent on activities that contribute to learning. Considering that U.S. schools already underperform when compared with other nations, why are we wasting money on sports equipments and stadiums? Sports equipment is expensive and needs constant replacement and updating. So, too, are sports venues. In an era where teachers are being fired or paid less because there isn't enough money for salaries, we cannot possibly justify such a strong emphasis on sports programs. In deemphasizing sports programs, some of the funds used for sports materials can be used for more important goals like teacher pay and more after-school help for struggling students.

Schools should encourage an academic culture over an athletic one. The purpose of schools is to educate youth, yet today in many schools, it as seen as "geeky" to be smart, while it is seen as "cool" to be a jock. With the current emphasis on sports, too many kids would much rather be a quarterback

going to play at home or on the playground with friends. When kids are doing sports on their own without the supervision of licensed teachers and coaches, the risk for injury increases. By keeping the emphasis on school sports programs, more students will be encouraged to engage in sports programs in supervised environments with proper equipment. Furthermore, the health benefits from physical exercise—such as reduced chance of obesity—help keep students safe from disease for their entire lives.

Sports cost big money, but they also bring in big money. Having a student get a perfect score on the SAT or ACT won't bring the same recognition as a team that wins the league trophy or a student who smashes a world record in sports. From the merchandizing of athletic T-shirts, to seats and treats in a stadium, sports teams earn back money in many ways. Successful sports teams also bring in donations from businesses and alumni that can be used to help schools overall. So, even though sports programs do take money from the budget, they have the potential to put lots of money back in.

Athletics can teach students a variety of important skills, all of which can be incorporated into academics and personal improvement. Sports teach young adults how to work as teams, develop leadership abilities, apply problem-solving skills to real-life situations, and work toward goals. It is true that the or team captain than president of the honor society. Such an attitude hardly encourages students to excel in classes or seek out higher-level and more challenging courses. Schools should celebrate academic achievement more than athletic achievement.

The idea that minorities and children from low-income families need sports to succeed is harmful. Saying that certain kinds of people are genetically better at sports is dangerously racist. The emphasis on sports in schools, especially for poor and minority students, needs to be combated because it suggests that the only way out of low-income neighborhoods is through sports superstardom, thus taking minority students out of programs that offer real opportunity for a better economic life with a greater number of choices.

main purpose of schools is to educate students, but athletic programs can certainly work in tandem and even support academic programs. Many coaches insist that their players keep up their grades.

Sports programs offer unique opportunities to minority and low-income students to attend really great academic programs for high school and college. Many high school and university sports programs are more ethnically and socioeconomically diverse than the schools themselves. In this case, sports programs actually help level the playing field by allowing access to a quality of education students might otherwise have been denied because of their lack of money or mainstream cultural capital.

OTHER MOTIONS:

Ban competitive sports in high schools

School sports programs do more harm than good

RELATED MOTIONS:

School sports programs are a waste of money

Government funding should not be used for school sports programs

WEB LINKS:

- Denhart, Matthew, Robert Villwock, and Richard Vedder. "The Academics-Athletics Trade Off." <http://www.centerforcollegeaffordability.org/uploads/athletics.pdf>. Analysis of college football programs.

- Edwards, Harry. "Are We Putting Too Much Emphasis on Sports?" <http://findarticles.com/p/articles/mi_m1077/is_n10_v47/ai_12511517/>. Article on the issue with an emphasis on the black experience.

- Myers, Linda. "CU Economist Shows Benefits from Big-Time College Sports Overrated." <http://www.news.cornell.edu/Chronicle/04/9.9.04/Frank-athletics.html>. Article summarizing research into the economics of college sports.

Swimming Pools, Private

Motion **Private swimming pools are unethical**

Introduction On a hot summer day, nothing is quite as nice as jumping into cool, clean water. For most people, this means a trip to the local pool, the lake, or the beach. A privileged few, however, need do nothing more than step out their back door and into a private pool. Private pools, common in some parts of the U.S. while rare in almost all other parts of the world, come with ethical concerns that many who have this luxury do not consider. Private pools hog vast quantities of chemically treated water for the personal pleasure of very few or even of only one individual. In the next hundred years or so, the need for fresh water will increase to the point where this seemingly endless commodity becomes precious—so, is it okay for people to fill entire swimming pools for their personal use?

Debating the Motion Both teams should research the availability of drinkable water and how availability has changed over time. In creating arguments, they should consider the consequences of using water for recreation versus using it for drinking. Both teams should remember to link the topic to ethics and not just to make arguments for and against swimming pools.

Proposition: The proposition might also want to research instances where private pools have posed a danger to local residents and environments. Remember that with any topic related to ethics, there are two options. The first would be to create arguments based on a single or several ethical theories, while the second would be to create arguments about why private pools are simply bad and then relate these arguments to ethics.

Opposition: The opposition need not argue that everyone should have private pools, but rather that a number of individuals having private pools does not create a moral harm. To do this, the team can show that the pools are actually ethically neutral or acceptable in certain circumstances.

PROS

Private pools can cause water shortages, especially in arid areas. Because water evaporates, pools must be refilled from reserves, thus preventing that water from being used

CONS

Pools can be filled with water that is not suitable for drinking or can be covered to prevent evaporation. Obviously private pools can be misused, but with the rise of green pools and for drinking. Indeed, the huge number of private pools was believed to be one of the factors in the 2005 French water shortage. Willfully ignoring ones' surroundings and climate limitations is unethical because the ramifications of acting selfishly could cause suffering to many.

Pools are unethical because they use water selfishly for the private pleasure and entertainment of the few when billions of people around the world lack clean drinking water. In this country, we already take more than our fair share of natural resources. Private swimming pools are the ultimate symbol of our excess—while someone elsewhere lacks clean drinking water, we splash around in thousands of gallons of water.

Private pools can be unsafe. Public pools must meet standards of safety, both in terms of personnel like lifeguards and in terms of water quality. Private pools are required to meet no such standards, thus increasing the risk of people drowning or suffering from injuries or illness related to improperly treated water.

Pools pose an environmental risk. Cleaning them requires many toxic chemicals that pollute the environment; pumps require lots of energy, releasing carbon emissions. Very few people benefit from private pools, since they are constructed for only a few people's use; accordingly, the harms outweigh the benefits. It is unethical to pollute the environment for such small returns.

pool maintenance techniques (such as pool covers), there is no reason pools must have an impact on drinking water.

The existence of private swimming pools does not affect the water level in far-away countries. To be sure, the lack of clean drinking water in other parts of the world is lamentable. However, banning private pools will not magically transport the saved water to people in need, thus, it is impossible to say that a moral harm comes from the pools themselves.

The fact that private swimming pools can be unsafe does not make having them unethical. We let people engage in all sorts of risky recreation, from drinking alcohol to trying extreme sports—individuals can choose for themselves what risks they wish to take. Furthermore, some areas do have swimming pool laws, such as an ordinance in Texas that makes it mandatory to place fencing around pools.

The alternative to pools in summer is lots and lots of fans and air-conditioning. The electricity required to run these and the Freon in air-conditioners pose a great risk to the environment. Taking away pools may simply encourage people to use these alternatives. In addition, as stated above, more "green"-friendly pools now exist, meaning there need not be such a great conflict between leisure and the environment.

OTHER MOTIONS:

Ban private swimming pools

Private swimming pools do more harm than good

RELATED MOTIONS:

Per capita water usage should be capped

WEB LINKS:

- Betts, Kellyn. <http://pubs.acs.org/cen/news/88/i26/8826news7.html>. Describes several studies conducted on the wastefulness of private pools.

- Lichfield, John. <http://www.independent.co.uk/news/world/europe/french-drought-looms-after-boom-in-swimming-pools-496077.html>. Argues that the boom in swimming pools in France was one of the factors making the 2005 water shortage especially bad.

- Practical Environmentalist. <http://www.practicalenvironmentalist.com/for-the-home/swimming-pools-and-the-environment-is-your-pool-eco-friendly.htm>. Explains how to make swimming pools more environmentally friendly.

Term Limits

Term limits do more harm than good

Term limits are legal restrictions that set a maximum number of years or terms an elected public official can serve. In the last decades of the twentieth century, many states and localities imposed term limits—a move fueled by general dissatisfaction with government and by the seeming lack of accountability of entrenched incumbents. But in light of experience, some people are rethinking these measures.

Both teams should research state and local term limits, focusing particularly on their long-term impact. Term limits have been around for decades, thus much information is available. Teams might also want to research other countries' experience with term limits. As in all cases where the motion speaks of harms and goods, make sure that arguments state explicitly where the harms and benefits lie as opposed to merely arguing whether term limits themselves are good or bad.

Proposition: The proposition may want to limit the scope of the debate to a particular office or level of government, however, they could also argue about term limits in general. Remember, the topic says they are more harmful than good but this does not mean that the proposition must argue that term limits are all bad, just that, on balance, they are more harmful than good.

Opposition: The opposition needs only to argue that, on balance, term limits are either good or neutral, both of which would counter the proposition's case. In addition, the opposition might want to propose a counter case in which they suggest uniform term limits for certain offices since current practices vary.

PROS

Term limits are inherently undemocratic. In a democracy, the people determine who should hold office. Term limits interfere with this right. Voters can always limit an official's term by voting her out, but, under term limits, they cannot always retain the individuals they want in office.

CONS

The core document of our democracy, the Constitution, limits our choices. It places age requirements on those running for Congress and it restricts those running for the presidency not only by age but by place of birth. Limits are not foreign to our political system.

PROS	CONS
Term limits are not necessary to overcome this advantage. Challengers win against well-known opponents all the time. Further, name recognition and popularity are likely indicators that the politician is performing well. And, as evidenced by recent political polls, incumbency can be as much of a disadvantage as an advantage. Americans do not like their politicians.	*Term limits eliminate the advantages that incumbents have in elections.* Most people recognize the name of a sitting politician and some may know her record. Over the years, she may have become extremely popular. Challengers who have not been in public life have difficulty overcoming this advantage. They must fight just to get voters' attention. And, because they are not widely known, they may have difficulty raising the funds needed to challenge an incumbent. Incumbents, on the other hand, have greater access to funding from the business and lobbying groups they may have helped while in office. Also, political parties are more likely to help incumbents.
Under term limits, we lose our most experienced politicians. Wisdom comes with experience; as in the work world, you only know how to do a job after doing it for a number of years. Term limits prevent incumbents from using their firsthand knowledge to work efficiently. As for diversity, studies have shown that while term limits have led to increased turnover, they have not resulted in a significant increase in the number of women and minorities in government.	*Term limits ensure a constant influx of new people and, therefore, new ideas.* Over time they can lead to more diversity, making government more representative of the population. Even the most well-meaning officials can become "stale" and out of touch with their constituents. We need new people to ensure that our elected officials are in touch with the times.
Term limits increase the power of lobbyists and special interests. Inexperienced legislators are more likely to rely on lobbyists, staff, and bureaucrats, thus increasing the power of unelected individuals.	*Term limits curtail the influence of lobbyists.* Meeting in a capital surrounded by lobbyists and isolated from their constituents often results in legislators getting a distorted picture of the world. Over time, legislators can develop close connections to lobbyists and special interests. They can end up working for these groups rather than for their constituents. Limits create the turnover necessary to put a stop to these relationships.

Term limits result in politicians thinking short term. They know they will be involved for only a short time, so they may avoid difficult decisions—leaving the problems for their successors, by which time the problem may be more severe.

This situation could arise without term limits. Politicians frequently put off making hard decisions for fear of voters' reactions at the polls. Look how long the Congress took to pass health care reform! Also, politicians who are term-limited may be more likely to represent their constituents and less likely to make decisions to further their careers. But, in any case, short term is not necessarily bad. Politicians who think short term are not committing government to policies that may not be appropriate over the long term. Times and circumstances change! What may have looked like a good idea may be a bad idea ten years later. We need new people to ensure that elected officials do the work of the people, not lobbyists.

OTHER MOTIONS:

Institute term limits for all elected offices

Term limits do more good than harm

RELATED MOTIONS:

Impose term limits on all House and Senate seats

Repeal the presidential term limit

WEB LINKS:

- BalancedPolitics.org. "Should Senators and Representatives in Congress Be Limited to a Certain Number of Terms in Office?" <http://www.balancedpolitics.org/term_limits.htm>. Site presents both pros and cons on the issue.

- The National Conference of State Legislatures. <http://www.ncsl.org/programs/legismgt/ABOUT/termlimit.htm>. Site documents recent developments on local levels to promote term limits.

- U.S. Term Limits. <http://www.termlimits.org/>. Site of a grassroots advocacy group that works to promote term limits at local, state, and federal levels.

Terrorists, Negotiate with

Motion   **The United States should negotiate with terrorists**

Introduction   We have heard governments say that they do not negotiate with terrorists. Yet, despite the rhetoric, many do, in fact, regularly engage in negotiations with terrorists—including the United States and Great Britain. Whether we do or not, however, is less a matter for this debate than whether or not we should. Is it ever advisable to negotiate with terrorists?

Debating the Motion   Both teams should research instances of nations negotiating with terrorists, focusing on how they justified doing so and the results.

Proposition: The proposition does not have to argue that the U.S. should always negotiate, although it could. The team might want to narrow this topic, setting out specific circumstances where negotiations would be used.

Opposition: The opposition does not necessarily need to speak to specific harms and benefits of negotiations; rather the team should aim to show why negotiations would not be a good public policy for the U.S. An ambitious opposition might want to differentiate between having a policy of negotiation, which it would argue is a bad idea, and being allowed to negotiate in secret or under very exceptional circumstances.

PROS

Terrorism poses such a grave threat that countries should use every tool at their disposal to stop it. The biggest danger is that terrorists might gain access to nuclear weapons. Since many terrorists are willing to sacrifice their own lives for their ideology, a real danger exists of their using such weapons, potentially killing millions. No national image or pride is worth more than millions of human lives. Even if negotiating with terrorists makes governments feel uncomfortable or "look bad," the lives of people threatened by terrorists are more important and no option should be off the table.

CONS

Negotiating with terrorists is too risky a path. Any organization crazy enough to blow up the world probably cannot be reasoned with through negotiation. Terrorists have different motivations and goals than rational governments and are often uninterested in self-preservation—thus, they have little or nothing to lose. Consequently, rational negotiation is unlikely to result in any gains. In fact, negotiations are likely to result in harms because they legitimize breakaway groups and publicly acknowledge them. Negotiating sends the message that violence and terrorism are effective ways to gain concessions, setting a dangerous precedent.

PROS

Some terrorist groups may have legitimate goals and ideas. For example, for years many people considered the African National Congress to be a terrorist group. However, history has shown that it was a legitimate organization fighting for a noble cause—the end of apartheid in South Africa. Furthermore, many terrorist groups have serious misconceptions about the positions taken by the United States. Discussions can create better understanding between opposing groups.

Negotiating gives us a platform to express moral superiority. Our nation's reputation for engaging in combat frequently and using our U.N. veto powers to support questionable causes lead many to view us in a negative light. By first trying a more peaceful path, we gain the high ground. Our national image will improve and we will counter the stereotype that we are too quick to military action. It also makes us look better than the terrorists, who may have begun the negotiations by killing or kidnapping.

If nothing else, agreeing to talk buys time to find alternatives in dangerous situations. We have all seen the movies where the sidekick just has to keep the bad guy talking and distracted long enough for the hero to come save the day. Agreeing to negotiations is similar—it can be a ruse that provides additional time to find information or set in play a plan that saves everyone.

CONS

The majority of terrorist groups are dangerous; they do not deserve to have their causes legitimized. The African National Congress is an exception—most terrorist groups today, such as Al Qaeda, are bent on killing and destruction. As stated above, we simply legitimize these goals by agreeing to negotiate with terrorists and accepting violence as a political tool.

Negotiating makes our country look weak. By reaching out to terrorists, we send the message that we are worried about our ability to protect ourselves from attacks. We must be as intimidating as possible to discourage terrorists from attacking us. Furthermore, negotiating suggests we doubt our military capability. If a nation has nothing to fear, then why is it willing to make concessions to its enemies? Finally, different governments have different views on negotiating with terrorists—there is no reason we will necessarily look better in the world's eyes by negotiating.

That is a brilliant plan, but the hitch is that it could only really work once. After such a ruse, terrorists will realize that they were tricked, thus encouraging them to become angrier and more bent on harming the U.S. They will also understand that they cannot trust the U.S. to negotiate and will probably refuse to enter discussions again.

OTHER MOTIONS:
Negotiating with terrorists compromises security
Negotiating with terrorists does more good than harm

RELATED MOTIONS:
It is ethical to negotiate with terrorists to save lives

WEB LINKS:
- Currie, Chris. "Should We Negotiate with Terrorists?" <http://www.mediate.com/articles/currie4.cfm>. Article in support of negotiating.
- PBS. "Should We Ever Negotiate with Terrorists?" <http://www.npr.org/templates/story/story.php?storyId=9078818>. Interview with proponents on both sides of the issue.
- Zalman, Amy. "Why Not Negotiate with Terrorists—Pros and Cons of Talking to Al Qaeda." <http://terrorism.about.com/od/globalwaronterror/i/NegotiateQaeda.htm>. Article providing background and arguments on both sides of the issue.

Torture

Motion

Torture is permissible for purposes of national security

Introduction

Despite the fact that domestic laws and the Geneva Convention of 1949 prohibit torture, during the Bush administration, the United States used torture, specifically waterboarding, to gain information from supposed terrorists. Many condemned these actions, but the administration defended waterboarding on the grounds of national security.

Debating the Motion

Both teams should research the definitions of *torture* as well as the Geneva Convention and U.S. domestic legislation prohibiting torture. They would also benefit from investigating how other countries handle the issue. Finally, advocates on both sides have written extensively to justify their position; both teams also need to review this literature.

Proposition: This motion is vague; the team needs to define it clearly: How does the proposition define *permissible* and *purposes of national security*? The proposition does not need to defend torture as good or in any way an ideal practice, but rather that the benefits the nation receives in terms of security far outweigh any ethical or legal objections.

Opposition: The opposition has several options in arguing this case. First, the team can argue against the motion on the basis of utility: torture does not provide any tangible benefits to national security. Second, the team could argue that torture is not permissible under any circumstances because torture is morally wrong. Finally, the opposition could argue acceptability. Most Americans do not condone torture under any circumstances—in a democracy, the people decide what is acceptable and, therefore, torture is not.

PROS

The use of torture is justified when many lives are at stake. If we believe that human rights are important, then logically we should try to protect as many as possible. If torturing one suspected terrorist can make him give information that will save many lives, the ends justify the means. To be sure, the terrorist's well-being is compromised, but since that compromise saves the actual lives of so many others, it is worth it.

CONS

It is never justified to use someone as a means to an end, and besides, we have no reason to believe torture would make us safer. Every person—even a suspected terrorist—has natural worth that ought not be compromised. If humans are seen as nothing more than tools, then they lose their special value and the whole concept of human dignity is undermined. Furthermore, even torture is risky. First, the United States is already struggling with a poor international reputation—every time a story leaks out about Americans using torture, more people turn against us, causing a security risk for all those millions we are supposed to be saving. Second and more important, torture is unlikely to yield significant information, since suspects will say anything to stop the torture.

Torture is not only permissible but necessary when time is a factor. In so-called ticking bomb scenarios, when only a limited amount of time is available to stop a disaster from occurring, governments should have and use every tool at their disposal. Yes, it would be nice to have the time for an interrogator to build a relationship with a suspect so he wants to talk, but if a threat is imminent and information is needed immediately, torture can provide quick information.

The ticking bomb scenario has never actually occurred. Furthermore, a reduced time frame would certainly not encourage prisoners to give accurate, or any, information. Presumably, the prisoner would also be aware of the time element and would know that any punishment or torture would be limited by the ticking bomb—when it went off, the justification for the torture would stop. Such knowledge would make it easier for prisoners to resist giving information

The Constitution grants the president powers in wartime to protect citizens; extreme circumstances make extreme measures more justified. We are at war with terrorist groups, although we cannot formally declare war because this type of warfare does not involve another nation-state. And, as Justice Antonin Scalia pointed out, technically torture is not the same thing as "punishment," meaning that the Eighth Amendment may not apply.

Torture is unconstitutional. The Constitution protects against cruel and unusual punishment; torture, by definition, consists of punishments that are both exceedingly cruel and unusual. Additionally, the war on terror, just like the war on drugs and other so-called wars, is not an actual war and special powers do not come in to play.

Publicly proclaiming that we are willing to use torture will deter our enemies. The sad truth is that a life in a U.S. jail might actually be easier than life in other countries. Jail means shelter, access to medical care, a place to sleep, regular meals, etc. This comparatively excellent treatment emboldens some to commit crimes against us if they know the consequence will be no worse than those mentioned earlier. Torture might act as a deterrent.

Our use of torture is a marketing tool for our enemies. In certain parts of the world, people already think the worst of us; the knowledge that we use torture will only confirm their opinions. We win no friends by torturing; people will want to join a crusade against us if we torture.

PROS

As a sovereign nation, we have the right to do whatever we deem best to ensure our national security. If this means torturing prisoners, so be it. A government's primary responsibility is to keep its citizens safe. If torture keeps them safe, then the government is not wrong to use it.

We maintain our standing in the world by showing that we will go to any lengths to protect our citizens. Certainly we should use torture only as a last resort, but we must show the world that we will use it if necessary.

CONS

No nation can do whatever it wants without regard to the rest of the world. As the world becomes increasingly interconnected, nations must cooperate to combat terrorism. Other democracies will be reluctant to work with us if they know that suspected terrorists they hand over to the United States may be tortured. Using torture makes us less safe, not more.

Torture undermines our moral standing in the world. Americans believe that our values set us apart from other countries. And, indeed, other nations look to the United States as a moral compass. If we use torture, we are just another bully state.

OTHER MOTIONS:

Torturing terrorists is constitutional

Torturing suspects does more harm than good

RELATED MOTIONS:

Torture is justifiable

Torture is never justifiable

WEB LINKS:

- BalancedPolitics.org. "Should High-ranking Captured Terrorists Be Tortured to Obtain Information?" <http://www.balancedpolitics.org/prisoner_torture.htm>. Pros and cons of using torture.

- Morin, Richard, and Claudia Deane. "Americans Split on How to Interrogate: Majority Polled Oppose Using Torture." <http://www.washingtonpost.com/wp-dyn/articles/A59631-2004May27.html>. Summary of a poll on American attitudes toward torture.

- Parry, John, and Welsh White. "Interrogating a Suspected Terrorist." <http://jurist.law.pitt.edu/terrorism/terrorismparry.htm>. Article opposed to the use of torture.

Trans Fats, Ban

Motion | **Repeal the ban on artificial trans fats**

Introduction | Artificial trans fats have long been a staple in fast foods and other junk foods, but the recent awareness of their potential health hazards has prompted some states, California is one, and cities, New York, for instance, to ban them in commercially available foods. Trans fats are a special kind of fat artificially created to extend the shelf life of food; however, its atomic structure is different from fats found naturally in food and this difference has been linked to increased heart health risks. Banning them is, nevertheless, controversial. While health advocates praise the move to ban trans fats, many store and restaurant owners fear a ban would hurt their business.

Debating the Motion | Obviously both teams need to research trans fats and their use. They should also research community bans and the debate surrounding the ban.

Proposition: Remember that in arguing for repealing the ban, the proposition is taking the position that trans fats are good, neutral, necessary, or some combination of these three stances. Their proposed repeal also can be total or partial. When the proposition team members research existing bans, they should examine what the bans cover and any exemptions. They can then decide whether they want to repeal the entire ban or only parts. Remember that while some narrowing of the topic is a clever strategic move, narrowing it too much will cost you the round: if you create a platform so narrow that the opposition cannot respond, there cannot be good clash and you will not win.

Opposition: The opposition is arguing to uphold trans fat bans, essentially arguing that trans fats are bad and need to be banned. In doing this, the opposition can simply defend the status quo. The alternative is to argue against repeal and for a reform of the ban: to do this, the opposition would need to create a counter case outlining their proposed reform.

PROS	CONS
This ban puts an unfair burden on small businesses and franchise owners. They are required to replace the cheaper artificial trans fats with more costly items that are more likely	*This ban does not put too great a burden on any one business because it applies to all.* Thus, everyone's costs will go up because everyone will be required to use alternatives. Therefore,

to spoil. Also, if prices go up, shoppers will flee to larger chains that can better absorb increased costs and keep prices down. The loss of business will further increase the hardship small-business owners face.

Individuals should be able to choose what they wish to eat—if it is junk food, then so be it. Try as we might, we cannot possibly ban all junk food. If a person wants to eat artificial trans fats, he should be allowed to do so. Likewise, a shopper should have the choice of purchasing items containing trans fats or not buying them. A business should not be placed in a position of not being able to sell goods made with trans fats.

People can eat junk food once in awhile. In moderation, these foods will not harm you if balanced by otherwise healthy food choices. Thus, rather than banning them, we should support education in healthier eating habits.

A ban on trans fats might be more harmful to health in the long run. As we know, replacing trans fats doesn't change the fact that fast food is unhealthy. The ban, however, may actually lead to increased consumption because people would think that fast food is healthy—when, in reality, it is just less bad.

This ban unfairly targets poor areas where cheap food dominates and healthy foods are hard to find. Such bans unfairly affect a population of both business owners and consumers who cannot afford the higher prices that come with the ban.

a bigger chain will also have to raise prices just as a small business would. Accordingly, customers won't be driven away from small businesses because the increases will happen all over.

We can ban foodstuffs that are unhealthy and we already do. We have placed limits and bans on all sorts of unhealthy items—drugs, tobacco, and alcohol, for example. Banning other items like artificial trans fats or even sugar-sweetened sodas is a natural extension of a well-established policy.

Sadly, people often are immoderate in their consumption. That is why some states, like Pennsylvania, ban the sale of alcohol during hours when it is most likely to be abused. Banning artificial trans fats will help those with limited self-control.

A ban on trans fats is a simple step to toward better health. Obesity and related problems like diabetes, heart disease, and cancer, have a pervasive effect on a person's life. They can limit a person's ability to work, increase medical costs, and even kill prematurely. A simple way to avoid these problems is to cut back on the availability of unhealthy food.

Given that some people only have access to fast food, we have a duty to make junk food as harmless as possible. Poor areas have some of the highest rates of obesity—this is no coincidence. If all that is available is junk and processed foods, no wonder many residents become obese. The ban does not target poor people; rather, it helps groups by removing a source of ill-health.

OTHER MOTIONS:

Ban trans fats

Junk food bans do more harm than good

RELATED MOTIONS:

The government has the right to legislate eating habits

WEB LINKS:

- American Heart Association. "Trans Fats." <http://www.americanheart.org/presenter. jhtml?identifier=3045792>. Site explains what trans fats are and discusses problems associated with their use.

- The Center for Consumer Freedom. "Delicious Trans Fat Wisdom from The Wall Street Journal." <http://consumerfreedom.net/news_detail.cfm/h/3084-delicious-trans-fat-wisdom-from-the-wall-street-journal>. Article opposing a ban on trans fats.

- Demare, Carol. "Trans Fats Are Back on the Menu." <http://www.timesunion.com/news/article/Trans-fat-issue-back-on-the-menu-574650.php>. Article discussing the impact of the ban on food quality.

U.N. Headquarters

Motion   **Move the United Nations headquarters**

Introduction   The current headquarters of the United Nations is comprised of some iconic buildings in New York that evoke images of bygone eras and dramatic Hitchcock films. Yet these buildings, as have many old buildings, have fallen into disrepair and rendered not only unusable but even dangerous from leaky roofs, unstable structures, and asbestos. As the United Nations embarks on a restoration project and debates what to do for a long-term fix, some are suggesting a move. Not just a move to a building elsewhere in New York City, but a move to a completely different city or even a different country.

Debating the Motion   Several countries have been suggested as hosts for the United Nations, so looking into these bids will give teams a foundation for starting to build their arguments. Additionally, looking into who pays for U.N. buildings and upkeep and the associated costs involved in running the U.N. and its missions will help both teams create arguments.

Proposition: The proposition needs to clarify what is meant by *moving* the United Nations: whether this means to new buildings, new cities, or new countries. The team should set out a concrete case recommending a different location and a time frame for moving or they can propose rotating the headquarters. In defending rotation, the team needs to propose a plan that outlines how often the headquarters will move and how the next location will be chosen.

Opposition: The opposition can argue for keeping the U.N. headquarters in New York City or it can launch a counter case. To do so, the team must maintain flexibility and rely on good research that anticipates possible proposition cases.

PROS

By putting the United Nations headquarters in another country, we could bring attention to needier parts of the world. The United States is a large and rich nation that does not really need the aid of other countries, so it seems a waste to have the U.N. headquarters here.

CONS

The very places that need the most assistance are probably also the least equipped to host such a large and complex organization. New York City has strong infrastructure, a low level of crime, good security, and an established international reputation. Accordingly, the

Putting it in, for example, sub-Saharan Africa, could draw attention to climate and health issues in that region; putting it in the Middle East could galvanize the world to try to solve geopolitical conflicts in that region.

U.N. does not impose a burden on the city. In a poorer, less-developed country, poverty issues or security could be problematic when hosting large numbers of heads of state and other dignitaries at conferences.

The headquarters should move from place to place so that every country has a chance both to host and to have their issues and concerns thoroughly addressed. Keeping the headquarters in one spot is inconsistent with the concept that the U.N. member nations are equal to one another.

While this is a beautiful idea, it is impossible to execute in practice. Nations struggling in the wake of wars and natural disasters would exhaust their limited resources in hosting the organization. New York City, a major transportation hub, is really a central place from which the U.N. can operate.

Keeping the U.N. headquarters in New York City taints the U.N. because the United States does not have the best international reputation. In fact, the U.S. is among the most controversial nations in the world. If the U.N. operates out of the major city in the U.S., its authority is undermined by association.

The United States certainly has its critics, but it is also one of the most democratic and prosperous nations in the world. Many of its core values—freedom of speech, the right to a fair trial, and the importance of elections—are contained in the U.N.'s charter. Often, the U.N. and the U.S. share goals, so it makes sense that they are located in the same place.

The United Nations should be moved for its own safety. The United States, especially New York City, is a target for terrorist attacks. By having the U.N. here, we put the delegates in danger of suffering as a result of attacks on New York and the U.S.

New York may be a terrorist target, but so is the U.N. headquarters. In fact, the 9/11 attacks were supposed to be followed up by attacks on the U.N., as well as on several other New York landmarks. The U.N. is always going to be at risk regardless of its location.

OTHER MOTIONS:

The United Nations should move to another U.S. city

The United Nations should move to another country

The United Nations should relocate to Dubai

RELATED MOTIONS:

The United Nations headquarters should rotate among different member states

WEB LINKS:

- GulfNews. "Dubai Invites United Nations to Set Up Headquarters." <http://gulfnews.com/news/gulf/uae/government/dubai-invites-united-nations-to-set-up-headquarters-1.568038>. Article supporting a move to Dubai.

- Howell, Llewellyn. "Move the UN to Jerusalem." <http://findarticles.com/p/articles/mi_m1272/is_2720_133/ai_n13683427/>. Article arguing for moving the U.N. to Jerusalem.

- Popp, Aaron. "Relocation of UN Headquarters." <http://www.uni.edu/ihsmun/archive/sc2006/SC-UNHQ.htm>. Site providing background and resources on the issue.

U.N. Security Council

Motion   Increase the number of United Nations Security Council permanent members

Introduction   The Security Council is one of the U.N.'s principal bodies, charged with maintaining peace and security. The Council is composed of five permanent members (China, France, Russia, the United Kingdom, and the United States) and ten nonpermanent members elected by the General Assembly for two-year terms. Its structure reflects the international situation at the end of World War II; the five permanent members were the victors. The organization has come under attack as ineffective and not representative of the twenty-first century world. Some have suggested that expanding the number of permanent members would help solve the problem.

Debating the Motion   Both teams need to research the history of the Security Council and the reasons for its structure. They also should look at the way the Security Council currently operates and if it has been effective in addressing security problems.

Proposition: Several large countries have been advocating for entrance to the Security Council, so research into their reasoning will help provide a framework for this case. Remember, also, that the members have not changed in many decades, so the changing face of politics over time will also provide fodder for arguments. The proposition might argue generally to increase the number of permanent members, but it might also want to create a specific case arguing for admission for a specific country or countries.

Opposition   The opposition might argue for the status quo or present a counter case. Creating a counter case is tricky since the opposition cannot know in advance what the proposition might set out as the terms of the debate, but a well-researched opposition team might prepare several possible counter cases and be ready to adapt them depending on the proposition's case.

PROS	CONS
The minuscule number of permanent members on the Security Council results in only a few countries having their political interests served.	*Realistically, expanding the number of countries in the Security Council is unlikely to change much.* First, the Security Council

PROS	CONS
The Security Council has voted to intervene in conflicts that affected members' financial or political interests, for example, Kuwait (which is known for being oil rich) during the Gulf War. On the other hand, it has ignored conflicts like the Rwandan genocide, which occurred in a region offering few economic or political benefits.	does not have the resources to intervene in every conflict. Second, even if it were expanded, the "selfish" nations could still veto intervention in countries where such action would not benefit them.
Allowing more permanent members could increase the efficiency of the Council and its ability to implement actions. The Council is limited by the personnel and funding of its members as well as political support and pressure that these members can offer. Increasing the number of countries could give the Council immediate access to both more people and political clout.	*The more people you have represented, the more interests that need to be considered, thus the more time needed to make decisions.* What makes the Security Council great is its small size, which allows members to really sit down and talk with one another. Adding more members will add more bureaucracy to the process and slow discussion and action, as well as make unanimous decisions more difficult.
The small size of the Security Council goes against the spirit and purpose of the U.N. The Security Council is supposed to serve as a representative body for the U.N. when quick decisions need to be made, yet it is composed of only five permanent members. It is not united—rather it is a conglomerate of the powerful keeping out the weak. The U.N. has grown over the years; the Security Council needs to be adapted so it adequately represents the U.N.'s total membership.	*All nations are included in the Security Council currently via a system that allows countries to rotate in and out of the Council, taking turns being temporary members.* This is the best possible solution because it keeps the size manageable while allowing everyone a turn to share their concerns.
The current composition of the Council is based on outdated prejudices left over from World War II. The major allies were given seats while countries like Japan and Germany (the aggressors in that war) were kept off for political reasons. Further, since then, other countries have risen to prominence, India and Brazil among them, in ways we could not have predicted 60 years ago. The Council needs updating. Germany and Japan are	*If more nations need to be included, then why not increase the number of temporary members?* Increasing the number of permanent members may result in unnecessary bickering and tension as countries bid for these new seats and harbor resentment against those who are selected. Increasing the number of nonpermanent members will allow more people more say without too much drama.

PROS	CONS
now two of the most peaceful and intelligently productive nations on Earth, Africa and South America deserve representation, and India and Brazil are two of the largest nations on the planet. The Security Council needs to change with the times.	

OTHER MOTIONS:

India should be a permanent member of the U.N. Security Council

Brazil should be a permanent member of the U.N. Security Council

Germany should be a permanent member of the U.N. Security Council

Japan should be a permanent member of the U.N. Security Council

RELATED MOTIONS:

Increase the number of nonpermanent members on the U.N. Security Council

Eliminate the nonpermanent members of the U.N. Security Council

WEB LINKS:

• Anbarasan, Ethirajan. "Analysis: India's Security Council Seat Bid." <http://news.bbc.co.uk/2/hi/americas/3679968.stm>. Overview of India's effort to gain a permanent seat on the Security Council.

• Global Policy Forum. "The UN Security Council. <http://www.globalpolicy.org/security-council.html>. Detailed resource on the Security Council and its activities.

• Highbeam Business. "Spain Opposes Adding Permanent Members to U.N. Security Council." <http://business.highbeam.com/436103/article-1G1-125525907/spain-opposes-adding-permanent-members-un-security>. Article reviewing reasons for Spain's opposition to increasing the number of permanent members as well as suggestions for reforming the Council.

Video Games

Motion   Video games are good for the United States

Introduction   When video games first appeared, few could have predicted how widespread they would become. What once could be played only on jumbo machines in special venues is now open to everyone in their home or on the go just about anywhere. Increasingly, game companies are trying to broaden their market from preadolescent and teenage boys to everyone, creating pastel and glittery handhelds to try to draw in girls and games that incorporate retro music for mom and dad. The reach of video games grows every time new markets are tapped. While the question once was whether or not they are good for boys, now we can ask whether or not they are good for the United State—so pervasive is their presence in society today.

Debating the Motion   When debating this topic, both teams need to pay special attention to the fact that the motion states that video games are good for the United States. While the tendency in these kinds of topics is for the arguments to devolve into why video games are simply good or bad, all arguments should relate to why they might be helpful, harmful, or neutral for the country in general. Solid research to back arguments is a must—ample material is available. In fact, the material is so extensive that teams might want to develop their arguments first and then search for evidence that support them.

Proposition: Remember that video games could encompass everything from violent war role-playing games to learning-focused systems like Leap Frog, so the proposition team should begin by narrowing the definition of the term. The narrow definition will limit the potential arguments the opposition can offer.

Opposition: The proposition's burden in this case is to prove that video games are good for the country, thus, the opposition can choose either to explain how they are bad or how they are neutral. If the proposition fails to narrow the scope of the term *video games*, the opposition should take advantage of that choice by focusing on the video games most often written about as harmful in the press. Find popular stories on violent games that promote crime, for example—they provide good examples. Additionally, current research showing that video games don't necessarily cause harm to children even though they provide nothing positive will help display neutrality.

PROS

Video games are beneficial to the U.S. because they get kids off the streets. Instead of idling after school in groups or gangs, causing and getting into trouble, many kids now head home as quickly as possible to get to their games. Fewer kids on the streets with nothing to do but get into trouble reduce potential crime, which is good for everyone.

Today's games are designed to bring families together—family unity is good for the U.S. While families used to eat dinner together every night and children came home to at least one parent, we now hear more and more about families where each member has a hectic schedule; family members scarcely see one another let alone sit down together for a meal. Family video games and systems are helping to combat these trends by creating activities that appeal to all ages and bring people together. These games are a simple way to reinvest in the family—the institution that is the cornerstone of our nation.

Video games can be used as innovative tools to educate. Standard education works best for those children who come from relatively well-off and educated families, but educators are still struggling to find systems that work for lower-income children or children with special needs. Educational video games can be used to engage students who might otherwise not pay attention. For a country that lags behind its peers in educational achievement, this is an enormous boon.

Video games expose people to new information and can thus contribute to a well-rounded and culturally aware citizenry. New games expose children to the music of bygone eras or the

CONS

The fact that video games keep kids off the streets is actually harmful to this country. They keep kids from walking around, playing games, going to the park, and generally getting any kind of exercise other than with their thumbs and forefingers. The sedentary nature of this after-school activity plays a huge part in the obesity epidemic that is wrecking this country.

These games are actually eroding the family structure. Games are beneficial for families who are inclined to take the time to hang out with one another. But if family members cannot even find time to see each other in the day, there is no way they will find time sit and play a video game together. Actually, in many cases, video games drive families apart, with younger members glued to their games while parents call in vain for them to come to the table. Kids also bring handhelds with them to meals, thus conversations that used to bring families together are now silenced.

Even if some games might be used to help in school, their effects on students outside the school remain a concern. Students are spending increasing amounts of time on video games instead of studying, doing homework, or engaging in independent reading. The presence of video games in the house is actually slowing the academic development of millions of children across the country, which will only serve to put them further behind their international peers.

The proposition is being unrealistic. Kids might learn the names of a couple of Greek gods or a classic rock song through games, but this pales in comparison to what they would gain

PROS	CONS

mythology of ancient civilizations; children learn about and become interested in subjects they never would have otherwise. This increase in knowledge helps them to become well-rounded and culturally sensitive.

No direct link has been shown between video games and poor behavior. We have long known, in fact, that the ability to act out abnormal behaviors in fantasy realms like video games helps confine such behaviors to the land of make-believe, thus keeping them out of the real world. Games can help us keep actual violence and crime down by allowing them only in the virtual world.

through spending their video game hours reading or engaging in after-school enrichment programs. The benefits of video games do not make up for everything that is lost as a result of the enormous amount of time kids waste on them.

Most of the best-selling video games promote violence and other antisocial behaviors. They only serve to teach the players that this kind of behavior, which is so detrimental to society, is acceptable and normal. The violence desensitizes people, while criminal activities are glorified and promoted. This will lead to increased violence and crime, which is bad for the country.

OTHER MOTIONS:

Video games do more harm than good

Violent video games should be banned

RELATED MOTIONS:

Video games are bad for boys

Schools should use video games as teaching tools

WEB LINKS:

- American Academy of Child & Adolescent Psychiatry. "Children and Video Games: Playing with Violence." <http://www.aacap.org/cs/root/facts_for_families/children_and_video_games_playing_with_violence>. Summary of the effects of excessive use of video games on children.

- CBSNews.com. "Violent Video Games Hailed as Learning Tool." <http://www.cbsnews.com/stories/2010/05/28/national/main6526866.shtml>. Article reviewing research on the benefits of video games.

- Fernandez, Alvaro. "Playing the Blame Game: Video Games Pros and Cons." <http://www.sharpbrains.com/blog/2008/09/26/playing-the-blame-game-video-games-pros-and-cons/>. Summary of research on the issue.

Voting, Mandatory

Motion **Voting should be mandatory**

Introduction Historically, the United States has had a low turnout rate in elections. In fact, based on turnout between 1945 and 2000, the U.S. ranked 20th among 21 established democracies. A democracy depends on its citizens to express their will, yet increasingly only a fraction of the population actually does so at the polls. Some argue that mandatory voting would solve this problem, while others argue that forcing people to vote is itself undemocratic.

Debating
the Motion Both teams should research mandatory voting in other countries: Australia is the most prominent democracy to require voting. Investigating who votes and why nonvoters do not participate in elections would also be helpful.

Proposition: The proposition should offer a plan explaining how they intend to implement mandatory voting. It should include information about in what elections voting will be mandatory, who must vote, who will not be eligible, who will be exempt from the law, and what kinds of penalties nonvoters will face.

Opposition: In the past, legislative bodies have tossed around this idea, but it has never been passed into law. Accordingly, the opposition may want to research why such measures did not pass as a way to build their own arguments.

PROS

In democracies with mandatory voting, the policy is largely supported by the public. Such laws lead citizens to view democratic participation as a duty, increasing appreciation for government by the people.

Mandatory voting will improve civic education and, eventually, the quality of government. Mandatory voting will encourage citizens to be more informed about governance and politics. Better-informed voters will make better electoral choices, improving our government.

CONS

The American people do not support such a policy. We are a democracy, which means citizens decide what is important. Laws should not be imposed on people with the justification that they will grow to like it.

Better civic education would lead to higher voluntary voter turnout, not the other way around. If citizens better understood politics, they would be more likely to vote. People who don't want to vote are unlikely to inform themselves about issues because they are forced to go to the polls. We should not force uninformed people to make poor electoral choices in hope that they will get better at it.

A *"none of the above" option on the ballot allows people who do not like any candidates to register this objection while still actively participating in the voting process.* Nevada already includes a "none of these candidates" option for all statewide offices on its ballots.

Compulsory voting would force people to vote for candidates they don't want. If they did not like any candidates on the ballot, they would have to choose "the lesser evil." They could not register a silent protest with the politics of the day by staying home.

Requiring everyone to vote would reduce political polarization. In most elections, less than half of eligible voters turn out, even fewer vote in primaries. Particularly in the primaries, those who do vote reflect the extreme ends of their party's spectrum. Thus, they support candidates who increase political polarization. In countries with compulsory voting, politicians know they have to appeal to the center to win. Mandatory voting will mean more moderate voters go to the polls and support more moderate candidates.

If people do not like the polarization of U.S. politics, they should vote. Inaction is an action; refusing to choose is itself a choice. If people are dissatisfied with extremism in both parties, they are responsible for electing more moderate candidates. The very premise of democracy is that citizens are capable of making competent decisions. To institute mandatory voting is to assume citizens are not capable of appropriately valuing their right to vote. If we cannot trust our populace to decide whether voting is worthwhile, why would we trust them to pick our democratic government?

Compulsory voting guarantees that all parts of society are represented in decisions. If everyone is required to vote, the outcome of an election will reflect the will of the majority, not just the few committed voters.

All individuals in society do not necessarily have views or interests at stake in a particular election. If people are forced to vote, those voters who are uninformed and apathetic will unduly affect the outcome of the election. The results would not necessarily reflect the opinions of those who have a genuine interest in an issue.

OTHER MOTIONS:
Mandatory voting does more harm than good
Mandatory voting does more good than harm

RELATED MOTIONS:
Mandatory voting is undemocratic

WEB LINKS:

- Qwghlm. "Why Compulsory Voting Is a Terrible Idea." <http://www.qwghlm. co.uk/2006/05/02/why-compulsory-voting-is-a-terrible-idea/>. Article presenting arguments against the motion.

- Weiner, Eric. "You Must Vote. It's the Law." <http://www.slate.com/id/2108832/>. Discussion of Australia's compulsory voting law.

Wiretaps, Warrantless

Motion   **Warrantless wiretaps are justified**

Introduction   In the aftermath of the terrorist attacks of September 2001, Pres. George W. Bush secretly authorized the National Security Agency to monitor telephone conversations and emails of Americans and other individuals originating in the United States without the court-approved warrants usually required for domestic surveillance. When the program came to light in 2005, it generated a firestorm of controversy. Critics claimed that it was unconstitutional and, in dismantling our rights, it was a victory for the terrorists. Others maintained that in times of crisis, drastic measures are necessary. The Bush administration contended that the president had the constitutional right as commander in chief to approve the program. Three years later, President Bush signed a law weakening the role of the courts in government surveillance. The Obama administration broadly continued to uphold the same position, arguing that the president must be able to exercise these powers.

Debating the Motion   A vast amount of material is available on this topic, so both teams need to think strategically when beginning their research. Teams need to research the history of wiretapping as well as the laws and constitutional protections that may limit its use, but the primary focus of research should be on finding arguments pro and con. Remember, the topic is not about whether warrantless wiretaps are good or bad but whether they are justified in certain, all, or no situations.

Proposition: The proposition does not need to argue that warrantless wiretaps are good or desirable under ideal conditions, but rather that their use is justified. The proposition could argue that all warrantless wiretaps are justified or that they are justified under certain circumstances. If the team chooses the latter approach, they need to outline a case describing under what circumstances wiretapping would be justified and who would be involved in using the wiretaps.

Opposition: The opposition has two overarching themes it could pursue: either to say that such wiretaps are never justified or to argue that they aren't justified under the circumstances set out by the proposition.

PROS

Post-9/11, drastic measures are necessary to keep the United States and its citizens safe. The Constitution provides for increased presidential power during times of war. In the twenty-first century, all war does not necessarily conform to a traditional definition of the word. In the war on terror, we are not fighting another government, but it is nonetheless a war. Warrantless wiretaps are a key tool for national security.

The rights guaranteed by the Bill of Rights apply only to citizens of the United States. The government is obligated to protect its citizens, not those from other nations with other systems of government. In using wiretaps on foreign nationals, we do not need warrants because, as noncitizens, they do not merit our protection.

The right to reasonable search and seizure only protects conversations where there is a reasonable expectation of privacy. This is a U.S. right guaranteed to people in U.S. territory. However, wiretaps used on individuals communicating with people in other countries are not unconstitutional because those who live outside the United States in countries where governments reserve the right to listen to their citizens do not have a reasonable expectation of privacy.

Ensuring the safety of the nation outweighs civil liberties in this case. Federal agents do not wiretap every person's home—even if they wanted to do so, they do not have the resources. Rather, they wiretap individuals and groups they suspect of engaging in terrorist activities. The effects of terrorism can be catastrophic; rogue actors can cause the

CONS

The war on terror is not a war as our Founders understood the term. The Constitution allows special presidential power when declaring war on other nations; however, these powers are deliberately limited to declared war. Benjamin Franklin once said, "Those who would give up essential liberty to purchase a little temporary safety deserve neither liberty nor safety." We are better off risking an attack than permitting the government to abuse its power.

Court rulings have interpreted the Constitution as applying to all residents of the United States. The Constitution does not specify citizens; the Supreme Court evaluates treatment of noncitizen residents in light of their presumed constitutional rights.

If at least one person is in the United States, then at least one person in the conversation has a reasonable expectation of privacy and thus unwarranted wiretapping is unconstitutional. The person outside the U.S. may not be entitled to privacy, but the person in the U.S. is. Certainly you cannot say wiretaps are not an intrusion into a person's privacy; for as long as wiretaps have been technically possible, warrants have been required for their use.

It is ridiculous to assume that a warrantless wiretap is really going to make the difference between the safety of a nation and its complete destruction. If reasonable cause to believe someone poses a danger can be shown, convincing a judge to issue a warrant should be no problem. We cannot allow infringements on people's rights with the justification that deaths of thousands, huge infrastructural damage, a crippling of the economy, and fear in the entire nation so that we are afraid to go about our daily lives. Terrorism is not like normal crime either in its intent or its effects and so it cannot be treated as such.

Federal officials may pay closer attention to individuals of certain backgrounds, but only because modern anti-American terrorism is based in the Mideast. Honest citizens have nothing to fear, but allowing the government to be efficient in identifying terrorists benefits everyone.

such infringements will probably only discover the guilty anyway—that kind of thinking defeats the purpose of having civil rights in the first place.

Unwarranted wiretaps are used to racially profile. Suspicions based on a person's ethnic background are insufficient to obtain a warrant. If a warrant is not necessary, the government can harass minorities.

OTHER MOTIONS:

Warrantless wiretaps are unconstitutional

Warrantless wiretaps do more harm than good

RELATED MOTIONS:

National security trumps the Bill of Rights

Forgoing civil liberties in the name of security is a victory for terrorists

WEB LINKS:

- Risen, James, and Eric Lichtblau. "Court Affirms Wiretapping Without Warrants." <http://www.nytimes.com/2009/01/16/washington/16fisa.html>. Report on a ruling by the Foreign Intelligence Surveillance Court of Review.

- White House. "President Bush: Information Sharing, Patriot Act Vital to Homeland Security." <http://georgewbush-whitehouse.archives.gov/news/releases/2004/04/print/20040420-2.html>. Remarks by the president justifying his actions.

- Yoo, John. "Why We Endorse Warrantless Wiretaps" <http://online.wsj.com/article/SB124770304290648701.html>. Essay by a Bush administration official in support of wiretapping.

Zero Tolerance in Schools

Motion   **Zero-tolerance policies in schools do more harm than good**

Introduction   Zero tolerance establishes a policy of punishing the breaking of any rule or law. Under zero-tolerance policies, principals, teachers, judges, and others cannot use their judgment in enforcing rules. They cannot consider a student's history, or whether the student understood the rule, and have no discretion over the punishment. Zero-tolerance policies are applied to a wide variety of illegal actions—particularly those involving drug possession or violence. Supporters say zero tolerance can make an individual think twice before disobeying rules. Opponents say that such policies are unfair and the punishments involved too severe.

Debating the Motion   Pay careful attention to the wording of this topic. It focuses on the harms versus benefits of the policy, not whether it is good or bad. Arguments must reflect this focus. Both teams should gather a number of examples of zero-tolerance policies, ranging from ones with narrow scopes that target only one issue such as drugs or weapons to broader policies that cover a number of actions and behaviors. In particular, look for cases that give information about the long-term impact of the policy.

Proposition: Because zero tolerance can apply in a number of different settings, the proposition should prepare a definition that explains what kinds of rules have zero-tolerance policies: Do they only apply to serious crimes, or minor problems like running in the hallway? The proposition should research what kind of schools tend to enforce zero tolerance and students' reaction to it. The team should focus on what kind of students are targeted under zero tolerance: Does the rule apply equally to all students or does the policy end up being more strictly enforced against certain students?

Opposition: Remember, that while the proposition must demonstrate conclusively why zero-tolerance policies do more harm than good, the same burden of proof does not apply to the opposition. The opposition has the choice of either defending the motion that zero-tolerance policies do more good than harm or they can put forth a more neutral position—for example, that while zero tolerance may not be good, it certainly doesn't impose undue harms.

PROS

Zero-tolerance policies do not stop violence or other harmful actions. Studies have not shown that zero-tolerance policies actually decrease misbehavior in school or crime outside of it. Since this is the stated purpose, zero-tolerance policies are not achieving their goal. Therefore, if zero-tolerance policies have any harms, they should not be put in place or implemented.

Zero-tolerance policies are enforced unfairly, often because rules are poorly written. Many ways are available to break a rule—zero-tolerance policies try to account for each one. The result is that students are often unaware they are breaking a rule. A prominent example is that of Kyle Herbert, a straight-A student who was suspended after a classmate dropped a pocket knife in his lap, or 6-year-old Zachary Christie, who faced reform school after bringing a Cub Scout knife with which to eat his lunch. (He was later reprieved.) Policies should be created with the understanding that life is not black and white, and school officials must use common sense in each situation.

Adopting a policy that inevitably increases the number of mistaken punishments is inherently more harmful than good. The U.S. justice system is based on the fundamental principle that it is better to let ten guilty men go free than send one innocent man to jail. Zero-tolerance policies do the opposite—they acknowledge that some well-behaved students will be unfairly punished but consider

CONS

We cannot say for certain that such policies do not work. Conclusive results are difficult to obtain because of the complexity of the issue. Many policy changes often occur at the same time, so it is difficult to know what effect any one change has. Furthermore, it is always difficult to evaluate preventive policies because we do not know what could have—but did not—happen. The opposition maintains that a well-planned and clearly explained policy requiring severe consequences for acts of violence and drug use logically decreases offenses.

Just because something is difficult does not mean it is bad. Students should be made aware that they cannot bring knives to school, but once the rule is in place, they must respect it. School board officials should put thought and consideration into zero-tolerance policies, but absolute enforcement makes students understand the importance of obeying school rules. Students should not think they may interpret rules as they see fit or only obey rules they approve of.

Students should take precautions to make sure they do not break rules. As long as students act responsibly, they should not get in trouble. Furthermore, schools have always had more discretion than the justice system—a person cannot be imprisoned for publishing offensive material, but a student can be prevented from putting it in the school newspaper. Students do not check all their rights at the that outcome to be acceptable in the greater cause of reducing violence.

Young people continue to mature through college; developing self-esteem during these years is critical. The severity of zero-tolerance punishments has huge psychological consequences: mistrust of authority, unwarranted guilt, anxiety about unintentionally breaking rules, etc. Many students commit a first offense because of temporary problems—anger caused by a parent's divorce, depression over a death in the family—and should receive help, not punishment. Categorizing all offenders as problem cases causes students to mistakenly believe there is something wrong with them.

If a school is to create a safe environment, it should do so in the least harmful and invasive way possible. Zero-tolerance policies cause unnecessary harm. While wrongdoers deserve punishment, the harm of excessive punishments goes against the goal of protecting people. Keeping students safe includes helping them feel secure in themselves; no child could feel safe if she is worried about a rigid zero-tolerance policy that threatens jail for minor offenses like littering or doodling.

schoolhouse doors, but they accept that they must obey stricter rules—including greater punishments for disobedience.

Using zero-tolerance policies on young people instills respect for rules. A punishment that is harsh in the short run sends a long-term warning to other students and citizens.

A school cannot serve any of its functions if it is unsafe. Zero-tolerance policies usually target serious offenses that endanger people—use of weapons, possession of illegal drugs, or offenses that predict bad behavior in the future. Students who break such rules are a serious threat to children around them and must be dealt with in a way that both punishes the individual student and warns others against copying his behavior.

OTHER MOTIONS:

Zero-tolerance policies in schools are unethical

Zero-tolerance policies do more good than harm

RELATED MOTIONS:

Zero-tolerance policies are unconstitutional

Zero tolerance makes zero sense

WEB LINKS:

- American Bar Association. "Zero Tolerance Policies." <http://www.abanet.org/crimjust/juvjus/zerotolreport.html>. Report on trends and consequences of zero-tolerance policies. The article also suggests alternatives.

- Cauchon, Dennis. "Zero-Tolerance Policies Lack Flexibility." <http://www.usatoday.com/educate/ednews3.htm>. Another specific case in which a teen violated a zero-tolerance policy on drugs and alcohol. This article includes interviews with various educators who both advocate and decry zero-tolerance policies.

- New York Times. "It's a Fork, It's a Spoon . . . It's a Weapon?" <http://www.nytimes.com/2009/10/12/education/12discipline.html>. A specific case in which a young child fell afoul of a policy pertaining to weapons when bringing utensils to school for eating his lunch.

Zoos

Zoos are unethical

Introduction Summertime trips to the zoo are as American as apple pie. Once a place to goggle at exotic animals, they have increasingly become a haven for endangered species and a place for high-tech scientific institutions to expand their commitment to responsible breeding programs and habitat conservation. However, criticism of zoos is on the rise. Opponents maintain that enclosing wild animals is wrong, no matter how big and how nice the enclosure. Supporters counter that zoos are often the last chance for severely endangered species. Most young visitors still enjoy these zoos, unaware of controversy that rages around them.

Debating the Motion This topic is about ethics, so both teams need to be careful to stick to ethical arguments and not allow the debate to simply become a list of characteristics that are good and bad about zoos.

Proposition: The proposition might begin by defining what they mean by *ethical*. For those just beginning with debate, it might be easiest to define *ethical* as an action in accordance with a major system of morality or ethics. By doing so, the proposition can simply develop arguments against zoos and tie each argument to one of these systems. A more advanced team can take the trickier route of picking a specific definition of *ethical*, for example, the ends justifying the means, and create arguments about zoos to match their chosen theory.

Opposition: The opposition has two options. They can either defend a neutral position, that is, that zoos are neither ethically harmful nor beneficial, or that, in fact, on balance, zoos are more ethical than not.

PROS

The way we treat animals reflects how we treat one another. Taking pleasure from zoos, where animals are sometime abused and often suffer, puts us at risk of feeling that such abuse and suffering are normal and that we can treat other human beings

CONS

Zoos actually promote a duty to others. We can learn from zoos how to care for others and the environment via the education programs many zoos provide on habitats and endangered species. Doing your duty is an accepted ethical practice.

in the same way. Treating others well is a key component of being ethical, and zoos undermine this.

Causing suffering to others is unethical. Animals suffer when they are captured and made to live in zoos, where they are often kept in small spaces or forced to perform tricks rather than living their lives in the wild. This is a form of enslavement—which we can always agree is unethical.

In this case, the ends justify the means, which is popular ethical theory. While in the past zoos may merely have been a series of cages for animals, most modern zoos provide appropriate space, habitat, and recreation for animals whose wild habitats have either been compromised or have vanished altogether. The activities that the animals engage in may seem entertaining to us, but they are actually for research to help animals.

Zoo animals should be released; this can be done responsibly in a way that would not be a death sentence for them. Training and reintroduction programs should be started immediately in all zoos, so we can treat other beings ethically by allowing them the chance to live authentic lives.

Even if zoos are unethical, it would be far more unethical to release animals into the wild. Zoo animals do not know how to exist in the wild and they would surely die. Such release would be a mass slaughter of innocent animals—which anyone can agree is unethical.

It is unethical to cause unnecessary unhappiness. Capturing wild animals or sending them to other zoos through loans and thus separating them from their mates and offspring cause great distress, which is unethical.

Placing animals in zoos is done for the greater good of a species and so is not unethical. Capturing endangered animals prevents the extinction of the species. As for moving zoo animals around, for those animals with some abilities to think and feel, most zoos are careful in moving them only when necessary for research or breeding. Diversifying the gene pool helps the species.

If the action is not one we could universally recommend for all animals, including human animals, it is unethical. No person would be content to be stuck in a small space, even if that space were well-designed. A gilded cage is still a cage. Therefore, we are not justified in confining animals in zoos.

Confining animals to zoos is more ethical than permitting a species to become extinct. The fact is that for many animals their habitat has been destroyed and they have nowhere else to go. We can either let them die out or bring them to zoos designed specifically to be as similar as possible to their original home. The latter option is by far the more ethical choice.

OTHER MOTIONS:

Zoos do more harm than good

Zoos are ethical

Zoos are a necessary evil

RELATED MOTIONS:

Animals should have the same rights as humans

WEB LINKS:

- American Veterinary Medical Association. "Is It Ethical to Keep Animals in Zoos?" <http://www.avma.org/onlnews/javma/dec02/021201d.asp>. Article describing how zoos are addressing the issue.

- "The Ethics Behind Zoos." <http://www2.dnr.cornell.edu/courses/nr201/research/examples/great3.pdf>. Student essay outlining the pros and cons of zoos.

Index

THE
WHITE PASS AND YUKON ROUTE
A Pictorial History

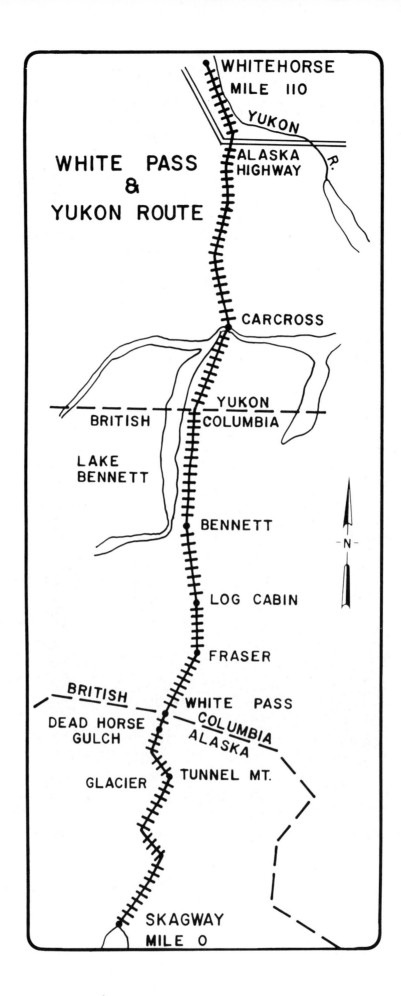

THE
WHITE PASS
AND
YUKON ROUTE

A Pictorial History

Railroad employees and passengers at Inspiration Point in the 1950s.   James Hamilton

by stan cohen

PICTORIAL HISTORIES PUBLISHING COMPANY

LIBRARY OF CONGRESS CATALOG
CARD NO. 79-90884

ISBN 0-933126-08-5

First Printing   March 1980
Second Printing   September 1980
Third Printing   January 1982
Fourth Printing   March 1984
Fifth Printing   March 1985
Sixth Printing   April 1987

PRINTED
IN CANADA

Printed by Friesen Printers
Altona, Manitoba

Cover: *The first passenger train to the summit enters the tunnel on February 20, 1899.*

Postcard from the author's collection

PICTORIAL HISTORIES PUBLISHING COMPANY
713 South 3rd West
Missoula, Montana 59801